WOMEN IN AMERICAN HISTORY

Series Editors

Mari Jo Buhle
Jacquelyn D. Hall
Anne Firor Scott

Women Doctors in Gilded-Age Washington

Women Doctors in Gilded-Age Washington

Race, Gender, and Professionalization

Gloria Moldow

UNIVERSITY OF ILLINOIS PRESS
Urbana and Chicago

Library of Congress Cataloging-in-Publication Data

Moldow, Gloria.
  Women doctors in gilded-age Washington.
  (Women in American history)
  Bibliography: p.
  Includes index.
  1. Women physicians—Washington (D.C.)—History—
19th century. 2. Sex discrimination in medicine—
Washington (D.C.)—History—19th century. 3. Professional
socialization—Washington (D.C.)—Sex difference—History—
19th century. 4. Women—Washington (D.C.)—Social
conditions—History—19th century. I. Title.
II. Series. [DNLM: 1. History of Medicine, 19th Cent.—
District of Columbia. 2. Physicians, Women—history—
District of Columbia. WZ 80.5.W5 M717w]
R692.M6 1987   305.4′3616′09753   86-19251
ISBN 0-252-01379-4 (alk. paper)

To the memory of my mother,
who shared the courage of these pioneers.

Contents

Acknowledgments

Several years ago, at a meeting of the Chesapeake Society of Women Historians held at the Smithsonian's Anthropological Archives, I learned about the manuscript collections of women who had served the Bureau of Ethnology in the 1880s. Intrigued, I spent several weeks poring through the papers of two of them, Matilda Coxe Stevenson and Alice Cunningham Fletcher. Their pioneering research on the Zuni and Omaha Indians, performed when Victorian women of their class presumably devoted themselves exclusively to domestic and pious duties, remained standard in the field for almost a century. Not surprisingly, the collections were as fascinating for what they told about the Indian tribes as what they revealed about the women themselves.

The manuscript papers also hinted at the existence of a vital community of professional women to which the anthropologists belonged. Stevenson's and Fletcher's correspondents and close friends included physicians, lawyers, authors, journalists, and scientists who met regularly at a number of all-women's organizations newly established in the city. The discovery of this lively community came at a time when those of us researching women's history were beginning to realize that the Elizabeth Blackwells and Maria Mitchells whom we studied were not anomalies in their generation.

Preliminary research into the lives of these professional women revealed a common pattern. Almost invariably, the women enjoyed acceptance and even a measure of success in their respective fields after struggling initially to gain recognition. But none achieved marked distinction in the male-dominated arena that she chose. Moreover, these women had few successors. Time and again the doors they struggled to open closed behind them. The experience of almost two hundred women physicians and medical students who lived and worked in Washington in this period demonstrated this pattern most clearly. I decided to use that experience to demonstrate my belief that although professional consolidation at the turn of the century aided women's entry into the professions in some ways, it ultimately hindered their progress. As the story unfolded, it testified not only to the "multiple lines of conservative defense" that women and other minorities confronted, to use Richard Shryock's phrase, but also to the tenacity of cultural sexism and racism.

My dissertation, submitted in 1980, profited from the guidance and patience of Hilda Smith, Jim Gilbert, and Myron Lounsbury and from the advice of John Duffy, all at the University of Maryland. Page Miller, Cindy Aron, Judy Markowitz, and others who shared a commitment to bringing a feminist perspective to contemporary scholarship made the research an adventure. An American Association of University of Women fellowship enabled me to finish an early version. Edna Stark, Dale Salm, Joan Antell, and Marilyn Brownstein, friends who share my interests, read portions of the manuscript, but I never would have considered publication without the encouragement of Mary Roth Walsh, who practices as well as researches the value of "feminist networks." Her monograph, *"Doctors Wanted, No Women Need Apply": Sexual Barriers in the Medical Profession, 1835–1975,* stands as a signal contribution to the field. Generous assistance from administrators at Iona College (especially from Dean John F. Noonan), who support the scholarly endeavors of administrators as well as faculty, enabled me to complete necessary revisions.

I wish also to acknowledge the assistance I received from numerous librarians, especially G. F. A. Key of the Martin Luther King Memorial Library in Washington, who at more than ninety is that library's most important repository of Washingtoniana; Annette D. Steiner of the George Washington University Special Collections Division; as well as librarians at the Washington Historical Society; the Moorland-Spingarn Research Center at Howard University; and the Georgetown University collection. Those who gave graciously of their time to reminisce about the women whose lives make up this book added to the richness of the available material.

This project grew up with my four children—Leslie, Andrea, Bruce, and Chip. Its various versions distributed themselves over dining rooms tables, playroom floors, and bedroom bureaus. The women doctors became part of all our lives. The children learned to respect a closed door and a deadline, but they more than stayed out of the way. They often shared in the project and transformed tedium into joy by trudging downtown with me to pore through census texts, count index cards, and check citations; more recently, they read and commented on chapters. I will always be grateful for their good will and affection. I hope they are none the worse for this family stepchild.

My husband Bert adjusted good naturedly to the inconveniences he never bargained for. He attended PTA meetings, drove carpools, and learned to fill in as Thanksgiving dinner cook, although he never did figure out how to operate the washing machine. He also read every chapter with a searing and critical eye, a job no one could have done as well. I think he's none the worse for this project either, and he knows I appreciate his love and support.

Introduction

The late nineteenth century was a period of dynamic social mobility, particularly for those aspiring to professional middle-class status. Until recently, historians defined the roles that emerged in this period strictly in male terms. If they focused on career-minded women at all, it was to examine their employment as school teachers, writers, librarians, or settlement-house workers. Moreover, analysts seldom attributed to professional women the impulses toward upward mobility and material success that men displayed. If there was no economic necessity, they accepted at face value Jane Addams's explanation of "subjective necessity" to account for women's attraction to nontraditional careers. Blind to women's participation in the professional upsurge of the 1890s, analysts also ignored the relationship between female aspirations and the emerging culture of professionalism.[1]

Within the last decade, historians have begun to address the experience of those Gilded-Age women whose careers defied preconceptions of the turn-of-the-century professional as a white, native-born, American male. Some analysts have focused on women professionals—single or married—who were as eager to succeed in the public sphere as their male counterparts. Others have examined the professional barriers women confronted. They point to how the male elite, consciously or not, structured professional institutions and societies to exclude women and other minorities.[2]

Studies of women's club activities have added yet another perspective to turn-of-the-century professional culture. The literature suggests that the urge to affiliate had implications for status affirmation that reached beyond the ostensible goals of organization. Contemporary analysts have referred also to the ways in which internalized cultural proscriptions created barriers to women's advancement in the period. They have demonstrated how educated and competent women, unlike their male counterparts, questioned their own abilities and gravitated toward exclusively female occupations or withdrew from the professions for which they had been trained.[3]

This book looks at one group of late-nineteenth-century professional women in light of these recent studies. It documents the ways in which the development of professional institutions at the turn of the century limited women's opportunities for advancement into professions. The locale of this study, Washington, D.C., was a center of scientific, educational, and cultural growth in the 1880s and 1890s and, reputedly, a "special center" for professional women. It drew scores of career-seeking women who intended to take advantage of the capital city's opportunties. Among them were some two hundred women physicians and medical students. With their female peers in law, science, letters, and education, these "new women" confidently expected a new age.[4]

Generational experiences differentiated between the "pioneers" and the "post-pioneers," groups with distinctly different motives and outlooks. The earlier group of women doctors entered the profession in the decades immediately following the Civil War. These women had come of age during the ferment of antebellum reform. Frequently women's rights activists, they were committed to securing equal rights for women of every class. Their successors, the "post-pioneers," were born after the war. The expansive social forces of the 1870s and 1880s shaped their formative years, and they viewed themselves differently from their predecessors. No less dissatisfied with traditional roles, they rejected the activist feminism of their forebears. Confidently they believed that the natural course of evolution would soon enable them to take their rightful place alongside their brothers, husbands, and fathers. Whichever their perspective, late-nineteenth-century professional women shared disappointment, as the experience of Washington's women doctors—both black and white—demonstrates.

In Washington, as elsewhere, ultimate career success depended upon integration into an emerging network of professional institutions that included medical schools, clinics, hospitals, and societies—all controlled by the white male medical elite. White women were able to effect breakthroughs in each of these areas. Time and again, however; disappointment followed initial success. Thus, during the 1880s when economic crises loomed, medical departments affiliated with Georgetown and George Washington Universities (the latter then known as Columbian University) admitted women. When their financial prospects brightened, these schools discontinued coeducation. Two other unaffiliated proprietary medical schools also accepted female candidates. But these schools, with shaky prospects from the start, succumbed to the high cost of medical modernization and closed at the turn of the century. A proposed female medical college, to be affiliated with George Washington University but funded and run by women, failed to materialize. Faculty opposition and women's uncertainty about the value of a segregated female institution undercut the school's proponents. One local school did provide women with a sustained opportunity for medical training. Scores of women, black and white, were graduated from the Howard University Medical Department between 1870 and 1900. Increasing racial prejudice in the city during the 1880s and beyond, however, drastically reduced white female enrollment. As a result of these setbacks, the city's female medical school population declined dramatically from a high of 20 percent of medical school students in the early 1890s to only 3 percent by 1900.

Washington women who did succeed in acquiring medical training before the turn of the century had difficulty securing supervised postgraduate experience. Barred from most clinic internships and hospital appointments, the city's white women established their own training centers. The success of these clinics varied. One was integrated into the male-dominated medical establishment at the cost of women's full participation. Another closed for want of funds. The third survived for several decades, largely because of the sustained support of a devoted handful of physicians. But that facility lacked resources and legitimacy, and women physicians graduating in the early twentieth century avoided affiliation. Only one of these clinics invited black women to participate—and that, on an extremely limited basis. Black women lacked opportunties within their own community as well as the resources to establish their own training clinics.

Medical women sought to overcome other barriers with mixed success. Denied licensing and consulting privileges, they appealed, successfully, to Congress for redress. After a fifteen-year struggle, white women—with the support of male allies—also gained entry into the local medical associations. Affiliation with these organizations did not signify women's acceptance into the professional elite, however, for by then power had shifted to the specialist societies and to the university hospital complexes then emerging in the city. These predictably barred women.

To compensate for their exclusion from such male-dominated professional societies, women established numerous broadly based organizations of their own. These racially and sexually segregated societies satisfied professional women's needs for intellectual companionship and moral support, but did little to promote their career aspirations;

indeed, such groups may have hindered women's integration into the professional community by institutionalizing the very distinctions they sought to erase.

A few women who possessed extraordinary talent, influence, and charisma transcended such obstacles to their progress and achieved moderate career success. None, however, reached the heights of the profession that men of comparable ability and training attained. Approximately 40 percent of the white women practiced for twenty-five years or more. Most black women were forced to create career alternatives. In the decade immediately following the Civil War, they were able to use existing networks developed by black abolitionists and reformers to establish themselves in the profession; later, they had to take advantage of such career opportunities as the racially segregated educational institutions in the city afforded. They were able to satisfy their social and professional ambitions—but not necessarily in the medical profession itself. Along with other "new women" of their generation, they watched the doors through which they had passed all but close behind them. Like the majority of Washington's career and professional women of the Gilded Age, they discovered that what one historian has called the "vertical vision" of career success was for men only, no matter how ardently women subscribed to its tenets. For most of these female Horatio Algers, the American dream remained a male prerogative.

1

Gilded-Age Washington and Careers for Women in Medicine

"More Opportunity for a Nobody to Become a Somebody"

In the last decades of the nineteenth century, social changes under way since before the Civil War gained momentum, transforming America's middle classes. Historians agree that these years represent a "crucial moment" in American social history, when the expansion of existing professional fields and the emergence of entirely new careers created a dynamic professional class. Members of this new class, largely recruited from the ranks of white, Anglo-Saxon, native-born Protestants, devised interlocking networks of institutions and organizations to enhance their newfound status and to give it form and permanence. Through university departments, government bureaus, hospitals, museums, libraries, charitable organizations, and professional societies, they created what one analyst has called the "vertical vision" of career success. By skillfully weaving their way through a given sequence of educational, occupational, and cultural institutions, aspiring elites could look forward to the material and social rewards of a professsional career.[1]

Blacks and whites, immigrants and native-born, the illiterate and the well educated joined these ranks, eager for the benefits that seemed tantalizingly in reach. The prospect of such benefits was not for men alone. Throughout the country, by the close of the century, growing numbers of women demonstrated their determination "to make more and be more" in the words of Josephine St. Pierre Ruffin, a leader in the black community of the period. Belva Lockwood, an ambitious Washington attorney, expressed this view clearly in a popular *Lippincott's* article in 1888. Because she "possessed all the ambition of a man," Lockwood said, she saw no reason to "ignore the gulf between the rights and privileges of the sexes." Lockwood left her teach-

5

ing job, with its meager earnings and low status, and became the first woman to practice before the Supreme Court and a leader of Washington's community of professional women.[2]

In no profession except teaching did women have better prospects than in medicine. Nationally, the number of trained women practitioners rose more than twelvefold between 1870 and 1900, from 544 in 1870 to 7,382 at the turn of the century. In 1894, 72 of 145 men's medical colleges enrolled 848 women, and 7 women's medical colleges enrolled another 541. Women made up 10 percent of the classes of nineteen coeducational medical schools and approximately 20 percent of the classes of other schools such as Howard University, Tufts College, the Massachusetts College of Physicians and Surgeons, and the University of Colorado Medical Department.[3]

Several factors contributed to women's remarkable advances in the profession. Women's rights activists, for instance, argued for greater participation of women in medicine and raised the issue to public notice. Elizabeth Cady Stanton, Lucretia Mott, and others protested in 1848 that men monopolized the medical profession and closed such "avenues of wealth and distinction" to women. In the 1850s and 1860s, women who held more traditional views of the female role objected to the increasing influence of "male midwives," or obstetricians, and sought to reverse the trend toward that specialty. Influential shapers of opinion, such as Sarah Josepha Hale, editor of the popular *Godey's Lady's Book,* declared male obstetricians to be an "outrage on female delicacy" and championed the cause of women doctors. The congruence of a belief in women's "innately" nurturant qualities and their traditional roles as midwives and nurses further strengthened the cause. Meanwhile, female physiological societies, established in the 1830s and 1840s to provide women with a greater understanding of their own health, enlightened a generation of women and even prompted some to seek formal training in order to instruct their peers. Together women from such diverse orientations helped to found numerous women's medical colleges, including the Woman's Medical College of Pennsylvania in 1850, the Woman's Medical College of the New York Infirmary for Women and Children in 1868, and the Woman's Medical College of Baltimore in 1882.[4]

Transformations in the medical profession, which were enlarging the base from which physicians were drawn, also facilitated women's entry into the field. Before mid-century, the so-called "regulars," elite physicians who had served their apprenticeships with men of their class and then trained at European medical centers, monopolized the formal practice of medicine. They relied upon such "heroic" therapies as bloodletting, blistering, and purging with large doses of toxic drugs. Not everyone shared their beliefs, and by the 1840s, numerous sects emerged to challenge their hegemony over the treatment of the middle class. These so-called "irregulars" included such sectarians as homeopaths, eclectics, water-cure proponents, and botanics, among others. Differing in many respects, they nonetheless shared a belief in the use of benign herbal remedies in contrast to the regulars' arsenal of more drastic measures. In an era of uncertain efficacies, these mild treatments often seemed to work as well as the harsher treatments of the regulars and won the sectarians a share of the regulars' clientele.[5]

The homeopaths and the eclectics wooed urban, middle-class women to the sensible therapeutics they espoused. Because of their antiestablishment challenge, the irregulars generally allied themselves with temperance, abolition, and women's rights crusaders and further gained the support of reform-minded women. In addition, they were more inclined to accept female practitioners into their ranks. Although at first, as one historian has noted, the faculties of homeopathic and eclectic schools "ran hot and cold" toward women students, opening their doors to them when it seemed expedient and closing them when male students objected, the majority approved coeducation by the late 1850s. By 1900, several hundred women doctors had graduated from such schools.[6]

At the same time, social changes within their own ranks challenged the elites' monopoly over the care of the urban middle and upper classes. The proliferation of commercial medical schools, resulting from demographic shifts, educational advances, and new modes of transportation, made it possible for men of every social rank to seek a medical diploma. The numbers of trained physicians swelled. By 1870, there were 55,000 trained doctors in the country, compared to 30,000 only two decades before. By 1900, the census reported almost 120,000 medical practitioners. The number of medical students alone doubled between 1880 and 1900, from almost 12,000 to more than 25,000, increasing ten times as fast as the nation's population.[7]

The regular doctors who operated profit-making, independent medical schools or university-affiliated medical departments opposed women's admission. But administrators of post-Civil War land-grant schools—especially those in the Midwest and the West—acknowledged the need for female medical education. Rather than establish expensive coordinate medical schools, leaders of these government-supported institutions admitted women to existing and newly created departments. The medical schools of the Universities of California and Michigan and Syracuse University admitted women in 1869,

1871, and 1870, respectively. By the late 1880s, numerous commercial medical schools followed their example. Coeducational medical training in the nineteenth century culminated in 1893 in the establishment of the Johns Hopkins University Medical Department in Baltimore. Mary Garrett of Baltimore and the Woman's Fund of the Johns Hopkins School of Medicine donated the $500,000 the school needed to open, with the stipulation that women be accepted on an equal basis with men.[8]

As a result of these converging trends, women physicians' prospects seemed bright by the 1880s and 1890s. Popular literature extolled this tendency. *The Woman's Journal* and the *Woman's Tribune* featured regular columns devoted to professional women's achievements—physicians among them—and urged readers to patronize doctors of their own sex. Authors of books directed toward female career aspirants echoed such sentiments. Annie Nathan Meyers's *Woman's Work in America* (1891) described the success of women in diverse fields and included a lengthy discussion written by Dr. Mary Putnam Jacobi about the status of women physicians. M. L. Rayne's *What Can a Woman Do: Or Her Position in the Business and Literary World,* published in 1893, also devoted a chapter to women doctors. Popular biographical dictionaries such as Frances E. Willard and Mary Livermore's *American Women: A Complete Encyclopedia of the Lives and Achievements of American Women in the Nineteenth Century* (1897) and Mary Logan's *The Part Taken by Women in American Society* (1911) listed scores of women physicians. Even widely read novels like Sarah Orne Jewett's *A Country Doctor* (1884) and Mark Twain's *The Gilded Age* (1873) featured women physicians as protagonists.[9]

Late-nineteenth-century Washington had its share of women doctors. They were part of a large and lively community of female professionals drawn to the capital by the postwar expansion of the federal government. Pre-Civil War departments enlarged, such as the Naval Observatory, the National Museum, the Census, the Treasury Department, the Post Office Department, and the Coast and Geodetic Survey. At the same time, agencies such as the Bureau of Ethnology, the Army Medical Museum, and the Department of Agriculture came into being. Along with a vast army of low-level civil servants, newly trained mathematicians, geographers, pathologists, and chemists migrated to Washington to work and study with such esteemed bureau chiefs as astronomer Simon Newcomb, geologist John Wesley Powell, bacteriologist Dr. Walter Reed, and chemist Harvey Wiley. Together they contributed to the status of Washington as a center of scientific learning "almost, if not quite, unsurpassed on the continent," according to a reporter in the *Nation*. [10]

Local educational institutions such as Georgetown College and Columbian College (later George Washington University) expanded to meet the needs of the hundreds of white-collar clerks who aspired to professional status. Administrators in these schools conducted classes in the late afternoons and evenings to attract such students, and for their corps of instructors drew on the talents of scientists and other professionals working in federal departments. Both Columbian and Georgetown advanced to university status in the 1870s and enlarged their facilities to accommodate more students. Howard University, which was established in 1869, also offered training in professional fields, as did the National University, which opened in 1884. Educators and entrepreneurs, eager to capitalize on the growing market of part-time students, opened new schools. The seemingly boundless opportunities in the capital prompted one journalist to comment that there was "more opportunity for a nobody to become a somebody" in Washington than anywhere in the country.[11]

Between 1870 and 1900, the scientists, administrators, physicians, lawyers, and educators working in this city, as elsewhere, created organizations that laid the foundation for twentieth-century professional life. At one level, these groups met important community needs; at another, they provided their members with opportunities for intellectual stimulation and social conviviality while heightening their professional identities. At still another, equally significant level, the associations promoted the particular interests of male leaders and inducted young men into the professional ranks. In 1871, Joseph Henry, director of the Smithsonian, Simon Newcomb, head of the Naval Observatory, and Dr. John Shaw Billings of the Army Medical Museum joined with others to found the Philosophical Society, the first group in Washington to bring together leaders of the new professional elite. In 1878, these same men, along with others from the Geological Survey, the Naval Observatory, and the Smithsonian, met with physicians Joseph M. Toner, Newton Bates, and Robert Fletcher to establish the Cosmos Club, a social group restricted to men who had achieved prominence in their fields. That same year, Toner joined with two anthropologists to organize the Anthropological Society of Washington, another organization that drew together members of the city's professional white male community.[12]

During this same period, a parallel professional elite emerged within the city's black male community. According to Gerri Major, a student of

9

late-nineteenth-century black society, Washington, the "heartland of black society," was then at the "height of its brilliance." There was not another place in the nation, she claimed, where so many "upper-class colored people were congregated." The educational opportunities provided by Howard University, combined with the patronage of Radical Republicans, enabled scores of black men—and women—to find relatively secure, well-paying jobs in government service. The city's segregated school system recruited the best-educated black men and women in the country and offered them one of the few intellectually stimulating environments then available. An impressive corps of black physicians were part of this community. Trained doctors who had served the troops in the Civil War remained in Washington after their contracts expired. There, they taught at Howard Medical School, the nation's first medical department to hire black physicians, and practiced at Freedmen's Hospital, the first hospital to admit black doctors. Barred from white organizations, these professionals formed comparable groups in their own community. Over the years, such associations as the National Medical Society, the Monday Literary Society, the Bethel Literary and Historical Society, and the Cosmos Club (different from that organized in white society) promoted the social and intellectual aspirations of the black professional and business elite.[13]

Women who aspired to professional status, whether black or white, recognized the unique economic and professional opportunities the city afforded. In 1891, newcomer Ellen Hardin Walworth wrote in the *Chautauquan* that Washington was a "special center" for professional and career women. "The women who are leaders in literature, art, Science, and patriotism congregate here," she boasted—and they did. Women active in public life—from political rights activists to founders of the Daughters of the American Revolution and the Colored Woman's League—made their homes in the city. Widely publicized annual meetings of the National Woman Suffrage Association fostered public debate on the status of the "new woman." Washington professional and career women were personal friends of Elizabeth Cady Stanton and Susan B. Anthony and entertained them when Congress was in session.[14]

Several of America's best-known novelists and newspaper correspondents belonged to this professional community. Mrs. E. D. E. N. Southworth, who earned as much as $10,000 annually for her works, held salons for the city's political and literary lights in her Georgetown home. Two physicians' wives, well-known novelists themselves, were members of this select group. Frances Hodgson Burnett, wife of Dr.

Swan Burnett, professor in Georgetown's medical department, had written *Little Lord Fauntleroy* and other children's classics; Jennie Gould Lincoln, wife of Dr. Nathan S. Lincoln, one-time president of the District of Columbia Medical Society, specialized in historical fiction.[15]

Columnists such as Mary Clemmer Ames and Abigail Dodge (Gail Hamilton), who reported on congressional activities, and Sara Lippincott (Grace Greenwood) and Kate Field produced widely read columns on politics and politicians. These women defended women's right to sit in the press galleries of the Senate and House and vigorously advanced women's rights, although only a few formally identified with the women's movement itself. In 1882, several of them formed the Woman's National Press Club in Washington in order to advance their professional interests through concerted action.[16]

Women were also able to take advantage of government expansion in the professional sector. Anthropologists Matilda Coxe Stevenson and Alice Cunningham Fletcher worked for John Wesley Powell of the Bureau of Ethnology. Mary Jane Rathbun, a marine zoologist, established the division of marine invertebrates at the National Museum and was responsible for much of its operation after 1886. Botanist Effie Southworth worked as a plant pathologist with numerous trained women botanists in the Department of Agriculture under Irwin Frank Smith. Mary Clare de Graffenreid, an instructor of mathematics and Latin at Georgetown Female Seminary, became one of the first statistical investigators for Carroll D. Wright, head of the Bureau of Labor. Several of these women published award-winning studies that brought them national attention.[17]

Women lawyers made up another segment of the women's professional community in the city. Belva Lockwood had studied at Howard and completed her training at the National University Law School. When National discontinued coeducation, she trained other women in her office. In 1896, Ellen Spencer Mussey, Marilla Ricker, and several other women lawyers founded the Women's Law Class. It later became the nucleus of American University's School of Law.[18]

Black women enriched the city's professional community as well. Mary Church Terrell, a member of this community, believed that "more educated colored women" lived in Washington than anywhere else in the country. Women filled the majority of jobs in the segregated black city schools: In 1913, thirty-three of forty-eight black principals were women. The majority had begun teaching in Washington during the 1880s and 1890s. Lucy Moten, a physician and the principal of the Washington Normal School from 1883 to 1920, reputedly earned one of the highest salaries in the black community. Terrell, a graduate of

Oberlin College, became the first woman to sit on the city's integrated school board.[19]

Medical women—both black and white—played an important role in these communities of professional women. Between 1870 and 1900, close to two hundred of them studied or practiced medicine in the city, a proportion comparable to the number in such cities as New York, and Philadelphia, centers of female medical education. These trained physicians began to practice in Washington during the Civil War. The first—Susan Edson, who graduated from the Eclectic College of Cincinnati in 1853, and Caroline Brown (later Winslow), who graduated from the Cleveland Homoeopathic Medical College in 1854—came to work in army hospitals during the war. Government officials refused to grant women the physician status or government contracts that their male counterparts received, but they did permit them to nurse the wounded. Edson and Winslow remained in the city after the war and helped to organize and staff the Homoeopathic Free Dispensary, the National Homoeopathic Hospital, and the Washington chapter of the American Institute of Homoeopathy. They were among the twenty women homeopaths who practiced in the city between 1870 and 1900, and who made up 20 percent of homeopathic doctors in Washington.[20]

The first white women regular doctors began to practice in the city somewhat later. They arrived in the 1870s. Isabel Barrows, an 1868 graduate of the New York Medical College for Women, opened her office in 1871 while teaching in the Howard Medical Department. Mary Spackman and Mary Parsons began practicing after their graduation from Howard in 1872 and 1874, respectively. In the next thirty years, approximately ninety white women trained in the regular practice of medicine entered the city's medical corps, their numbers and proportions increasing with each decade. The majority had graduated from local schools: forty-three from Howard, twenty-one from Columbian, and approximately twenty from National University and the Washington Homoeopathic College. Graduates of women's medical schools in New York, Philadelphia, and Baltimore, and from the coeducational medical departments of the Universities of Kentucky and Michigan as well as from several smaller proprietary medical schools also practiced in the city during those decades. Although their numbers increased steadily over the years and reached forty-two active practitioners in 1900, women regulars never made up more than 6 percent of Washington's regular medical corps. Before 1900, another one hundred women had enrolled in different medical, dental, and pharmacy departments in the city without ever graduating. Their annual enrollments also increased over the years. Altogether, approximately thirty women studied medicine in the 1870s, forty-two in the 1880s, and one hundred ten in the 1890s.

Black women formed a very small part of the corps of practicing women physicians and were almost always isolated from the activities of their white counterparts. Sarah Marinda Loguen, an 1876 graduate of the Medical College of Syracuse, was the first trained black women to practice in Washington. She established her practice as a regular in the city in 1880. Of the twenty-three black women who graduated from Howard between 1870 and 1900, approximately one-half, practiced medicine in the city at some time.[21]

At the time when trained women doctors began practicing there, Washington, like other cities in the United States, had an amorphous system of medical health care. On the eve of the Civil War, thirty to forty regulars had listed themselves in the city directory, along with five homeopaths, one or two eclectics, and scores of irregulars who offered their services as magnetic healers, cuppers and leachers, and Indian doctors.

A skeleton of medical associations and institutions existed, established by regulars earlier in the century. In 1817, a group of men who had been trained in Edinburgh and at the University of Pennsylvania Medical School organized the District of Columbia Medical Society. Congress chartered that group to license—or refuse to license—all doctors who wished to practice in the city. Some of the same physicians formed the District of Columbia Medical Association fifteen years later, in 1833, to set fees and maintain a code of ethics, functions that the society's charter did not permit.[22]

Elite doctors affiliated with these societies had established two medical schools before the Civil War: the National College of Medicine (1825), a proprietary or commercial medical school affiliated with Columbian College, and Georgetown Medical Department (1830), a school similarly run for profit and affiliated with Georgetown College. As was common at the time, administrators of both liberal arts colleges welcomed such departments. They gained the distinction of hosting a medical department while incurring no financial obligation for its operation.[23]

The prewar regulars also participated in the founding and staffing of several of the city's public health charities, including the Washington Asylum, the Government Hospital for the Insane, and the Washington Infirmary. These institutions reinforced the bonds between the regulars affiliated with the medical schools and public health administrators and brought added distinction to participating doctors.[24]

The Civil War years brought dramatic changes to the city and altered the composition and structure of the medical profession itself. Between 1860 and 1870, the population increased from 75,000 to more than 131,000. (Freed slaves, many of them needing medical care, comprised almost one-half of that increase.) The number of doctors rose correspondingly. The 87 physicians who were practicing in the city in 1860 almost doubled in number, to 161, by 1867. The majority who listed themselves in the city directory were regulars who had been military surgeons in city hospitals; 15 percent were homeopaths. Over the next three decades, the number of regulars increased tenfold and the number of homeopaths sixfold.[25]

These doctors contributed to the formation of several new medical institutions. Medical schools, dispensaries, clinics, hospitals, and associations all multiplied over the next thirty years. By the turn of the century, Washington boasted ten general and specialty hospitals and more than twenty clinics and dispensaries, all founded by doctors affiliated with the city's medical schools.[26]

The growth of these institutions was largely a response to the increasing numbers of those seeking medical education and training. Between 1870 and 1894, the number of medical students in the city grew by significant proportions as new schools opened and existing departments expanded. The medical department of Howard University, founded in 1869, joined Columbian and Georgetown. It averaged twenty-five students per year in the 1870s, and increased to more than one hundred students per year in the 1890s. Between 1870 and 1900, more than a thousand medical students trained at that school. In 1885, local physicians who were unable to secure posts at Columbian or Georgetown founded a rival school, the National University of Medicine. This small college added several hundred more students to the local medical school population before it closed in 1903. Georgetown University, which enrolled approximately forty students per year in the 1870s, admitted more than one hundred students each year in the 1890s. With Columbian's figures comparable, these two schools accounted for more than one thousand medical students training in the city in the last third of the century.[27]

Homeopaths did not remain idle. In 1870, in response to the adamant refusal of the Board of Examiners of the District of Columbia Medical Society to continue licensing members of their sect, homeopaths inveighed Congress to charter a sectarian medical association with the right to license qualified homeopaths. In 1882, these physicians organized the Homoeopathic Free Dispensary, and in 1885, the National Homoeopathic Hospital. In 1894, a few homeopaths also es-

tablished a short-lived independent medical school, the National Homoeopathic Medical College. Although only lasting three years, this
school also contributed to the upsurge in the numbers of trained physicians in the city.[28]

Women appeared to be gaining ground in the medical profession
just when their male colleagues were growing concerned about overcrowding in the field. Physicians in the nation's capital—as elsewhere
—began to take actions to limit the number of graduating doctors in
order to sustain a fair income and a high level of status within the profession. Women were primary targets among those considered super-
fluous. Beginning in the mid-1890s, a reaction against the training of
women physicians took shape in medical schools across the country—
even as women appeared to be winning coveted medical society memberships and hospital appointments. Numerous private colleges, like
Columbian in Washington, bowed to male student and faculty pressure and discontinued coeducation. As the cost of equipping medical
laboratories and surgical amphitheaters became prohibitive and the
need for hospital experience became essential, several women's colleges that had been operating on limited budgets closed as did other
marginally operating medical schools like the homeopathic college in
Washington. Between 1894 and 1904, enrollment of women in American medical schools dropped by one-third. Although women had begun to account for 15 to 20 percent of some medical school departments in the 1890s, they represented only 4 percent of all medical
graduates in 1905 and only 2.6 percent in 1915.[29]

Female registrations in Washington followed this pattern. In the
first quarter of the twentieth century, the proportion of women entering the medical community dropped almost 50 percent. In 1929, a
full generation after Washington's 1890 women doctors had entered
the practice of medicine, only thirty-one women practiced in the city,
down from forty-two in 1900. These physicians comprised 3.4 percent of all Washington doctors, compared to more than 6 percent at
the turn of the century; more significantly, half of the women had entered the practice of medicine before 1900. As the late-nineteenth-
century women physicians retired, there were few to take their places.
As the history of women's participation in the medical profession in
Washington demonstrates, the future that women's increasing numbers
seemed to promise in the nineties never materialized. The achievements of the women who trained in the last decades of the nineteenth
century, anticipating a new age for women, all but disappeared with
time.[30]

2

Demographic Characteristics and Motivations of Pioneer Women Doctors

"I Had All the Ambition of a Man."

"Humankind might be divided into three groups—men, women, and women physicians," Professor William Osler of the Johns Hopkins School of Medicine would say, teasing his women students in the 1890s. Osler's perception that women doctors were "a class apart" may have held some truth, especially in terms of the earlier women physicians whose activities on behalf of women's rights distinguished them from their contemporaries. But the majority of late-nineteenth-century Washington women who sought medical training were much like the men of their day. Principally white and native born, ranging in age from the mid-twenties to the mid-forties, undistinguished by superior education or elite social class, they were the daughters, sisters, wives, and widows of ambitious men who were creating the expanding ranks of the professional middle class.[1]

Generational experiences created important differences among these early medical women. The first group, the pioneers, were born before the Civil War and came to maturity during the ferment of antebellum libertarian movements. The nine black and thirty-seven white women for whom such information is available came to Washington to study or practice between 1865 and 1884 (the year Columbian University opened its medical school to women). The majority were devoted to such causes as abolition, universal suffrage, women's rights, and moral reform. Yet they differed in their family backgrounds and motivations. Young, reform-minded black women from the most elite stratum of antebellum black society made up one segment of the pioneer group; older white women's rights activists (primarily homeopaths) comprised another portion; and white women of various ages who had come to Washington alone and with their families to search for job opportunities made up the remainder.[2]

The later group, the post-pioneer women doctors, were born after the Civil War. Their life experiences and motivations, shaped by the heady expansiveness of the postwar years, differed markedly from those of their predecessors. The one hundred twenty-two women whose lives could be traced—twenty-three black and ninety-nine white—considered themselves "new women." More concerned with their status as professionals than with their identity as women, they rejected the model of sisterhood to which many of their predecessors had subscribed and sought instead the social and material rewards that the profession promised.

Washington was undergoing a vast demographic transformation when the first women seeking to be physicians arrived. The city's population almost doubled between 1860 and 1870. In that decade, white population increased 40 percent while the proportion of blacks rose 203 percent. Like their fellow white immigrants, a majority of white medical women came from mid-Atlantic or New England states. Seventeen of thirty-one women for whom such information is known were in this group. Five others were born in central states such as Ohio, Indiana, and Michigan, and six were foreign born (most in the British Isles or Canada). Significantly, only one of these women was a Washington, D. C., native; two others came from nearby Maryland.[3]

The early black women doctors, on the other hand, differed sharply in geographic origins from the vast majority of blacks settling in the city. Only one medical woman came from the South, the area that contributed the vast majority of newly arrived black residents. Another was born in Illinois. The rest came from three communities renowned for black abolitionist activity in or near Philadelphia, Pennsylvania, Ontario, Canada, and central New York State.[4]

Whether they were white or black, however, these women—and their families—were responding to the job opportunities that the burgeoning Washington economy afforded. Of the thirty-two white women whose economic backgrounds could be traced, the largest number, eleven, were single and self-supporting. They came alone to the city in search of a livelihood. Four of them had earned medical degrees even before they had arrived. Among them were Caroline Brown (later Winslow), an 1856 graduate of the Western College of Homoeopathy, and Susan Edson, an 1854 graduate of the Cleveland Homoeopathic College. Both women came to Washington to nurse the wounded during the war and remained to form the nucleus of an active female homeopathic community.[5]

17

Another five women also came to Washington alone, but they had been previously married and were widowed, separated, or divorced when they arrived. One of these, Mary Walker, had prior medical training. She had graduated from the Rochester Eclectic Medical College in 1855. When the war began, Walker left her physician husband to lead an independent life and work in army hospitals. She later took courses in the Howard Medical Department. Anna Bensich, another of these, was the widow of a medical practitioner. She enrolled in Howard shortly after her husband died. Although Benisch never graduated from the Howard medical program, she listed herself as a physician in the city directory and registered as a midwife with the Board of Health.[6]

Eight of the thirty-two pioneer white women doctors had come to Washington as young children. One of them, Lily Dent, was only four years old when her father, a physician from an elite Maryland family, accepted a clerical job in the Federal Register's Office. When Lily became eighteen, she worked as a counter in the Treasury Department, and three years later, while still employed, she entered Howard's medical program.[7]

Another eight women in the pioneer medical group were married and arrived in Washington with their husbands and children. Like some of their single colleagues, three had earned medical degrees before coming to the capital. Isabel Barrows, for example, was graduated from the Woman's Medical College in New York in 1868 and studied in Europe before joining her husband, who was stenographer to Secretary of State William Seward. New York native Francis Hillyer was one of the five married woman who studied medicine after they arrived in the city. Despite the problems of settling in a new city and caring for her two young children, Hillyer enrolled in Howard's medical program the same year that she arrived.[8]

Like most of these white women, many black women interested in medical study came to Washington because of available job opportunities. But the city's lively black community and opportunities at Howard University afforded additional inducements. In the 1870s, Sarah Marinda Loguen, a student at the Syracuse Medical College, corresponded with friends who had moved to Washington from Rochester, Albany, and Ontario. They lived with a local minister, Dr. Alexander Crummel, and his wife. The young women taught in the city's segregated school system and attended Howard University. They were "having the time of their lives," they wrote Loguen. In 1880, after completing her medical internship, Loguen joined them and lived with her married sister. At least one other pioneer black woman

18

came to Washington to live with members of her family. Eunice Shadd left her parents' home in Canada and moved to Washington to be with her brother Abraham and her older sister, Mary Ann Shadd Cary, a Washington elementary school principal. Shadd enrolled in the Howard University Normal School in 1870 and taught in the city's segregated school system before entering the medical program at Howard.[9]

Most of the pioneer women doctors came from middle-class or incipient middle-class households. Three of the twenty-eight white women, however, enjoyed upper-economic status. Annie Rice was the most elite of these three. Her father had been first consul to Japan during the Civil War and settled his family in Washington in 1875 when his term of office ended. Rice studied with private tutors in Japan and graduated from a female seminary in San Francisco. Jeannette Sumner, another student of means, lived in Washington with her brother, a commander in the United States Navy. Her father practiced medicine in Michigan. She and Rice studied medicine at Georgetown University and transferred together to the Woman's Medical College in Pennsylvania.[10]

A larger proportion, fourteen of twenty-eight, came from families where fathers, brothers, husbands, or the women themselves held jobs that reflected more modest middle-class circumstances. Cora Bland's husband, for instance, was a journalist, while Frances Mann's husband worked as a clerk in the government. Nine women were government clerks or school teachers. One, Ellen Sheldon, was her aged mother's sole support. She worked for the War Department as a copyist before entering Howard in 1879. Mary Spackman, widowed shortly after she and her husband moved with their young children to Washington in 1868, worked in the Federal Register's Office for two years before she entered Howard's medical department. She held that job while she went to school and until she established her practice.[11]

Only two of these white pioneers came from families that might be characterized as working class. Mary Hart's father was a janitor, and Mary Wooster's father, who raised six children after his wife died, was an unskilled laborer and drayman. Mary, the eldest of the Wooster children, studied in a business school and worked as a government clerk before she enrolled in the medical school. While employed during the day, she earned both medical and dental degrees. Two of her brothers also studied medicine while in government employ.[12]

An important difference in status distinguishes white women from black. Whereas white pioneers came largely from undistinguished middle-class households, Washington's black pioneer medical women all belonged to the most privileged stratum of postwar black society. Loguen's background was typical. Her father, the Bishop Jermain Loguen, had escaped from slavery to join John Brown in Canada. He later studied at the Oneida Institute and married a classmate. They prospered and owned their own home as well as several other properties near Syracuse, New York. The Loguens operated the most active station of the Underground Railroad on the East Coast. (During the war, they reputedly hid 1,500 runaway slaves in their "fugitive room" on the second floor.) Caroline Still was another Washington medical student from an elite black family. Her father, Benjamin Still, a wealthy sailmaker, had organized the Pennsylvania Society for the Abolition of Slavery, formed the Underground Railroad in Philadelphia and, with Robert Purvis, established the American Abolition Society. Eunice Shadd's background was equally distinguished. Her father, Abraham Shadd, a well-to-do property owner, rose to prominence as delegate to the American Anti-Slavery Society and president of the National Convention of Free People of Color. He was township counselor in Chatham, Ontario, and published a free press when Eunice was born.[13]

The privileged education that black pioneer medical women enjoyed also denotes elite status. Still, the best educated of the group, had been privately tutored at Mrs. Henry Gordon's school in Philadelphia and then attended the Friends' Raspberry Alley School and the Institute for Colored Youth. Before she studied medicine, she earned a B.A. from Oberlin and taught music and drawing at Howard. Three other pioneer medical women, Nanette Stafford, Georgiana Rumbley, and Rebecca Cole, also attended the Institute for Colored Youth in Philadelphia. Another, Kate Beatty, graduated from the Michigan Female Seminary.[14]

Such economic and social factors affected the ages at which pioneer medical women began to study medicine. Generally, white women were older than their black counterparts. The ages of twenty-seven white women that are known averaged thirty-one years at the start of their medical education. (Married women differed hardly at all in age from single women, but women homeopaths were among the oldest in the pioneer group.) Eleven of the white women were in their twenties when they started a medical program, twelve were in their thirties, and four were more than forty. Mary Parsons, one of the youngest of this group, entered Howard's medical school at the age of twenty-two after graduating from a New Hampshire seminary. She planned to study in New York with Elizabeth Blackwell but decided instead to enroll in the Howard program, which she considered superior. Mayne Marshal Pile was thirty-two when she embarked on a medical career. She had been married for fifteen years and was a mother when she enrolled in the Woman's Medical College of Baltimore. Pile and her husband moved to Washington following her graduation. Mary Eliza Hartwell, one of the older women to enter medical school, was in her mid-forties. She came to Washington from Ohio for a government job, then worked as a clerk in the Pension Office for three years before she enrolled in the Howard Medical Department.[15]

In contrast, all six black women whose ages are known started medical school when they were in their teens or twenties; their ages ranged from nineteen to twenty-eight, with an average of twenty-four years—seven years less than the ages of white pioneer medical women. Rebecca Cole, the youngest of this group, was only nineteen when she entered the Woman's Medical College of Pennsylvania in 1866. She served as a "sanitary visitor" in Elizabeth Blackwell's New York Infirmary before settling in Washington as physician to the Home for Dependent Colored Women and Children. Caroline Still was the oldest of the group, and her circumstances were unique. She graduated from Oberlin when she was eighteen, taught school for a year, and then married a minister. When she was twenty-five, widowed, and had a child, Still began her medical education.[16]

The attitudes toward women's rights that prevailed in many of the black pioneer women's households influenced the ages at which they began medical study. Most grew up in abolitionist households where spirited discussions of women's rights and social reform were daily fare. Loguen's home, for example, was a meeting place for social reformers of every philosophy. Frederick Douglass, a founder of the National Woman Suffrage Association, and activist Frances Watkins Harper were regular guests. (Douglass later hung Loguen's shingle outside her Washington office.) Both of Loguen's parents were active women's rights supporters.[17]

Still, who studied medicine at Howard for one year before transferring to the Woman's Medical College in Pennsylvania, also came from a household where women's rights were stressed, as did Eunice Shadd. Still's mother was closely associated with women from the Purvis and Forten families who, with Lucretia Mott and Angelina and Sarah Grimke, founded the Philadelphia Female Anti-Slavery Society. Eunice Shadd's sister, Mary Ann Shadd Cary (an abolitionist and women's rights activist like her father), became one of the first black female law graduates in the country. She organized the Colored Woman's Progressive Franchise Association in 1880, helped to found the American

Equal Rights Association, and held office in the National Woman Suffrage Association. She was involved in several of these organizations when her younger sister Eunice lived with her in Washington.[18]

Some of these early black women doctors received support from other quarters as well. When Caroline Still, Rebecca Cole, and Nannette Stafford attended the Institute for Colored Youth in Philadelphia, Sarah Mapps Douglass (no relation to Frederick Douglass) headed the girls' primary department there. Before assuming that post, Douglass had studied at the Ladies Institute of the Pennsylvania Medical University in a program that prepared women to lecture before female physiological reform societies. After her graduation in 1858, the first black woman to complete a medical program in the United States, Douglass introduced courses in anatomy and physiology into the institute's curriculum and may well have encouraged her young charges to pursue medical careers.[19]

The reform networks to which the families of black medical women belonged reached throughout the East Coast and further nourished their medical aspirations. Shadd and Still studied with Charles Purvis, professor at Howard's medical school. Purvis's family was part of the Philadelphia abolitionist community. His father worked closely with Shadd and Still's parents, and both father and son were ardent supporters of women's rights. Dr. Purvis often attended women's rights conventions in Washington with his wife and his daughter Alice, later a physician herself. The Loguen family also participated in this network through their Underground Railroad activities. Jermain Loguen frequently corresponded with Benjamin Still. Their daughters met when Sarah was a medical resident at the clinic of the Woman's Medical College of Philadelphia and Caroline was a student in that school.[20]

There is little evidence that white women enjoyed such family and community support for their unorthodox aspirations. Barrows was one of only four pioneers whose parents probably endorsed their daughters' medical aspirations. Her mother was an outspoken proponet of suffrage and dress reform, and her father was a Grahamite physician who lent his support to many social causes. As a child, Barrows often accompanied him on his rounds and assisted in surgical work. Although she served two years as a missionary in India, she was only twenty-three years old when she returned to America after her husband's death to study medicine.[21]

Ellen Sargent was another pioneer who enjoyed her parents' support. Her father, Senator Aaron Sargent of California, was a friend of Elizabeth Cady Stanton's and had introduced an early suffrage amendment. Young Ellen attended National Woman Suffrage Association meetings with her parents and decided at an early age to train herself for self-fulfilling work. She graduated from the Washington Business College when she was eighteen and entered the Howard medical program two years later with her brother. Shortly before her father finished his term of office, Sargent transferred to a women's medical college in San Francisco and there completed her degree.[22]

White women such as these came from exceptional families. For most, adult experiences rather than childhood socialization prompted a medical career. Caroline Brown Winslow, for example, grew up in Utica, New York, in an area noted for its ferment of antebellum reform. Her parents, who, according to one of Winslow's contemporaries, were "cultivated, intellectual, and highly respected" members of that community, opposed women's rights activities. They expected Caroline to remain in the family home until she married. When Winslow was in her late twenties, she spent several months at a water-cure resort frequented by women reformers. Her interest in a medical career stemmed from that experience and the influence of her doctors, Rachel and R. D. Gleason, trained eclectics committed to women's rights. They encouraged Caroline to enroll, against her parents' wishes, in the Eclectic Medical College of Cincinnati.[23]

Burghardt, another older student, was born in 1834 in Vermont and worked as a school teacher and then as a governess in the home of the poet William Cullen Bryant. When the war began, she answered the call for volunteer nurses and trained for three months at Bellevue Hospital under Dr. Elizabeth Blackwell. Assigned to Washington hospitals, Burghardt reportedly became one of Dorothea Dix's youngest and hardest working recruits. She remained in the capital after the war. Over the next several decades, Burghardt worked for the government and participated actively in women's rights organizations. It was not until 1876, when she was forty-two years old, that Burghardt enrolled in Howard's medical department.[24]

Unlike the black women who were linked by family connections to networks of support and encouragement, white medical women who emigrated to Washington alone or with their immediate families had few social resources upon which to draw. At least one group, the women homeopaths, created their own community of mutual support. It centered around meetings of the Homoeopathic Free Dispensary, a group established by women physicians and lay supporters, and the Moral Education Society (MES), a reform organization with a strong women's rights orientation. Almost every woman who entered the practice of homeopathic medicine in the city belonged to one or both of these groups. Residential patterns and informal networks of mutual aid reinforced the organizational commitments which these associations represented. In 1875, for example, Grace Roberts, an unmarried woman in her early thirties, came to Washington. She moved in with Winslow and her husband and enrolled in the Howard Medical Department. At the same time, she joined the Moral Education Society and served on its board. Mary Hart, another society and dispensary board member, followed Roberts into Howard and shared an office with Burghardt (also a member of both groups) upon her graduation a year later. Ellen Sheldon worked in the War Department for several years before she, too, decided to enroll in Howard's medical school. The year she entered Howard, she and her mother moved next door to Winslow. Margaret Hislop already possessed a medical diploma from the Hahnemann Medical College and Hospital in Chicago when she came to Washington. Before she opened her own office, she shared an office with Edson and Minnie C. T. Love, both homeopaths active in the Homoeopathic Free Dispensary. Between 1870 and 1885, nine such women joined the trained homeopathic ranks that centered around Winslow and Edson and these groups. An analysis of male physician and medical student residences fails to show a comparable pattern.[25]

Even as the number of activist homeopathic women physicians was increasing, their proportion of Washington's female physicians was declining. Beginning in the 1880s, the number of women entering the profession as regular practitioners began to rise. These newcomers represented the forward edge of a group of career-oriented, postpioneer regulars whose numbers would peak in the 1890s. The generation of the 1890s shared different values and espoused different motivations for studying medicine than had their predecessors. Unlike the pioneers who sought medical careers because they believed in the power of sisterhood to liberate women from social and economic oppression, the post-pioneers studied medicine to join the growing ranks of Washington's professionals; they believed they possessed all the rights they needed. Rejecting the woman-centered orientation of the immediate postwar generation, they sought acceptance into the medical fraternity as qualified equals.

Anna Garland Spencer, a women's rights activist of the period, remarked on a comparable shift in the membership of the women's movement itself. The early activists, she maintained, had regarded themselves as "martyrs and heroines" and relished their pioneer roles. They supported women's rights to secure not only their own advancement, but the advancement of others as well. When the next generation came of age, "learning [for women] . . . had become fashionable," she said. "Professional life [was] easy and attractive." The women who came to maturity then avoided women's rights activities. They considered political goals irrelevant to their personal and professional ambitions. Medical women among them, they sought instead the financial and status rewards that the professions seemed to promise.[26]

The post-pioneer generation of women doctors differed from their predecessors in numerous other respects as well. Far more had been born and raised in the Washington area than had been the case in the past. Of the ninety white women whose geographic backgrounds could be determined, twenty-six, or almost 30 percent, were native Washingtonians or came from nearby Maryland communities, compared to fewer than 10 percent of the earlier medical women. Mabel Cornish Bond was typical. Her father, a major, had settled in the capital during the war and stayed on as a clerk in the Treasury Department. Bond was born in the city and attended local public schools and Vassar College before she enrolled in a New York medical college.[27]

Another twenty-nine white women doctors and medical students, slightly more than 30 percent, came from the New England and the mid-Atlantic regions that had contributed more than half of the white pioneers. Amelia Frances Foye, a post-pioneer in this category, was born in upstate New York. She moved with her sister and her widowed mother to Washington when influential friends secured federal clerkships for her and her sister.[28]

The numbers and proportions of women who came from the West also shifted in the postwar decades. Earlier, only 15 percent of white women doctors came from Ohio or states and territories west. Now, twenty-four of ninety, or about one-fourth, came from that region of the country, with several from states beyond the Mississippi. Carrie Davis, for example, was born in Ohio, received her early schooling in Missouri, and attended normal school in Kansas. She was homesteading there when she decided to move to Washington to study medicine with her sister, May Davis Baker.[29]

The distribution of white women from the South also changed. Among the post-pioneers, six white women came from cities below the Mason-Dixon line, but not one white woman had originated there in the earlier group. One such southerner was Margaret Magnon York, a Louisiana native of French Creole and Scotch-Irish descent. She taught school in Galveston before she moved alone to Washington to work in the Post Office Department. After her marriage and the birth of her daughter, York entered medical school.[30]

As with the early group, foreign-born women were minimally represented (only five of the ninety). But more of the post-pioneer women traced their origins to Germany, where a tradition of trained midwives prevailed, rather than to the English-speaking countries from which the foreign-born pioneer doctors had originated. They included Mary Strobel, a graduate of the National University Medical Department, Amelia Ehrbach, a graduate of Columbian, and Anna Bartsch (Dunne), a graduate of Howard.[31]

The shift in geographical origins is notable for black post-pioneer women as well. Here, too, more women were natives of the Washington, D. C.-Maryland area than before, six of twenty-three, or approximately 25 percent, compared to none of the earlier group. Jane Eleanor Datcher was the daughter of freeborn blacks who had long resided in Washington. She studied in private schools run by the city's black community and then attended Cornell University before she entered the Howard Medical Department. Significantly, the New England region and Canada, which had contributed the majority of black pioneer medical women, played an insignificant role in the origins of the later group. Now only one of the twenty-three black medical women came from this area: Harriet Riggs, a native of Maine. When she secured a teaching job in the city school system, Riggs moved to Washington with her widowed mother.[32]

The shift in black post-pioneer women's southern orgins was also striking. Whereas only one black woman had come from a southern state in the early group, almost half, eleven of twenty-three postpioneers, were born there, several in Virginia. Ionia Whipper was not among these. She was born even further south, in South Carolina in 1874. Her father, a member of the elite Philadelphia black community which advocated women's rights, had moved to South Carolina after the war. There he became a respected circuit court judge and married Francis Rollins, a member of the prewar free black community of Charleston.[33]

The shift in the proportion of black women originating from the West is as notable for the states from which they came from as for the increase from that region. Earlier, one medical woman had been born in Illinois. Later, five women came from such states as Iowa, Tennessee, Wisconsin, and Ohio. Artishia Gilbert, one of these, was born in Kentucky, where her father was an itinerant miner. She received her M. A. from the state university there and her M. D. from Louisville National Medical College before she moved to Washington to study at Howard.[34]

A more subtle shift is apparent in the social class origins of postpioneer black and white women. Like the earlier medical women, a majority of these came from, and were contributing to, the city's growing white-collar and entrepreneurial middle class; few traced their origins to the wealthy classes from which the male leaders of Washington's white medical community came. For late-nineteenth-century women, black or white, the more elite the family, the more likely the opposition to a medical career—or to any career. In Washington's white community, for example, Madeleine Dahlgren, author of *Etiquette of Social Life in Washington*, the society matron's bible, epitomized this view. She insisted that her daughter Ulrica withdraw from the Washington Committee for the Woman's Medical Fund of Johns Hopkins, a group raising money to ensure the opening of the Johns Hopkins University Medical School to women. Even though the philanthropist and socialite Phoebe Apperson Hearst coordinated the Washington branch of the Hopkins plan, Dahlgren found the notion of women physicians untenable.[35]

The situation of Rosalie Slaughter Morton, a white physician who practiced in Washington in 1903, demonstrates this attitude. Born into an aristocratic Virginia family, Morton became a physician despite her parents' strenuous objections. In her autobiography, *A Woman Surgeon*, she relates how her mother refused to allow her daughter to "move in constant danger of contagion" and be "at the beck and call of rude, uncouth people." Her father voiced other objections. "I do not want my daughter to earn money," he declared. "Your field of service is to keep on making us happy, and later to marry a man of your own class. It is essential," he continued "that society's standards be maintained." To Morton's plea that she wanted to be of service to society like her brothers who were physicians, her father responded, "I would feel that all my efforts as a lawyer, banker, citizen, and father were defeated if my daughter prepared herself to go to work. It is unthinkable that you should do so."[36]

Morton put aside her dream of becoming a physician, although she had received encouragement from one of her brothers and from her Quaker aunts. But when her father died, she returned to her original plan. Ironically, his failure to provide adequately for her in his will— assuming she would marry and be cared for—forced her to become self-supporting. Morton refused aid from her brothers and used a small annuity to cover her medical school expenses at the Woman's Medical College in Philadelphia.

Financial exigency thrust one Washington woman from this elite class into a medical career. Emily Cowperthwaite, a student in Columbian's medical school in 1890, was the daughter of a Philadelphia publisher. Before the war, contemporaries considered her father "one of the most respectable merchants of high social power in the city."

Forced to find employment for himself after he lost his fortune, he prevailed upon his contacts to secure positions in the government for his daughters—"ladies of real refinement." Emily taught school, worked in a federal office, and graduated from the Washington Training School for Nurses before she enrolled in Columbian's medical department.[37]

No black post-pioneer medical women came from a comparable level of society. Black men of this postwar economic elite—the so-called *creme de la creme* of black society—were as vehement in their opposition to daughters' or wives' career aspirations as were their white counterparts. The attitude of Mary Church Terrell's father, a member of this new class, epitomizes the views of his peers regarding professional employment for women. Terrell, a Washington educator, was a close friend of several of the city's post-pioneer black women doctors. After her graduation from Oberlin in 1884, she considered accepting a teaching job at Wilberforce College. Her father, reputedly one of the wealthiest men in Memphis, threatened to disown her. "Since he was willing and able to support me," Terrell explained in her autobiography, "he did not understand why I wanted to teach or do any kind of work." He was a former slave, she said, who had adopted the aristocratic prejudices of his past masters. "In the South for nearly three hundred years," Terrell wrote, "'real ladies' did not work and my father was thoroughly imbued with that ideal. He wanted his daughter to be a lady." Terrell disregarded her father's wishes and suffered his displeasure. She had been reared in the North by her mother, "among Yankees," she said, and she embraced the "Yankee respect for work [and] a life of usefulness."[38]

The wealthy may have rejected careers for women, but some families comfortably settled in, or aspiring to, the expanding professional and entrepreneurial ranks encouraged that option. Approximately 35 percent of white post-pioneer medical women, twenty-seven of seventy-eight whose backgrounds could be traced, came from families headed by high-level professional men like physician Robert Reyburn and astronomer Simon Newcomb. Reyburn, the son of a widowed Scotch immigrant and later a professor of medicine at Georgetown and Howard medical schools, had struggled himself to achieve professional distinction from modest beginnings. Both of his daughters graduated from the National University Medical Department in 1895; one of them, Eugenia, entered her father's medical practice.[39]

Newcomb, another celebrated Washington professional, directed the Naval Observatory in Washington, taught at the Johns Hopkins University, and helped to establish several of Washington's most prestigious professional associations. He, too, rose above his humble beginnings. The son of a tanner and saddle maker in Nova Scotia, he served an impoverished apprenticeship to a botanic physician before coming to Washington and marrying Caroline Hassler, daughter of a Washington physician. The Newcombs cultivated the career aspirations of their eldest daughter, Anita, later a physician. Simon Newcomb frequently took Anita with him on scientific expeditions and to professional meetings and regarded her achievements with pride. After she presented a well-received paper at the national conference of the American Association for the Advancement of Science in 1888, Newcomb told a colleague that he felt as elated as a "medical student who just experimented with hasheesh."[40]

The twenty-seven women in these comfortable white middle-class ranks included ten women who joined their professional husbands as professionals in their own right. May Davis Baker, for example, entered Columbian's medical program the same year that she, her husband, and their child moved to Washington when he accepted a position as assistant director of the Washington Zoological Park.[41]

As with women of more secure means, unforseen circumstances thrust some women of this advantaged class into the ranks of the employed. Jessie Kappelar, for instance, had to support herself and her two young children when her husband, a prominent real estate attorney, died suddenly. Capitalizing on his former political connections and on her fluency in languages, Kappelar secured a job with the Census Bureau at the same time that she enrolled in medical school. She wrote her supervisor when she graduated that "every beginning is hard. . . . But mine has proved as successful as I could possibly expect." Clara Bliss Hinds, the daughter of a prominent Washington physician, found herself in similar straits when her husband deserted her and their three-year-old daughter. "A degree meant bread and butter to me," she told a reporter.[42]

A similar proportion of black medical women, seven of the eighteen whose status could be determined from city directories and the census, came from comparably situated families—despite the recent emancipation of their race and the economic and educational restrictions confronting them. Although not among the most well-to-do of their race, members of this group still enjoyed a comfortable lifestyle and community status. A contemporary reported that they "live in fine houses and surround themselves with luxurious refinements of life." "They dress in the latest styles," the observer noted in 1883, "and attend influential churches, frequent the concert, lectures, and theatre."[43]

Alice Waring was one of this group. Her father, the Reverend

William Waring, moved to Washington in 1872 from Oberlin, Ohio, shortly after his daughter was born in order to accept an appointment as clerk in the Treasury Department. During the next twenty years, while his children were growing up, he managed a construction business and started one of the city's first black-owned banks even while he worked at his government job. Alice Waring was one of several Waring children to achieve professional status. Her sister became a Washington principal; her brother graduated from the medical school, became a principal in the Washington school system, and was ultimately appointed superintendent of the Baltimore segregated schools. Other women in this group included Sarah Garland Jones, whose father was a well-known building contractor in Richmond (her sister also became a doctor and her husband studied medicine), and Ionia Whipper, whose father was a circuit court judge.[44]

Because professional opportunities in areas other than the ministry were just materializing for American blacks, some fathers in these ranks were preparing themselves for medical careers at the same time as their sons and daughters. The family of Mary Louise Brown is illustrative. Brown's father, the Reverend John Mifflin Brown, attended Howard's medical school soon after the university opened, only two years before his sons enrolled. Frequent reassignments, during which he helped to organize several southern black colleges, prevented him from finishing a degree, but three of his sons as well as his daughter did complete their professional schooling at Howard. One son became a minister, another a doctor, the third a teacher.[45]

Unlike these women from privileged ranks in both the white and black communities, the majority of Washington's ambitious post-pioneers came from more modestly situated middle-class or working-class families: fifty of seventy-eight white women for whom such information is known. The majority worked in white-collar jobs as clerks, school teachers, bookkeepers, and salespersons as did their fathers, brothers, sisters, or husbands. Mary Holmes, a graduate of the National University Medical Department, for example, was a government clerk as were her father and sister. Another sister taught school. The Holmes family rented quarters in a neighborhood with other clerks, bookkeepers, printers, and petty bourgeoisie businessmen. The fathers of Pearl Gunckel, Alice Koogle, and Augusta Pettigrew (the women, Columbian students in the early 1890s) were, respectively, a bookkeeper, a bill collector, and a draftsman.[46]

Only five white women came from families considered working class. Louease Lenman, a graduate of the National Homoeopathic Medical College, fits that description. Lenman's mother, the widow of a fireman, kept house for her son, a blacksmith, and for her two daughters. One daughter was a bookbinder in the Government Printing Office. The other, Louease, was a dressmaker and sold women's "fancy goods" and perfumes while studying medicine. Amelia Ehrbach's background is also illustrative. Her father, a German immigrant, was a cooper and brewer. She worked as a servant before she attended nursing school and enrolled in Columbian's medical department.[47]

Given the limited occupational opportunities that blacks experienced, several of those considered working class by virtue of family members' occupations actually held higher status in the black community. Fathers and sons in this group worked as barbers, waiters, bartenders, and draymen; wives and daughters were seamstresses. Sons and daughters from these ranks became leaders of Washington's professional middle class. The father of Louise Tancil, for example, was a barber, her mother a dressmaker. Tancil graduated from Howard's medical program and married a physician. (Her brother became a doctor in Washington as well.) Lucy Moten was the most distinguished of Washington's professional black women. She was the principal of Howard University Normal School and a medical school graduate. Her father had been a messenger in the Patent Office and a barber.[48]

Just as differences emerged in the social status and geographic backgrounds of the post-pioneers relative to their predecessors, so too did a shift in the ages at which they undertook medical study. Once again, black women were younger than their white counterparts when they entered medical school. The average age for twenty-three black women was 26.4 compared to 29.5 for sixty-two white women. This 3.1 year difference, contrasts sharply to the seven years that separated the ages of black and white pioneers. (The average age of the black post-pioneers was 26.4 compared to 24 for the pioneers; the average age of white post-pioneers was 29.5 compared to 31 for their predecessors.)[49]

The ages of the post-pioneers were not tending toward a mean. On the contrary, quite young black women and older white women were still enrolling in medical schools just as they had before. But now, more older black women and more young white women were joining them, creating a bimodal age distribution. Young women, black and white, primarily single and ranging in age from eighteen to twenty-four, made up one segment of the post-pioneer female medical student body; older women, black and white, married and single, primarily in their mid-thirties, comprised the other.

Several factors contributed to the increase of women from different age cohorts into the pool of female medical students. Favorable publicity about women doctors, especially items featured in women's rights journals and local newspapers, enhanced the legitimacy of medical careers for women; too, Washington women doctors' increasing numbers and their greater visibility enabled them to serve as role models for women of all ages; finally, medical educational opportunities for women expanded in the city. Medical study came within reach of many more women with Columbian's admission of women in 1884, National University's initiation of coeducation in 1888, and the opening of the coeducational National Homoeopathic Medical College in 1892, in addition to Howard's long-standing program.

These factors, combined with the exuberance with which women in the 1890s had begun to consider higher education and professional training, created a growing cadre of women who looked upon themselves as "new women" with the "new woman's characterisitcs and ambitions," in the words of Julia Pearl Hughes, a black medical student who graduated from Howard in 1897. Married and single, black and white, youthful and middle-aged, they desired a life's work from which they could earn a comfortable income, enjoy the respect of their neighbors, and engage in work more satisfying and remunerative than the teaching, clerking, and nursing then available.[50]

When Dr. Bertha Van Hoosen outlined her reasons for seeking a medical career in her autobiography, *Petticoat Surgeon*, she probably voiced the sentiments of many of her Washington contemporaries. Van Hoosen, a graduate of the University of Michigan Medical School in 1888, freely admitted that she sought a medical career because she desired the "material necessities" a physician might own: "a horse and buggy, an office, a home and personal servants." She also valued the "social status a member of the learned profession" earned. But, most important, Van Hoosen wrote, she longed for the independence that a medical career made possible, the chance "to be [her] own boss, . . . to be able to say . . . [as had her father], I can speak my mind on any subject . . . I am a free man." Alice Hamilton, another contemporary, echoed similar sentiments in her autobiography, *Exploring the Dangerous Trades*. She chose medicine above careers then available to women, she said, "because as a doctor I could go anywhere I pleased. . . . I should meet all sorts and conditions of men, I should not be tied down to a school or a college as a teacher, or have to work under a superior, as a nurse must do."[51]

Two Baltimore physicians of the 1890s, Lilian Welsh and Mary Sherwood, recalled being drawn to medicine by the excitement of scientific undertakings. "We were two ordinary women who had looked forward from early girlhood to the possibility of self-support," Welsh wrote in *Reminiscences of Thirty Years in Baltimore.* We "had gone into teaching because it was the only profession with any intellectual outlook." The two doctors tired of teaching and, with a keen interest in "science and human nature," Welsh said, they followed their "intellectual bent" and entered medical school.[52]

Like these women—all single—a growing number of late-nineteenth-century women pursued medical study because they regarded independent, self-supporting careers as a positive alternative to marriage—not as a necessary fallback in the event they failed to marry. In 1888, a contributor to the *Alpha,* the journal of the Moral Education Society edited by physician Caroline Winslow, forcefully expressed that notion. "A woman who has open before her the broad avenues of usefulness, who has ambition and energy to develop her powers, will not be satisfied to tie herself down in the soul-cramping marriage," the author wrote. The new woman, she added, "has learned woman's highest duty to herself and humanity demands her full development as a *Woman,* not as a *Wife* or a *Mother.*"[53]

Women in the black community shared this attitude. Many faced the prospect of having to "marry down" in social class or educational attainment because the pool of men of comparable status was limited. Anna Cooper, a friend and colleague of Washington's black women doctors, encouraged her contemporaries to pursue careers instead of marriage, especially since their marital prospects were bleak. In an essay published in 1893 entitled "The Higher Education of Women" the Oberlin graduate and teacher in Washington's elite M Street High School wrote that "the old subjective, stagnant . . . life for woman has gone." No longer do women have to marry because they lack the resources and opportunities for independent self-support, she said. Education and "the self reliance which it gives, renders woman less dependent on the marriage relation for physical support" which, Cooper emphasized, "does not always accompany it." Indeed, in 1896, a contributor to the *Bee* echoed that sentiment. "Working women don't care to marry," the author wrote, "because the inducement is very poor and the man they may tie to gets only starvation wages. Women should look out for their own future happiness," the author concluded.[54]

Some married women of the period embraced the ideology of financial independence and self-reliance as ardently as did their single colleagues. They, too, regarded themselves as "new women" and sought opportunities for personal growth through higher education and rewarding, productive work. Anita Newcomb McGee, a married physician, was one of their advocates. McGee urged "intelligent wives and daughters of well-to-do business and professional men" to consider careers and meaningful work when she spoke at women's clubs on women's "progress toward self-respect and individuality." Addressing the Daughters of the American Revolution on one occasion, McGee expanded on her view that the woman who devoted herself exclusively to domestic duties and failed to develop her own potential endangered her physical health and "dwarfed and narrowed" her intellect. Speaking as a physician, McGee urged the woman of talent and ability to pursue a career or other activity outside the home in addition to the "wifely and motherly duties which she now performs in return for her husband's support." Her unborn children—even the "nation and the whole of her race"—McGee prophesied, would profit from the "Woman who raised herself above the average."[55]

McGee credited her husband, William J. McGee of the Bureau of Ethnology, with providing the support necessary for her professional undertakings. "One of the first things I learned," the newly graduated physician told a group of women on another occasion, was that "distinguished man as he is, [he] expected his wife to have an identity of her own." He was one of a growing minority of men, she boasted, who supported their wives' ambitions with "no fear of being a nonentity in the family."[56]

Surveys of the period indicate that Anita and W. J., as he was known, were not unique; approximately one-third of all nineteenth-century women doctors were married. (These studies are based primarily on data for white women.) Washington's female medical school graduates reflected this pattern. Among white post-pioneer women, at least twenty-five of eighty-three students whose marital status was known had married before entering medical school. (Eight of these had been widowed or divorced before they started medical training; the other seventeen were living with their husbands.) At least another eight married after graduating. Of the black post-pioneer women for whom such information is known, five of twenty-one married before entering medical school, four married later, and twelve remained single.[57]

Married women's reasons for entering the medical profession hardly varied from those expressed by single women: They needed to contribute to the family income, or they desired challenging, self-fulfilling work. Some shared the feelings expressed by Sara Newcomb Merrick, Anita McGee's aunt, when she complained to Simon Newcomb, her brother, just a few months before her niece's graduation from Columbian that she felt stifled by her domestic routine. "I cannot be satisfied as most women are with household and social duties," she wrote; "I am doing nothing now but existing." Less than three years later, Merrick shared the news that she had "resolved at last to gratify the burning desire of her life." "I am taking a medical course in one of the most highly scientific colleges in the country," she wrote Simon. "The wonders revealed by the microscope and in the Physiological laboratory as well as in the dissecting room are a never ending source of enjoyment." Merrick was fifty years old at the time. I "utterly disprove the assertion that you cannot teach an old dog new tricks, in other words, that one cannot successfuly take up a new line of life or study when past middle age," Merrick added. She later graduated with "honorable averages" in thirty-four exams and practiced in Boston.[58]

If, like Merrick, a married woman eschewed club and philanthropic activities, few avenues for self expression or remunerative work outside the home—other than writing or operating a school (both of which Merrick had tried)—were available. Salaried jobs for married women were all but impossible to obtain. In Washington, government departments and private-sector offices hired married women only under the most extenuating circumstances. The Washington public school system followed an unwritten policy against hiring married women and, on more than one occasion, discharged women who married.[59]

Flexible medical schedules permitted women to combine family life with a career. Anita McGee, for example, not only conducted office hours in her home during hours compatible with the family's schedule, but during the summer months she closed her practice so that she could take her young children away from the stifling city. A medical career also allowed married women to earn additional income for the family. Wage-earning employment—if it could have been obtained— would have detracted from a couple's social status and cast doubt on a husband's ability to support his family. A private practice could have been justified on humanitarian grounds without jeopardizing the couple's standing in the community.

Other women sought medical careers because of the examples of male—and female—relatives. Fathers and brothers served as role models for daughters and sisters as traditionally they had for sons and brothers. At least nine white women were the daughters of trained physicians, and six were the sisters. In the black community, it was the brothers, rather than the fathers, who preceded the women into the medical fraternity. The brothers of Louise Tancil, May Louise Jones, and Alice Waring all studied at Howard before their sisters enrolled. Another three medical women had grandfathers who practiced medicine. Two of Amelia Erbach's uncles were healers of a different sort; one was a "cupper and leecher," the other a "dentist-surgeon." Even

35

husbands' medical careers influenced wives' decisions. Five pioneer and nine post-pioneer white women were married to doctors when they entered medical school.[60]

Female relatives provided equally valid role models, although they lacked formal training themselves. Among the white women, Mary Parsons's grandmother had been a midwife or "granny" in northern New Hampshire. Mary Strobel's mother considered herself a physician, but she was probably a midwife. The family's neighbors in Laurel, Maryland, regularly called upon Isabel Haslup's mother for her herbal remedies and surgical skills. Among black medical women, Sarah Loguen's mother had provided essential medical care for many of the seriously ill and wounded fugitive slaves who sought refuge in her home, and according to some accounts, Ionia Whipper's mother had studied medicine. Sisters were equally influential. In the white community, Haslup's sister studied nursing along with Daisy Orleman's before the younger women entered medical school. May Baker was studying at Howard when her sister joined her there, and Adeline E. Portman willed her medical instruments to her sister, a Michigan physician. Alice Burritt, who graduated from the New York Medical College and Hospital for Women, influenced her sister-in-law to study medicine at Howard. Both practiced homeopathy. Sarah Garland Jones, the black physician who practiced in Richmond, Virginia, had a sister who was a physician.[61]

In maintaining a family custom as in other respects, women doctors resembled their male counterparts. But whether late-nineteenth-century women were carrying on a family tradition or initiating one, they blazed new trails. Undoubtedly, they were above the average in ability, energy, and ambition. Many were neither content to achieve vicariously through their husbands, fathers, and brothers, nor satisfied with the traditional remunerative work and leisure activities assigned to their sex. They wanted "to make more and be more" at a time when new horizons appeared to be opening for women and men alike. Although their numbers were small, they were increasing. Unfortunately, women doctors found themselves embarked on a collision course with male colleagues who believed that the profession already suffered from oversupply. The struggles late-nineteenth-century women doctors faced in wresting concessions from men in the profession foreshadowed the difficulties their successors would encounter for decades to come.

3

The Howard University Medical Department

"Without Regard to Race or Sex"

Howard University offered women—both black and white—the first opportunity for medical study in the Washington area. Between 1869 and 1900, 103 women enrolled in the medical school (30 black, 57 white, and 16 whose race could not be determined.) Approximately half graduated (23 black and 25 white). The proportion of women in the medical school reached 24 percent in the 1870s (6 of 25 in 1875), but dropped to 2 percent in the early 1890s (2 women of 110 students) when white women abandoned the school. They chose to attend newly available programs in segregated white institutions rather than study at Howard's medical department, which by then had become disproportionately black and male.

Segregation at Howard in the 1890s contrasted sharply with founders' intention of creating a coeducational, racially integrated institution that would rank among the first in the nation. At first, founders had a more limited goal in mind. In 1867, members of the Missionary Society of the First Congregational Church of Washington met to establish a divinity school for black men only. But with support from the Freedmen's Bureau and from Radical Republicans in Congress, they broadened that goal and decided to set up a university with preparatory, teacher training, and agricultural schools, and departments of law and medicine. General Oliver Otis Howard, director of the Freedmen's Bureau and the school's leading proponent, and Senator Samuel Pomeroy of Kansas, an advocate of women's rights, convinced their cosponsors to admit whites as well as blacks, women as well as men, to the school.[1]

Soon after the medical department opened in 1868, the faculty placed notices in local newspapers and in the school's catalogs inviting women to attend on the same basis as men. Victorian norms of propriety, however, dictated separate dissecting rooms and "other conveniences" for women. The faculty also delivered separate lectures to women in subjects "unsuitable to the general class." The first woman enrolled in 1869.[2]

Despite such apparent support for female students, faculty members were actually divided in their attitudes toward medical coeducation. Black physician Charles Purvis was one of women's chief supporters. A member of an illustrious Philadelphia abolitionist family committed to women's rights (his own father opposed the 14th and 15th Ammendments because they disenfranchised women), Purvis attended annual meetings of the National Woman Suffrage Association with his wife. He later encouraged his daughter to become a physician. Abolitionist Robert Reyburn, a white colleague of Purvis's on the medical school faculty, also supported women's rights and, like Purvis, encouraged his daughters to pursue medical degrees.[3]

Other faculty members harbored reservations about coeducation, and were even opposed to the principle of higher education for women. Silas Loomis, for example, dean of the faculty and a founder of the medical school, was a former abolitionist who championed black education. Yet he vigorously opposed female higher education. In 1870, a few weeks after the first group of female medical students completed their first term, Loomis presented a paper, "Longevity of Women," to the District of Columbia Medical Society. In it, he blamed a seeming increase in maternal mortality during childbirth and a decline in American fertility rates on young women who pursued higher education. Like others of his time, he believed that intellectual activity during puberty competed biologically with the maturation of the female reproductive organs and caused irreversible damage. Anticipating Edward Clarke's *Sex in Education: A Fair Chance for the Girls,* a highly influential condemnation of higher education for women published in 1873, Loomis declared that "forced activity of the brain" during puberty sapped the "vitality of the developing sex organs." Loomis was willing to acknowledge that women students could excel in their studies, but he warned that they would pay the price of being incapable of bearing and nursing normal children. Even more ominously, Loomis introduced the specter of abortion and feticide in his text, subjects that preoccupied many physicians of the time. He claimed that an educated mother's "enfeebled condition" inclined her toward committing such acts. Because male physicians of the period accused women doctors and midwives of performing abortions and used that pretext in their attempt to drive women from medicine, Loomis's criticism had a double edge when viewed from the vantage point of his women students.[4]

Another faculty member expressed his hostility toward women students more openly. According to formal charges brought against Alexander Augusta by two women students in February 1873, the black director of the anatomy laboratory regularly denied women the materials they needed to perform dissecting assignments. Augusta's attitude apparently reflected male student sentiment, because the women also complained of "ill treatment and insults" from the men in their class.[5]

Such treatment was hardly unique. In the late nineteenth century (and beyond), female medical students experienced disruptions in their daily educational routines and harassment both in and out of class. Dr. Isabel Barrows, a member of the Howard faculty who had resigned just weeks before the incident involving Dr. Augusta, complained of similar treatment in her own school days in New York. The "dignified medical students of Bellevue," she said, showered spitballs on the women in their medical class and made their studies painfully difficult. Barrows observed that her professor invariably "laughed at their insults." She was convinced that he had a "sneaking desire to do the same, not approving of petticoats coming to his clinic."[6]

Medical women recorded similar experiences elsewhere. Cora Hawkins, a medical technologist whose father taught at the University of Michigan during this period, reported in her autobiography, *Buggies, Blizzards, and Babies,* that "in the early years it was the honest conviction of male medical students everywhere that women had no place in their school." They literally sought ways of "smoking the girls out," she said, by "blowing cigar smoke in their faces." Men also monopolized scarce material, equipment, and working space, and neglected to "pass along word about any change in schedule or a special assignment." On occasion, male students used more direct means of ridding a school of women. Threatening a boycott, men at the Chicago Medical School petitioned the faculty in 1869 to dismiss the women who had been admitted the previous year. The faculty capitulated, ending that school's short-lived policy of coeducation.[7]

Howard faculty members, however, refused to condone such behavior. After investigating the complaints, they formally directed the dean of the medical school to inform all parties guilty of these "discourtesies" of their "disapprobation" in the "strongest terms" and to "announce their inflexible determination to carry out to the letter, the spirit and the intent of the organic law of the university." The women's interests, they declared, "shall be equally cared for under any and all circumstances." The faculty replaced Augusta soon thereafter.[8]

The school's newly formed alumni association also took a direct interest in the controversy. The group read a strongly worded resolution before the assembled class, which condemned discrimination against women students as "unmanly and unworthy of the profession." Discrimination rested upon "selfish interest or ignorant prejudice," the resolution stated, and it had to be abandoned. "We highly appreciate and honor intellect and capacity . . . without regard to nationality or sex," the alumni declared and concluded their statement by demanding for women "the same rights and immunities that we demand for ourselves."[9]

Those rights, however, remained elusive. For twenty years, the faculty denied senior women students three-month residency appointments to Freedmen's Hospital and assistantships in the dispensary and laboratories. They also refused to grant laboratory or clinical appointments to women until 1897, although women had formally complained since 1876. Similarly, the faculty denied women teaching appointments usually granted to new graduates. A woman had been appointed to the staff in the early years, however. Imbued with the liberal vision of the founders, the faculty risked the censure of the American Medical Association by hiring Isabel Barrows in 1871 to teach ophthalmology and to supervise all treatment of eye and ear disorders at Freedmen's Hospital. Although Barrows, an 1868 graduate of the Woman's Medical College of the New York Infirmary, had studied in Vienna and qualified for the Pomeroy Professorship in Opthalmology, she served at the level of instructor, in part—some said—to avoid the AMA prohibition against employing female medical professors. The ploy failed to satisfy the ethics committee of the AMA, however. At its annual convention in 1872, AMA officials barred Howard's biracial delegation and used Barrows's appointment to justify their action. Samuel Busey, a Washington doctor who served on the national board, warned Howard's staff that continued defiance of the AMA's prohibition against hiring women would jeopardize the medical department's status in that body.[10]

The AMA's chastisement served its purpose. After Barrows resigned in January 1873, the medical school replaced her with a male physician. Although the AMA soon thereafter changed its policy regarding women instructors, the Howard staff did not appoint another woman to the faculty for more than twenty years, despite the presence of numerous qualified women doctors in Washington. In 1893, they elected Mary Morrison, a white graduate, class of 1886, to teach pediatrics in the nursing school affiliated with Freedmen's Hospital. The following year, the faculty engaged Julia Hall, a black graduate of the class of 1892, as instructor of gynecology. Isabel Haslup, a white alumna—Howard '97—held that post between 1898 and 1900. None of these women ever held the title of professor.[11]

However ambivalent the faculty's attitude toward the female presence, women appreciated the opportunity available, and their numbers rose. Between 1870 and 1880, five or six women matriculated in each medical school class, thirty women in all. Because class size averaged thirty-five students, women accounted for approximately 15 percent of each class. In some years, 1875 and 1876 in particular, women comprised more than 20 percent of the class (24 percent and 22 percent, respectively).[12]

During the late 1880s, however, women's enrollments began to decline numerically and proportionately. By 1890, two women—both black—comprised 1.7 percent of a class of 115 students. The following year, two women registered with 124 men. A sharp decline in white female enrollment largely accounted for this decrease. In the 1870s, most of Howard's female students had been white (twenty-two white, four black, four whose race is not known). A similar proportion of white women attended in the early 1880s. But after the Columbian and National Medical Departments opened to women, the number of white women at Howard declined. At the same time, the number of black women students increased. Between 1890 and 1894, three white and thirteen black women attended Howard's medical classes. The number of white women rose slightly between 1894 and 1898, when Columbian University medical school closed its doors to women, but it soon declined again.[13]

White male enrollments also declined during this time. The exact racial mixture of Howard male medical students is difficult to determine until 1891, the year for which precise figures are available, but incomplete records suggest that white men comprised between 50 and 70 percent of the medical student body during the 1870s and for much of the 1880s. Minutes of the 1881 faculty meeting, for example, show that 65 percent of the class of 1881–82 was white. Records for 1887–88 indicate a slight decline to 59 percent. In 1891, the proportion of white men dropped further, to 33 percent. By 1897, white students made up only 14.1 percent of the class.[14]

Several factors contributed to the declining number of white students at Howard, not the least of which was the worsening quality of medical education at that institution. At its beginnings, the Howard

Medical Department had been a source of pride to its founders—and of envy to its rivals, the medical school faculties of Georgetown and Columbian Universities. The school's organizers developed an ambitious program of medical study that included a five-month term and a graded course of study. The longer term gave students two months more of medical study than other local schools offered. More important, the graded program enabled them to choose from a wide selection of courses. Thus, first-year students studied anatomy, physiology, microscopy, chemistry, and toxicology, while second-year students took more advanced courses in materia medica, advanced chemistry, medical jurisprudence, advanced anatomy, pathology, and diseases of women and children. Such grading of classes, from elementary the first year to more advanced the second year, represented a pedagogical departure. Most medical schools of the period, even those offering high-quality education, offered courses in no particular sequence. During the second year, students repeated courses they had attended during the first with the hope of acquiring a better grasp of the material at the second sitting.

General Howard's supplement of the school's operating budget with Freedmen's Bureau funds made such a curriculum possible. In 1868–69, for example, the cost of salaries and lecture material amounted to almost $8,000, whereas income from tuition totalled only $700. The Bureau made up the difference. Bureau funds also helped the medical department recruit experienced and well-trained faculty members. Unlike proprietary medical schools (such as Columbian and Georgetown) where professors shared income from tuition after deducting expenses, Howard's medical department guaranteed its instructors an annual salary. Few schools could match the $1,000 the department offered most of its part-time staff. The school had such excellent financial resources that it tried to lure a professor from Harvard, Dr. George F. Barker. (He refused the $3,000 full-time offer, demanding at least $5,000 to compensate for Washington's high cost of living.) Several Georgetown faculty members responded to such inducements, among them Silas Loomis and Robert Reyburn, key faculty members on the Georgetown staff. Reyburn's appointment to Howard's department was particularly critical, because as chief medical officer of Freedmen's Hospital he guaranteed a reciprocal relationship between the school and the hospital.[15]

Bureau funds also enabled faculty members to introduce innovations into the plan of study. Freedmen's Hospital facilities gave doctors the opportunity to offer surgical, diagnostic, and treatment clinics. Members used stereopticon slides—a marvelous novelty—to illustrate diseases and microscopical organisms. General Howard also used federal funds to construct a hospital and medical classroom building worth $150,000 at no cost or obligation to the school. Rival medical faculties, struggling with mortgage debts and expansion costs, could hardly conceal their envy.

At the outset, affiliates of local medical schools regarded the newcomer as "a much more dangerous rival" than its neighbors, according to Joseph Taber Johnson, a professor at both Georgetown and Howard. He reported that Georgetown faculty members feared that within a few years, Howard would "have more endowments and more students" than their own school. To a degree, such fears were justified. In 1875, for example, Arthur Glennon, the son of a local white doctor, switched from Georgetown to Howard, where he believed "the best clinical facilities were afforded." Other white students attended Howard because the bureau subsidized reduced tuition fees.[16]

Johnson warned General Howard that Georgetown staff members planned to discharge Loomis for having affiliated with the new school. Because of Reyburn's access to Freedmen's Hospital clinical facilties and his excellent reputation, Johnson said, the Georgeown faculty were loath to lose him. They planned instead to coerce Reyburn into resigning from Howard by presenting him with an exceptional offer combined with an ultimatum. Johnson feared that Reyburn's departure would deliver a "staggering blow" to the new medical school, and he prevailed upon General Howard to intercede. Forewarned, the general and the board of trustees offered Reyburn a higher salary to remain with the Howard Medical Department and give up his Georgetown post.

Unfortunately, the medical school's reputation was short-lived. Within a few years of its founding, Howard fell victim to changing race relations and the animosity of rival faculties. White doctors in Washington deliberately isolated physicians affiliated with the interracial medical college. Fear of economic competition as well as racial antagonism motivated their behavior. In his 1874 report, Gideon Palmer, a former abolitionist who was dean of the Howard medical faculty, complained of the difficulty in hiring medical faculty. Several doctors who had consented initially to be candidates, he reported, later declined. "Discouragements were thrown around those physicians who were solicited to fill the chairs," he wrote. Moreover, he said, "prejudice which still exists among the medical profession, at least, against those who are connected with this institution," had damaged private practices as well.[17]

The local medical society also made it difficult for black doctors to practice or to consult with white colleagues on the same faculty. Members of the segregated medical organizations in the city denied membership and attendant consultation privileges and professional courtesies to Howard's black faculty members. Dr. D. Willard Bliss, a highly respected member of the white medical community, publicly defied the ban and consulted with black physician Alexander Augusta. The District of Columbia Medical Association, the official body of the profession, promptly expelled him. Five years later, his lucrative practice severely reduced and his livelihood threatened, Bliss apologized publicly to the society and requested reinstatement.[18]

Howard's faculty members discovered that opposition to racial integration and coeducation isolated them even at the national level. National associations used published regulations against the hiring of female teachers and the admission of women students as the justification for imposing sanctions against the school. Conventions of the American Medical Association in 1870 and 1872, for example, refused to seat Howard's interracial delegation on that pretext. The Association of American Medical Colleges, which had accepted Howard's delegates in 1872, denied recognition to that group in 1877. Again, antagonism against women rather than against blacks formed the basis of stated objections. The association accused Howard's medical staff of violating the groups' ethics by instructing women and men in the same classrooms, avoiding entirely the issue of race which many felt was at the heart of the complaint.[19]

Such prejudice affected the students as well. Faculty members of Georgetown and Columbian denied Howard medical students access to medical lectures and clinical demonstrations, both because of their rivalry with Howard and because of their prejudice against black students. Eventually, white Howard students did receive permission to attend those sessions; black students were able to attend demonstrations at Freedmen's Hospital only. Howard's faculty withdrew the names of the offending hospitals from the medical school catalog.[20]

The closing of the Freedmen's Bureau in 1872 and the economic depression the following year had an even greater impact on the quality of medical education at Howard. The withdrawl of bureau funds left the medical school with few financial resources upon which to draw. At first, faculty members hoped that rising enrollment would compensate for the loss of their backers, but the depression eliminated that possibility. The number of students in the medical department, which had doubled after the first two years and then increased sixfold by 1871, dropped 60 percent in 1873 at the height of the financial panic.

All departments of the university suffered from the drastic curtailment of funds. The school itself seemed on the verge of dissolution. The trustees reduced by half the salaries of members of all departments and cut off entirely all funds to the medical and law departments. Based on past enrollments, they calculated that the professional schools could survive on tuition alone. Medical and law faculty were forced to accept a percentage of net income after expenses instead of a guaranteed salary. The majority of the medical staff, Reyburn and Johnson among them, objected to those terms and left the institution. Their departure left gaps in the medical curriculum that remained unfilled for almost two decades, seriously weakening the school's offerings.

The remaining faculty took a bold step that kept the medical program alive—but barely. In a radical departure from practice anywhere in the country, they recommended that the school eliminate tuition altogether but retain matriculation and graduation fees. Members hoped that the federal government ultimately would endow the school on a permanent basis. Between 1874 and 1880, Howard Medical Department charged no tuition whatsoever. By 1880, economic conditions in the city improved sufficiently to allow the trustees to reinstate a modest tuition fee, which was still well below the school's needs. Two years later, the executive committee allocated funds for medical school expenses and salaries. The infusion of money helped the department stay afloat; it did little to improve the deteriorating quality of the medical facilities, however.

During the years of economic crisis, 1873–82, faculty members had no choice but to minimize expenses even at the risk of seriously undermining the quality of medical education. In 1873, the staff reduced clinical instruction to two times instead of five times weekly and limited laboratory work to instruction in the operation of a microscope. Even securing cadavers for dissection proved prohibitively expensive. At times, twelve students instead of the customary four shared one corpse.[21]

Despite these problems, student enrollment remained relatively constant after 1873. Because the Howard faculty maintained a low tuition policy relative to other schools, it managed to attract government clerks who could not otherwise have afforded medical school. A medical education at Howard from the 1870s to mid-1880s cost almost nothing during some years, or at most only half as much as at Georgetown or Columbian during other years. The Howard faculty's decision to retain a two-year course until 1883 and a five-month term until 1889 also increased Howard's attractiveness to students more concerned with earning a degree quickly than with the quality of their education. (Columbian and Georgetown had adopted three-year, seven-month programs in 1878 and 1879, respectively.)

Howard's fortunes began to improve in the early 1890s. As the economy rose in the 1880s, the trustees authorized several tuition increases. In 1892, students paid the same for a Howard medical education as did students at other local schools. Income from investments and a successful contribution campaign enabled the medical school to build a surgical amphitheater and a histological laboratory and to modernize the bacteriological laboratory. Concerned for quality, the faculty extended the term to six months in 1889, and adopted a four-year course in 1890.

These improvements came too late, however. The Howard medical program had fallen too far behind by the 1890s to recoup the losses that it sustained. From a racially integrated medical college whose student body was almost equally divided between whites and blacks, Howard had become an almost wholly black institution. After the mid-1880s, white students who could choose schools of considerably higher quality—at the same tuition—found little advantage to enrolling at Howard. Black students, male and female, had no local alternatives. Howard remained the only area school that would admit them.

The proportion of black students at the college would have increased merely by the attrition of white students. At the same time, however, a whole generation of black men and women came of age who had been born into freedom after the Civil War. Spurred on by what they viewed as an opportunity to secure a foothold in the middle class, they began to enter Howard just when white students began to transfer away. At some point near the end of the eighties, a critical moment was reached when black students constituted more than one-half of the medical school student body. From that time, enrollment of whites decreased even more rapidly each year. By 1897, only twenty-two white students enrolled in a class of 156.[22]

As white male enrollment dropped, white female enrollment declined as well. Fewer white women attended Howard, not only because of the changing racial composition of the school but also because they could now attend the more prestigious Columbian Medical School or the young National University. Degrees from those schools ensured greater status than a Howard medical diploma, both because they were all-white and because Howard's early reputation for quality had deteriorated. Indeed, proponents of female medical education argued that it would "do injury" to the quality of medical care in the capital if Columbian's discontinuation of coeducation limited women to Howard, an "institution of lower grade."[23]

When Columbian did close its doors to women in 1893, Howard's medical department reaped temporary benefits. In 1894, eight white women matriculated in a class of seventeen women, more than had attended in any one year in the 1870s or 1880s. Similar numbers registered each year for the next few years. By the end of the decade, however, white female enrollment dropped again. By then, women who had originally planned to study medicine at Columbian—some of whom had come to Washington and taken federal jobs for that purpose alone—either fulfilled their ambitions at Howard or found other alternatives. After 1895, white women interested in medical training knew well in advance that Columbian was closed to women and made arrangements elsewhere. After 1900, the proportion of all women attending medical classes at Howard varied from 2.5 percent to 7 percent, far from the former high of 24 percent. White women were scarcely represented in those classes. The number of black women enrolled in the department simply could not compensate for their loss. Thus, although Howard's policy toward women remained steadfast, the school played a diminished role in female medical education after 1895. Increasing prejudice that drew the color line at Howard drew the line against women doctors as well.[24]

4

Proprietary Medical Schools

"The Line Is Drawn Against the Women."

The history of coeducation in Washington's proprietary medical schools during the 1880s and 1890s demonstrates the role that finances played in determining women's opportunities to study medicine. During the last decades of the nineteenth century, each one of Washington's four proprietary schools experimented with coeducation. Georgetown, Columbian, and National medical schools admitted women during periods of real or imagined fiscal crises, Georgetown in 1880, Columbian in 1884, and National in 1889. Georgetown and Columbian discontinued coeducation, Georgetown after one year and Columbian after eight. Opponents of coeducation in those schools regained the upper hand when it became clear that the departments would survive unaided by women's tuition. National collapsed in 1903. Women's added tuition proved inadequate to ensure the school's survival. The fourth proprietary school, the National Homoeopathic Medical College, a small medical department that had admitted women from the outset, closed after three years because it was severely undercapitalized.

To their dismay, women discovered that no strategy dissuaded faculties from ending coeducation once they set upon that course. Neither behind-the-scenes pressure, pledges of financial support, nor public expressions of outrage affected the decision to rid a school of the female presence. A plan to establish a women's medical college connected with Columbian (with $15,000 pledged to ensure its opening) also failed. Never fully endorsed by the faculty—nor by medical women themselves—the proposal lost momentum when Johns Hopkins opened in nearby Baltimore as a coeducational school of the first rank. Hopkins, however, proved not to be the wave of the future that women had hoped. Instead, the policies that Washington commercial

48

schools pursued anticipated the course of female education over the next few decades.

Georgetown University became Washington's first commercial medical college to admit women when the faculty experimented with co-education in the 1880–81 school year. Before they made that decision, the faculty and the Jesuits who ran the preparatory school and liberal arts college had witnessed severe retrenchments. Following the Civil War, the school lost its traditional southern constituency. Located on the outskirts of Washington, it failed to attract civil servants interested in upgrading their positions by attending college courses in the evenings. The medical school, located near downtown, fared somewhat better than the college, but its federally employed students were subject to political vagaries and easy dismissal.[1]

By the mid-1870s, college administrators were seeking desperately for a solution to the school's economic problems. Provoked by a further downturn in enrollments in the wake of the 1873 economic crisis, Joseph E. Keller, father provincial of Georgetown, and Patrick Healy, vice-rector, met with the faculties in "extraordinary consultation" to explore ways of meeting the crisis. Healy took the initiative. Instead of counseling further retrenchment, he urged the departments of the college to expand and seek a national constituency. Healy's daring plan required an additional outlay of funds at a time when the college was already burdened with debts, but he convinced the representatives of the liberal arts, law, and medical departments to borrow money to enlarge their departments and improve their facilities.[2]

As a chemist himself, Healy took a personal interest in upgrading the medical department. The medical faculty, however, bore the entire risk and expense. In 1876, at his urging, the senior faculty adopted the first of several innovations. Several retired with the rank of professor emeriti, and the department hired younger physicians to take their places. Joseph Taber Johnson of Howard's medical department and Samuel Busey, founder of Children's Hospital, were among the rising stars the faculty hired. Both were prominent in emerging specialties —Johnson in gynecology, and Busey in pediatrics. These men brought renown to the college while adding vigor to the medical curriculum.[3]

The faculty instituted even more daring revisions the following year. They extended the course of study from two to three years and lengthened the semester from five to seven months, steps that premier institutions such as the University of Pennsylvania and Harvard had reluctantly undertaken. Schools were loath to adopt the longer term recommended by the American Medical Association with good reason: Sharp enrollment declines forced departments that had adopted such schedules to retreat to the shorter term. By 1880, only 8 of 128 medical colleges in the country offered a three-year course.[4]

Georgetown's action increased the direct costs of medical study for students by at least $125 and raised indirect costs for the extra year of medical study, factors that threatened to drive away all but the most determined and well-to-do. Healy and the medical faculty accepted those risks. They recognized that premier medical schools would have to adopt the AMA's recommendation or be at a serious competitive disadvantage.

At Healy's instigation, the faculty introduced other changes designed to improve the quality and the reputation of medical education at Georgetown. They scheduled courses in an ordered sequence of difficulty instead of allowing students to repeat the same courses each year in no particular sequence, and they instituted examinations at each level to ensure that only those who had mastered the material could proceed. The faculty also offered new courses in areas representing the specialties of the younger men, enhancing the scope of the medical program.

These innovations considerably reduced the already low registrations. The first year they took effect, 1876, enrollment dropped by half, from eighty to thirty-seven. In 1878, only four medical students graduated from the department, down from seven the year before. Enrollments rose slightly in 1879 but then dropped again in 1880. Faculty members took small consolation from the congratulations that they received in 1883 from the secretary of the Illinois Board of Health, who cited "the small percentage of your graduates to matriculate" as a mark of the program's excellence.[5]

In 1880, with no improvement in sight, coeducation's proponents convinced their colleagues to consider two women who had applied to the medical school, Annie Rice and Jeannette Sumner. Rice and Sumner were ideal candidates in many respects. Both were well-educated women from comfortable professional families. Rice, who was twenty-eight, lived with her father, a retired lawyer who had served as first consul to Japan in 1862. Her brother Nathan lived in the same household. He was recently graduated from Georgetown medical school at the top of his class. Sumner, who was thirty-five, lived near Rice with her brother, a lieutenant commander in the Navy. Her father practiced medicine in Michigan.[6]

At least two doctors on Georgetown's staff lobbied for women's admission. One, Joseph Taber Johnson, professor of obstetrics and gynecology and, in 1880, president of the faculty, had taught women at Howard's medical school before joining Georgetown. There, he had worked alongside ophthalmologist Isabel Barrows, a physician whose training exceeded that of most doctors on Georgetown's staff. Johnson was also active in the effort to admit blacks and women into Washington medical societies in the 1870s. In addition, his wife, Maud Bascomb Johnson, was a member of a family prominent in female education: Her father, a founder of Howard University, helped to ensure that school's policy of coeducation, and her sister had just graduated from Vassar.[7]

Samuel Busey, women's other proponent, was also a physician of considerable influence. A former president of the elite Medical Society, he supported medical coeducation partly because of his own experiences as an undergraduate, when he had trained with women preparing to be midwives. With Johnson, he had encouraged the local medical societies to admit women, and just two years earlier, in 1878, he had attempted to amend the bylaws of the Washington Medical Society so that women doctors could consult professionally with society members.[8]

Other faculty members appeared more ambivalent. Dr. James W. Lovejoy, for example, the professor of materia medica and a former president of the District of Columbia Medical Society, was unsure about women's future in the profession, but recognized that justice demanded that they be accorded certain rights. Earlier, he had insisted that medicine "was not the calling of women" and went on record opposing the training of women doctors in "mixed" classes or coeducational medical schools. He even declared their increasing numbers "an evil." Yet at Medical Society meetings in 1874, Lovejoy defended the rights of practicing women physicians by supporting consulting privileges for them. Justice for women physicians—and for their patients—demanded such professional courtesies, he said. Lovejoy's ambivalence toward women doctors, combined with Georgetown's bleak prospects, may well have prompted him to accede to the admission of Rice and Sumner to the medical class of 1880.[9]

All evidence points to the women's successful completion of the first year of medical study. But at the end of that year, they transferred to the Woman's Medical College of Pennsylvania. There they received full credit for the year spent at Georgetown. Available records offer no clue to their decision to leave, but the Georgetown faculty may well have decided to simply discontinue the experiment. After the women's departure, they refused all other female applicants. In 1884, for example, they turned down a request for transfer from a first-year student of the Woman's Medical College of Pennsylvania whose father was a physician. Several years later, in 1898, the faculty also denied the application of a woman who had a B.A. from Wellesley and an M.S. from Columbian, although they did permit her to attend a special class in anatomy. (The applicant, Louise Tayler-Jones, later earned the M.D. from Johns Hopkins.)[10]

Registrations in the medical school showed little improvement after Rice and Sumner's departure. The faculty blamed low enrollments on the lengthened course of study and the lack of adequate facilities. Rather than increase their numbers with women's enrollments, they decided to upgrade the school to attract more men. For this, they turned to the Jesuits. In 1886, the host college agreed to invest $18,600 in a new medical building and to pay the interest on a $50,000 loan that the medical department had incurred. These changes and improved economic circumstances in the city eventually provided the outcome that the medical faculty sought. In 1890, the department boasted a student enrollment of more than one hundred men. Barely a memory remained of women's presence in the medical school ten years earlier.

A comparable experiment with coeducation at National University's College of Medicine took a different turn. National was founded by a group of doctors, covetous of the status of physicians affiliated with Georgetown and Columbian medical schools, who had joined with others in a plan to create a comprehensive, government-supported graduate and professional institution for white students only. When fulfillment of these plans seemed too distant, the physicians involved in the project proceeded with their own school. Confident that the government would ultimately adopt the comprehensive university scheme, they persuaded then-president Chester A. Arthur to sign their diplomas.[11]

National's faculty lacked the status and financial advantage that colleagues at the other proprietary schools gained from university affiliation. At the outset, they were unable to raise sufficient capital to meet the competitive challenge of their rivals. As a contemporary observed, the failure of "a very elaborate scheme . . . involving the outlay of a considerable sum of money" forced National to postpone indefinitely the construction of laboratories and clinics. Student tuition, the only source of income, barely met expenses. Between 1885 and 1890, twenty to twenty-five students attended per year, compared to almost one hundred at the other schools. With tuition at $100 per student, approximately the same as at Howard, Columbian, and Georgetown, National's corps of fourteen professors had little to invest or to share after they paid expenses. The National faculty's decision to admit women to medical classes in 1889—women had been successfully attending Columbian since 1884—was consistent with its need for additional revenue.[12]

At first, National's commitment to women was less than wholehearted. Faculty members prohibited women from attending classes they deemed immodest for mixed groups, but failed to schedule comparable courses for them. After 1892, however, when Columbian discontinued coeducation, the National faculty redoubled its efforts to attract women. A notice in the *Woman's Journal* in 1893 announced that the "National Medical and Dental University has thrown its doors even wider open than before and cordially invites the women to share all its privileges equally with male students." That year, "to accommodate the female medical students," the faculty appointed two women doctors to the staff. Mathilda Gallagher, an honors graduate of the previous year, became demonstrator of obstetrics, and Mary Morrison, one of Howard's most promising alumna, became assistant demonstrator of anatomy. While these positions were the least prestigious on a medical staff, they did represent a concession to women students and the only opportunity in the city for women doctors to acquire faculty positions. Faculty members abolished Morrison's job the following year but retained Gallagher in her post until 1903, when the school merged with Columbian.[13]

National's efforts to attract women students succeeded. Only three women had enrolled in National in 1891, but fourteen registered in 1892 following Columbian's dicontinuation of coeducation. They made up 21.4 percent of the class of 1892–93 compared to 6 percent the previous year. Thirteen enrolled in 1893–94, the last year for which figures are available. Approximately ten of Washington's women doctors graduated from National before it closed.[14]

In the beginning, women found the students and the faculty courteous. In 1892, Ella Marble, one of the school's first-year women students, noted that the young men "spring . . . quickly to place a chair for a lady when she enters the room, assist the ladies on with their wraps and lift their hats to them gracefully." One would never suspect, Marble tellingly observed, that these women were "their competitors for college honors, and possible rivals in their profession." As the novelty of women students wore off, however, men awoke to the significance of the female presence. Three years later, Marble wrote in a letter to the *Woman's Medical Journal* that every woman could tell "a tale of persecution, injustices or insult . . . because of her desire to learn to care for the sick and suffering in an intelligent and scientific manner." Marble did acknowledge being well treated "by every *intelligent* male student," however.[15]

Despite such difficulties, Marble appealed to readers to aid the "young college struggling for a place among the older and more favored ones." "It needs money very much to provide such equipment as a first-class college should have," she repeated elsewhere. "It would be nice if women could help them in return for their helping woman." National, however, could not attract benefactors. Its financial problems continued unabated, and in 1903, the school merged with Columbian's all-male medical department. Columbian refused to accept National's female students. Some women transferred to Howard, the only remaining coeducational medical department in the city; others left Washington to study elsewhere or abandoned medical study altogether.[16]

Like National University, the National Homoeopathic Medical College, another school that admitted white women before 1900, succumbed to undercapitalization and the rising costs of medical education. The school opened in 1893 and closed three years later. Its brief existence was clouded with controversy. In 1895, the city's dentists hired an attorney to take the dental department to court. In a legal manueuver, the faculty changed the school's name to the Washington Homoeopathic Medical College. When officers applied in 1896 to reincorporate, the District of Columbia Board of Health officer successfully opposed that action. He claimed that the National Homoeopathic College had been discredited, and he demonstrated that the same men were planning to operate the new school without any changes in curricula or facilities. The school closed that year, but during its three years of operation, it did graduate several medical doctors, two women among them. Its truncated history—like that of National's—demonstrates how dependent women were on the financial status of the marginally operating schools that were willing to admit them. The inferior quality of education at those schools and their uncertain status proved more problematic than helpful to women's entry into the profession.[17]

One commercial medical school in Washington, the National College of Medicine of Columbian College (not to be confused with the National University College of Medicine), did offer white women an extended opportunity for superior medical education. The success women enjoyed there beginning in 1884 made it that much more difficult for them to accept the school's abrupt cancellation of coeducation in 1892. A group of prominent physicians organized the medical department in 1825, four years after the college itself opened. The undergraduate and preparatory schools depended primarily upon southern students (most from Virginia) and the school found itself with a vastly reduced student body at war's end. The medical department fared somewhat better than the college, but throughout the 1870s, when bankruptcy plagued the host institution, the medical staff took an active interest in the affairs of the college. Affiliated physicians recognized that their future lay in the continued operation of the college.[18]

By 1880, a worsening situation demanded action. Both the college and the medical school were in serious straits. The college's debts had climbed to more than $10,000. With taxes unpaid, bankruptcy loomed. At the same time, medical school salaries reached the lowest point in the school's postwar history. As a stopgap measure, the college officially adopted the medical school and declared it an "integral part of the university system" in order to save money on taxes by securing tax-exempt status for the medical school property. School officials also fixed faculty salaries at $1 per year. But medical faculty and college adminstrators sought even more comprehensive measures. "We must remodel our course of instruction, adapt it to the wants and surroundings of the city and bring it into the midst of those we would instruct," President James Clarke Welling declared, as he called for a "plan for the entire reconstruction" of all the departments of the university.[19]

Welling constituted a special committee for this purpose and in 1883 appointed Major John Wesley Powell, popular chief of the Bureau of Ethnology, to direct its efforts. Powell's own background inclined him toward favoring higher education for women. He counted several women scientists among his professional staff, and both his wife and sister were active suffragists. After weeks of deliberation, Powell's group presented its formal recommendations. As mandated, the plans did promise to alter the very nature of the institution. Central was a proposal to sell the existing undergraduate college campus at the outskirts of the city and move classes to a downtown location near the medical school. Funds from the sale would defray some of the school's indebtedness, and a downtown campus would enable the departments to attract white-collar clerical workers who could attend late afternoon or evening classes. Members of the panel also urged all of the departments to reevaluate their curricula and offer "what people will pay for learning." Their recommendation that the college recruit "people of every class" similarly reflected a major shift in emphasis to broaden the student base.[20]

The admission of women to the school was implicit in these recommendations. The committee stopped just short of recommending that policy schoolwide, however. "The admission or exclusion of women students should not be decided by a hard and fast line applying indiscriminately to all the Schools and Departments of the University," members stated. Rather, each department was urged to base its decision on "comparative expediency" following "an expression of opinion . . . from all the members of each Faculty."[21]

Responses varied. Columbian's law department rejected the committee's recommendation outright. Its faculty maintained that the "admission of women into the Law School was not required by any public want." The Corcoran Scientific Department, scheduled to open in 1884, decided under Powell's leadership to admit women. Simon Newcomb and Lester Frank Ward were on that department's staff. The faculty of the other major department, the medical school, vacillated. Without a doubt, the faculty recognized that the school could use an infusion of students. The immediate postwar spurt of enrollments had steadily fallen from about seventy students in 1870 to slightly more than forty after the financial panic of 1873, where it remained until the late 1870s, when it dropped once more. At that time, the department, in response to Georgetown's challenge, lengthened the school's term to five months and the program to three years. Part-time students who worked as government clerks switched to Howard University's medical department, where the semesters were shorter and the two-year program less costly.[22]

Faculty salaries at Columbian, reflecting declining enrollments, averaged less than $300 per year between 1870 and 1882 in contrast to salaries of the law deparment faculty, which averaged $2,400 annually. Full-time liberal arts professors earned $2,000 a year. Medical professors did expect to supplement their teaching with income from student tutorials and from their private practices, but by 1875, a smaller proportion of students sought faculty preceptors. Even with income from private practices, the return from the medical school was disappointingly inadequate. Modest increases in student enrollment in 1883 and 1884, the result of an expansion in the size of the Pension Bureau staff, raised each doctor's share to $350 and then to $425, figures still far below comparable salaries in other college departments.[23]

Dim enrollment prospects and a critical need for funds to improve the facilities encouraged the Columbian medical faculty to consider coeducation, a possibility not entirely alien to the participating doctors. In 1855, two women had requested admission, but the department had turned them down. The issue arose again in the late 1870s, when enrollments had dropped sharply. At that time, some Columbian faculty members had admitted women to their classes—unofficially. According to reports, the women had fit comfortably into the medical school routine, and the faculty had recommended to the board of trustees that the department formally adopt coeduction. The trustees, however, hestitated to go that far. As one of them later recalled, we "hum'd and haw'd . . . and squirmed in our seats, as men do when they do not know what to do." "Every one of us was in favor of the higher education of women," he said, but when it came to the vote, "the vote was 'No!'"[24]

Ironically, in 1883, when Columbian's board of trustees was willing to approve coeducation, it was the medical faculty that hesitated. Although they acknowledged that "woman has a mission in the medical service of the future," faculty members officially denied the applications of four women candidates, citing inadequate facilities as the reason for their refusal. Faculty members were far from united in their decision, however. Several did permit the applicants—Clara Bliss Hinds, Sarah Scull, Ellen Cathcart, and Alice White—to attend their lectures "without matriculation or other official recognition."[25]

Like the women admitted to Georgetown, Columbian's first female students came from the same class of people as the doctors themselves. Hinds, the daughter of popular Washington physician D. Willard Bliss, had been one of Washington's most popular debutantes. She had always wanted to become a doctor, but her father had refused to allow her to consider that possibility, even though both of her brothers attended medical school. Courting her father's disapproval, Hinds had applied to medical schools when she was a young woman. After she received "many rebuffs," she said, she gave up hope for a medical career and married. Within a few years, however, after she divorced her husband, Hinds again applied to the Columbian Medical Department (with the encouragement of Dr. Mary Parsons). At the time, she was thirty-two years old and responsible for her young daughter's support. Alice White, another applicant, had also been married previously. Little else is known about White, but she chose William Lee, an advocate of women physicians, as her preceptor.[26]

The other two candidates, Scull and Cathcart, apparently had no intention of practicing medicine. Single, self-supporting teachers, they undertook medical study in order to follow their scientific interests and to advance their careers. When Scull entered the program, she was a teacher at the exclusive Mt. Vernon Seminary for girls. She later became its associate principal. Her intellectual interests were highly eclectic and included a year of archaeological research in Greece. Cathcart, forty-four years old, taught in the public schools of the District of Columbia. Several years of medical study enabled her to leave teaching for a job in the prestigious scientific Department of Agriculture.[27]

The four women had successfully completed the first term by December. On December 10, 1884, they applied once more for formal admission. Couching their letter in terms guaranteed to reassure rather than alarm fellow students and faculty, they stated their purpose was to "make a thorough and progressive study of Biology, the physiological relations of Psychology and of medicine," and to benefit by the "superior advantages otherwise unattainable, [that] would open to them in the Lectures of members of your distinguished body."[28]

This time, the faculty approved their petition. Members forwarded the letter to the board of trustees with their recommendation that the trustees admit women "on the same footing" as men. Apologizing for their apparent inconsistency, faculty members acknowledged that it "may appear somewhat wayward on the part of the Faculty to have changed its decision." But since their earlier response in September, they said, they had discovered that coeducation was workable. The women had demonstrated that "the inconveniences from want of proper retiring rooms [which the faculty thought would be an obstacle to their attendance] is not in reality an insuperable difficulty, but one with which they [the ladies] are quite willing to put up with." More significantly, the faculty concluded that "no objection on the part of the male pupils has been made to the admission of females."[29]

The united front that the medical faculty presented belied differences among the members. The dean of the faculty admitted to the college president that "a bare majority" favored the admission of women. "For the sake of harmony," he said, "the vote was made unanimous." William Lee, Elliott Coues, and Edward Fristoe were probably three of the seven voting members who supported coeducation. Lee, professor of physiology, served as preceptor for Hinds and White and remained a loyal supporter of women. In 1890, he helped to incorporate and consulted at the Woman's Clinic, a facility staffed entirely by women. In 1892, when Columbian discontinued medical coeducation, Lee remained loyal in his commitment to coeducation. He was the only faculty member who refused to sign the order to make that decision unanimous.[30]

Coues, another ally of women students in the department, created a sensation and gave up his position over the issue of coeducation, however, when he delivered an inflammatory commencement address in

March 1887, the year Hinds graduated from the medical school. In his speech, "A Woman in the Case," Coues, an advocate of women's rights, questioned what had taken the school and American society so long to allow women "to do and be all that she would were she free to act out her whole nature." He answered his own question by attacking religious and social conventions in such an inflammatory manner that the faculty refused to publish the professor's address as was customary. Coues printed the essay at his own expense and resigned in protest. Advocates of medical coeducation lost a much-needed ally in the process.[31]

Fristoe, professor of chemistry and dean of the soon-to-be-opened coeducational Corcoran School of Science of Columbian, was women students' third ally. When he died in 1892, women mourned his loss, recalling that he had been a generous "friend and advocate" from the start. D. Webster Prentiss may have been the fourth member to support women's admission. The year before women's admission, Prentiss, professor of materia medica, had agreed to serve on the board of the Women's Dispensary, a clinic established by Rice and Sumner when they returned to Washington after graduating from the Woman's Medical College of Philadelphia.[32]

These men had adversaries among the faculty. According to a contemporary, "there had always been three members . . . who were bitterly opposed to allowing women to study medicine on any terms." Albert Freeman Africanus King, dean of the faculty and professor of obstetrics and the diseases of women, may well have been one of these. In 1887, for example, a few years after women began attending the medical college, King delivered a diatribe against female higher education. In his presidential address before the Washington Obstetrical and Gynecological Society, he asserted that civilization and higher education had "perverted and misdirected" women's natural instincts. Menstruation, the travails of childbirth, and the high incidence of female sterility, he maintained, were contemporary pathological phenomena, in part attributable to the "subversion of natural instincts, growing out of education." Such a view of higher education, combined with his propensity for telling bawdy jokes about women in his gynecology classes, suggest that King viewed women students from a less than favorable perspective. When King resigned in 1894 as dean of the medical faculty, he cited as one of his major accomplishments the "satisfactory adjustment of the 'woman question' in the department." Coeducation was discontinued during his tenure.[33]

Women's early enrollment confirmed neither the highest expectations of their proponents nor the worst fears of their detractors. Between 1884 and 1888, only four to five women registered in each medical class; their numbers constituted between five and six percent of the pre-1889 classes. As the school's medical facilities improved and women's faith in the school's commitment to coeducation increased, female numbers increased. Between 1889 and 1892, a total of thirty-five women registered, raising the proportion of female students in the school to 11.2 percent. Male enrollment rose as well during the same period. In 1886, the number of medical students reached one hundred for the first time in the school's history. (A rise in civil servants employed by the Pension Bureau—that department required the training of large numbers of medical examiners—contributed also to that increase.)[34]

Throughout this period, relations between the women and their male professors and fellow students remained strained. Women knew that they were "on trial," in the words of Edna Clarke, a medical student who later registered in the school of science. Clarke felt that they were all "looked upon as a problem." Women doctors outside the Washington community reported rumors of occasional conflicts between the staff and the female students. Dr. Maria Zakrzewska, a founder of the New England Hospital for Women in Boston, remarked in her autobiography that faculty members at the medical college opposed to coeducation "made the path of the women students as rough and stoney as possible." The male students, "taking their cue from these professors," she said, "added discourtesies and affronts to hostilities." Even fifty years later, Hinds recalled that "they were grinding years. . . . We asked no favors," she said, "and would receive none."[35]

Tensions between the male students and faculty members and the female students increased as the proportion of women in the medical department rose. According to a female medical student, male instructors voiced concerns that with "female students . . . increasing in much greater ratio than the male," men would soon desert the school. Some professors began lobbying against coeducation. They made it clear that they "did not care to lecture at a women's college."[36]

In the spring of 1892—a semester that saw record registrations—an incident occurred that brought tensions to a head and gave the faculty an excuse to discontinue coeducation. Significantly, no direct reference to the incident itself appears in numerous local sources that discuss the faculty's action. One commenter writing in the *Woman's Journal* hinted that there was more than met the eye. To the Columbian faculty's claim that "coeducation in medicine is a failure," she countered that some "hint, and above a whisper, too, that this is not the true reason. But as it is so much easier to punish the women than men, the women must go." Zakrzewska referred more pointedly to the event in her autobiography. Improprieties had taken place in the dissecting lab, she said. A few male students "debased themselves by offering insult, not only to the women medical students, but also to the helpless bodies." The men involved received no punishment, she noted; instead, the faculty used the incident to expel the women students who were involved and to punish the "whole sex of innocent victims" by barring women from the school. In Zakrzewska's view, the medical staff had been planning to end coeducation anyway and used the incident as a pretext for their action. Women students shared that assessment.[37]

Notice of the faculty's intent sent shock waves through the community of women students and alumnae. Immediately, the women met to consider ways to dissuade the faculty from taking the planned action. Representing the women students on an executive committee formed for that purpose were Daisy M. Orleman, a graduate of the class of 1890, Anita Newcomb McGee, a medical senior, and Margaret Magnon York, a second-year student. All of these women were outstanding students. Orleman later enjoyed an extraordinary medical career, earning special awards from the French Academy of Science for her work in dermatology. York and McGee were both married students who soon graduated with honors. York practiced medicine for more than fifty years, first in New York then in California, and McGee distinguished herself for special services rendered the American and Japanese governments in supervising nursing corps during the Spanish-American and Russo-Japanese wars.[38]

Formally, the women's committee presented a petition to the faculty board stating their opposition to the proposed exclusion and requesting a hearing. Informally, they interviewed faculty menbers to discover where their allegiances lay and to persuade them to defeat the proposal. Threats, pleading, outrage, and shock alternated with rational argument in their petition. First, McGee, the committee secretary, warned the faculty that they could suffer retaliation for such an untoward action. "All friends of the higher education of women, of whom there are many in this land, especially in this city," she claimed, would hold the faculty members, all practicing physicians, individually responsible for the school's action. Shifting mood, she called upon the faculty's sense of civic duty, declaring that the "standard of the medical profession in the District" would be jeopardized if women were "force[d] . . . to take their diplomas from institutions of lower grade," referring to Howard's and National's medical departments, both considered inferior to Columbian's.[39]

With these preliminaries addressed, McGee focused on the pre-cipating event—without, however, referring directly to the incident itself. (Some time later, however, she did consider mentioning the incident when composing a letter to the editor of the *Washington Post*, but decided not to. A sentence beginning, "To mention the reason for this action is quite beyond. . . ." was struck over and the incident ignored.) In the petition, McGee did state the committee's concern that women students' reputations would be "tarnished" if the planned action caused reports of the incident to reach the public. She urged the board to ignore the unchivalrous behavior of the male students. Such behavior, she argued, was "contrary to the spirit of the times" and was "diminishing in practice." Acknowledging that the women students involved might have contributed to the problem, she forwarded her committee's offer to form an alumnae-senior women's association to screen prospective female applicants and to "maintain harmony." Future problems could easily be "overcome," McGee explained, "by intelligent cooperation between the faculty and the female students."[40]

Having offered what seemed to be a sensible solution to the immediate problem, McGee went on to address the apparent underlying issue, the faculty's fear that women were driving male students away from Columbian into the arms of its rival, Georgetown. Privately, some faculty members had complained to the women's committee that male enrollment at Columbian was failing to keep pace with enrollment at Georgetown's all-male medical college. They laid the blame on steadily rising female enrollments.

In their petition, the women vigorously denied that assertion and presented evidence to the contrary. It was relatively easy to discount faculty concerns when it came to the earliest years of coeducation, 1884–86. For those years, Columbian's registration rose by twenty-four students to Georgetown's three, a proportional gain of 30 percent for Columbian compared to 11 percent for Georgetown. Explaining the figure for subsequent years, 1888–92, presented a greater challenge. McGee, therefore, enclosed the following table.[41]

"Session	Columbian	Georgetown
"1888–'89	125 (12 women)	83
"1889–'90	128 (10 women)	89
"1890–'91	155 (16)	124
"1891–'92	15?	107

These figures did show a proportional increase of 49 percent for Georgetown compared to 24 percent for Columbian between 1888–89 and 1890–91. The women claimed, however, that Georgetown's increase was "largely fictitious," and could be attributed to a change in their method of counting students. In actuality, they said, Columbian grew by more than thirty students during the previous three years, while Georgetown acquired, at most, only twenty-four students, "and probably, in fact, only half of that number." Thus, between 1888 and 1892, the relative rates of growth of the two schools was similar, McGee claimed: 26 percent for Columbian and 29 percent for Georgetown. Whatever gains Georgetown did make, she argued, resulted from improvements in the program and the facilities. "The statistics show," McGee pointed out, that Georgetown did not experience the steady growth in students that would have resulted from "a constantly acting cause." Rather, enrollment increased by spurts, each one following improvements to Georgetown's program.[42]

The petition mentioned Georgetown's construction of a new $50,000 building with "comfortable clean, and well-ventilated lecture rooms," improvements in clinical advantages, and the addition of well-equipped chemical, physiological, and bacteriological laboratories. Where Georgetown previously was "inferior in every way to Columbian," McGee maintained, "today it claims to be decidedly its superior." To add to their argument, women students interviewed Muncaster Magruder, dean of the Georgetown Medical Department. He acknowledged that "no student in that college has ever expressed a preference for his college because women were not admitted there."[43]

The women next raised the issue that struck at the heart of the problem—increasing female enrollments. Naively, they reassured the faculty that the steadily increasing number of women students, which had already tripled from 1888 to 1891, would more than offset any future "assumed loss" in male student enrollment at the medical school. To "deliberately cut off this certain and growing source of income for the sake of supposition seems inconsistent," they reasoned. Their argument had an ominous ring, for women were confirming the faculty's worst fear: If the current rate of female registrations continued, women could one day dominate Columbian's medical student body.[44]

Columbian's medical school administrators already feared that their department was undergoing what contemporary scholars label "feminization," a term used to refer to a reduction in prestige or wages that occurs in male-dominated fields when women enter in large numbers. Just the year before, in 1891, noted physician Mary Putnam Jacobi commented on this tendency in an essay about women physicians. Jacobi expressed chagrin at the "odd idea advanced . . . on so many occasions, that whenever a woman should prove herself capable of an intellectual achievement, this latter would cease to constitute an honor for the men who had previously prized it." Jacobi cited the experience of London University, which had been "flooded" with letters from "indignant physicians" when that school opened enrollment to women. The doctors declared that "their own diplomas, previously obtained, had been lowered in value, their contracts violated, and their most sacred property right invaded."[45]

Doubtless, medical faculty members were also aware that a male reaction against coeducation had begun to manifest itself in institutions of higher learning throughout the United States. According to one of the women involved in the attempt to overturn the decision, the year before, Harvard students had threatened to "withdraw in a body to Yale, if women were admitted." The "compliant Faculty" yielded, she reported. In addition, just a few weeks before the Columbian faculty's decision, newspapers across the country reported an incident in St. Louis, where male medical students opposed to coeducation picketed a local medical school to "rid the institution of what they considered a handicap to the profession." They similarly threatened to desert the department for neighboring rivals. Indeed, Columbian students had already threatened similar action if the faculty failed to provide them with adequate clinical opportunities in obstetrics. From this perspective, the women's emphasis on the benefits of increasing female enrollment may well have inflamed rather than allayed faculty fears regarding coeducation.[46]

Still, the petition forced the faculty to reconsider its decision. Members agreed to meet in special session in June but refused to allow women to present their case in person. Much to the women students' and alumnae's dismay, board members reaffirmed their earlier decision to discontinue coeducation. The faculty's vote was unanimous with one exception: William Lee cast a dissenting vote. Reportedly, however, the staff was far from agreed in its sentiments. McGee later discovered that two professors who opposed the decision had voted with the majority, "with the view of making the action unanimous." She also learned that the entire dental faculty voted "against their convictions" to promote unity in the department. It is interesting to note that with the exception of Coues and Lee, the board that welcomed women in 1884 consisted of the same men who dismissed them in 1892. Attempts in July by some faculty members to delay implementation of the decison for another year also failed.[47]

Although dismayed by the faculty's vote, Columbian's female medical students and graduates continued to seek redress. They appealed next to the board of trustees, a body composed of the president of the university and the overseers. Traditionally, this group seconded the recommendations of the medical school faculty in any action regarding the governance of that department. King, the dean of the medical school, raised women's hopes by referring to the time, fifteen or twenty years earlier, when the trustees had overruled the faculty's recommendation, thereby establishing a precedent that could work in the women's favor. Ironically, the issue was the same, but the positions were reversed: On that occasion, King said, the medical faculty had favored the admission of women, but the trustees had "refused to sanction the step and thus debarred women from the college for several years." Women hoped to use the precedent to persuade the board to overrule the medical faculty once more, this time in their favor. Accordingly, they submitted a letter to the trustees, enclosing the petition previously sent to the faculty.[48]

The second letter presented a more restrained and dispassionate appeal than the first, even though it addressed many of the same issues. Once more, the women questioned the grounds for their dismissal and appealed for the restoration of coeducation in the best interests of the college. Convinced that they could garner community support for their cause, the women's group warned the trustees that the reputation—and the enrollment—of the entire college would suffer if the trustees proceeded to implement the medical faculty's request. "In the eyes of the public," wrote McGee, speaking again for the women's committee, "the Medical Department is an integral part of the University. That which injures the part, injures the whole." More pragmatically, the petition focused on the key issues at hand— the supposed decline in the rate of growth of the college—and its corollary, the predicted abandonment of Columbian's medical school by present and prospective male students. "Do men shun this college because the presence of women has diminished the proverbial rudeness of medical students?" they questioned. "Can one man be named who has avoided Columbian because of the presence of women?"[49]

The women once more pressed their argument that rather than constituting a liability, female enrollment represented an asset. "The revenue of the Medical Department would be curtailed" rather than enhanced "by excluding women," they argued. Extrapolating from current income, the authors calculated that if the college turned women away, it would lose "at least $5,000 a year for the next four years," or $20,000—a sum that the medical school could ill afford to forego. Concluding with a plea for reconsideration, the women rested their case.[50]

Their second appeal suffered the same fate as the first. The board of trustees officially affirmed the medical faculty's right to end coeducation by the fall of 1892, citing economic pressures as their reason. Privately, board members confided that they had been "almost unanimous in their opposition to the exclusion of women," but their own preferences had been "overborne by the financial control exerted" by three members of the medical school's staff.[51]

Unwilling to accept defeat, members of the women's committee adopted a new strategy and sought support from Washington residents interested in professional education for women. In May 1892, they asked leaders of several Washington women's organizations to mobilize community support to pressure Columbian into reinstating coeducation. Lucia Eames Blount, president of ProReNata, a local women's rights society, coordinated the petition and letter-writing campaign to rally Washington's influential elite and leaders of women's clubs throughout the country on behalf of Columbian's medical women.

Blount was the logical person and ProReNata the appropriate group to undertake such an effort. Married to a wealthy industrialist, Blount directed numerous civic and women's club activities from her Georgetown home, Dunbarton Oaks. A friend of Susan B. Anthony's and an activist for women's rights, Blount had acquired lobbying skills and knowlege of parliamentary procedure from her work on behalf of women's suffrage. It was through these experiences that she recognized that women's cause suffered from female inexperience in public debate and women's naivete regarding legislative protocol. In 1889, to remedy such deficiencies, she founded ProReNata, an organization whose name she derived from a medical term meaning "to do what must be done."[52]

Members of ProReNata devoted their efforts to the advancement of women's civil and political rights. At meetings, they debated sample bills in mock congress to improve their ability to speak extemporaneously and promote legislation. Subjects of their bills ranged from women's suffrage and jury service to immigration restriction and the prohibition of female figures in front of tobacco stores. Papers written and distributed by members, which included "Principles of Law Women Ought to Know," "Rights of Ownership, Contract, Deeds, Bonds, Wills, Executors, and Mortgages," and "Has a Knowledge of Germ Theory Benefitted People?" reiterated such concerns.[53]

With her talent for organization and her abundant energy, Blount launched a petition campaign aimed at the audience she hoped would influence the trustees and the medical faculty. Working among her own friends, she and the women medical students and others interested in medical coeducation at Columbian gathered the names of more than two hundred "of the *best citizens* of Washington, including senators, representatives, judges, newspapermen, and District officials," according to a published report. In January 1893, they presented the petition to the medical school faculty with the request that the professors reinstate coeducation. "The protests of all the leading women's clubs in the country . . . including Sorosis of New York, the Women's Club of Massachusetts, etc." accompanied the appeal, according to one newspaper.[54]

Conspicuously absent from the letters of appeal were the names of such political activists as Susan B. Anthony, Blount's personal friend, and Elizabeth Cady Stanton, as well as representatives of local and national suffrage associations to which Blount belonged. Anthony, a visitor to the Blount home during this period, remained publicly aloof from the controversy. Even her private diaries written during the winters of 1892 and 1893, when she was in Washington on suffrage business, bore no mention of Columbian's action or of the petition campaign. Yet during this time Anthony was frequently in the company of Blount and another suffrage colleague, Ella Marble, a medical student who was secretary of Blount's committee. Similarly, women's rights newspapers such as the *Woman's Journal* and the *Woman's Tribune* failed to mention the coeducation debate until well after the campaign had ended, even though the *Woman's Journal* had announced Anita McGee's graduation in May 1892, when the controversy was at its height.[55]

The omission of suffragists from the debate may well have been deliberate. As part of their strategy, women doctors could well have avoided involving women's rights activists, fearing their involvement could backfire and alienate the trustees. McGee later acknowledged that she refrained from "noising abroad the contemplated unpopular action" in order to avoid "dragging the name of Columbian in the dust." The women hoped that logical argument and reasonable pressure tactics would ultimately succeed.[56]

The women doctors involved in the controversy could have rejected the public support of suffrage leaders for other reasons as well. Unlike the pioneer women doctors who had linked suffrage and women's rights activities with their own success, few post-pioneer women doctors and medical students supported suffrage or the women's rights movement. Although they staunchly endorsed the principle of enlarged educational and economic opportunities for women, they rejected the organized women's rights movement as a means for achieving such goals. Women students in the medical school, for example, dismissed the efforts of early activists who made their achievements possible. Some told Ella Marble that women owed their advances in the professions to evolutionary social forces, not to female activism. McGee, leader of the women students and alumnae, openly criticized the organized women's movement herself. "'Advancement of Woman' Associations and 'Woman's Council' . . . do harm, not good," she insisted, because such groups emphasized "the very distinction which ought to be obliterated."[57]

Post-pioneer medical women also feared that activities that identified them with the suffrage movement or with women's rights activities could jeopardize their status in the profession. Already risking social censure for seeking unorthodox careers, they had to choose their allies with care. Most late-nineteenth-century Americans still regarded "manly" women who actively supported suffrage with disdain. Even though some prominent Washington women supported women's rights activities, Washington's professional community identified the cause with such eccentric practitioners as the pioneer homeopath Caroline Winslow or the better known Mary Walker whose bloomer-style costume provoked ridicule and criticism.

The women's decision to disassociate themselves from the suffragists had no effect on the outcome. The petition campaign failed to move either the faculty or the board of trustees. As Coues had predicted in a letter to Blount, "Petitions, no matter by whom signed are generally pigeonholed. . . . In this case, nothing short of an electric shock as we discussed will awaken the sleepy old fogies to the signs of the times."[58]

The publicity that the women's petition provoked, however, did force the faculty to defend their decision publicly. In a letter to the *Washington Post* in January 1893, the medical professors asserted that barring women from the school after an eight-year trial resulted from a "lack of accommodations" and not from "any spirit of discrimination against the sex." Because the medical school "cannot accommodate all of the men who apply for admission in its present quarters," the doctors claimed, "the line is drawn against the women."[59]

This published excuse provoked quick and incredulous responses from several women. In the letter she wrote to the editor of the *Washington Post*, published with slight revisions over the name of Ella Marble, secretary of ProReNata, McGee asserted that the faculty was being less than honest. Columbian was far from overcrowded, she insisted. "It is only necessary for a visitor to attend a lecture . . . to observe that all the seats are not occupied." One could hardly cite "crowding" in the laboratory as a problem, she went on, "as no laboratory work had hitherto been offered to students . . . (unless a little looking through a microscope may be called such)." If the faculty were truly sincere in claiming that the lack of space forced them to exclude women, she demanded to know why they did not institute a rigid entrance examination instead of barring women. Such a measure, she noted, would improve the quality of the school without discriminating against one group.[60]

Other women on the committee responded to different excuses that faculty members had offered. Members of Columbian's staff had complained that coeducation was "a strain on modesty," and that they suffered "restrictions in lecturing to a mixed class." Ella Marble countered that there was nothing "immodest or indelicate in the study of medicine." "The restraint felt," she maintained in her published rebuttal, "was in the matter of telling exceedingly questionable stories upon the ladies' frowned and decided disapproval." The antics of Dr. King, the corpulent dean of the medical school who delighted male students with his classroom antics—especially with his imitations of pregnant women—constituted only a small part of the behavior that women found offensive.[61]

Such retorts enabled the women involved to vent their disappointment, but they had no effect on either the faculty or the trustees. In the fall of 1893, the medical department at Columbian University settled into its new routine without first-year women students. The faculty permitted those women already enrolled to complete their training. Sixty percent of these eventually completed their degrees, most from other institutions.

For a while during this crisis, those interested in female medical education explored the possibility of founding a women's medical college linked to Columbian. In the spring of 1892, when the faculty first threatened to exclude women students, a group of Washington women approached the medical school with an offer of $15,000 to establish a coordinate department. Several of Washington's most prestigious doctors had acknowledged that there was "need of a medical college where women alone shall be taught." An article in the October 1892 issue of the *National Medical Review,* the organ of the District of Columbia Medical Society, later supported that view. Its author recommended establishing a high-caliber midwifery school where a woman could receive "special training under special teachers for that practice which would most naturally come to her."[62]

Women had a far different training institution in mind. Their proposal, as outlined by McGee, envisioned a department "free from any ties that would prevent its progress, managed by women and the friends of women, and maintaining the highest possible standards." With regard to the male doctors' plan, women retorted, "It is one thing to speak of a medical school for women of high character; it is a very different thing to suggest an annex of doubtful standing, appended as a side show to a medical night school."[63]

Negotiations led nowhere. "The necessary funds were within our reach," McGee declared, but Columbian University "failed . . . conspicuously to avail itself of this opportunity." Moreover, by early 1893, women themselves began to lose interest in the project. Anticipating the opening of the "magnificent Johns Hopkins" and of a coeducational medical department affiliated with a proposed Methodist university in Washington (one that never did materialize), women felt that "conditions [had] changed materially." "It is the unanimous opinion of those interested in the matter," wrote McGee in the spring of 1893, that there is no longer a "field whatever in this city for a medical school for women alone."[64]

Thus, by the spring of 1893, with all of their efforts exhausted and with no prospect for a women's medical school, Washington women who had been interested in studying in Columbian's medical program began to seek other alternatives. If the profile of Columbian's previous women students is any indication, many aspiring women doctors could not go elsewhere for medical study because they depended upon their salaries from local jobs. Others were married or supported family members living in Washington. Such women had to make the best of local opportunities. A few enrolled in other area medical schools. Beginning in the fall of 1893, white female enrollment at Howard and National increased by almost twenty-five women; this represented a rise of several hundred percent at each of those schools.

A few women rejected that alternative. For them, Howard's predominately black male student body and National's inadequate facilities represented undesirable alternatives. They chose instead to pursue different degrees, either in the newly established Corcoran School of Science or in one of Columbian's new graduate programs. In 1893, women comprised nine of twenty-one "special students" enrolled in the chemistry program of the Corcoran School of Science. They were hopeful, perhaps, that the medical school would reverse its decision and allow them to transfer to that program the following year. Others matriculated in graduate degree programs. Between 1893 and 1900, twenty-seven women earned advanced degrees in Columbian's graduate school. None had attended previously, although technically eligible to enroll. Women comprised almost one-fourth of all master's degree candidates in the science program alone during those years (ten of forty-seven). A few of those women, such as Louise Tayler, were premedical students who undertook graduate study expecting the Columbian Medical Department to restore coeducation in the interim. When Tayler completed her M.S. in psychology, she still could not matriculate in the medical school. Instead, she applied to Georgetown's medical program—also without success—and eventually earned her medical degree from Johns Hopkins.[65]

Other potential Columbian students shifted their career plans and committed themselves to careers in the sciences. This decision radically affected the options open to them. Other than teaching in women's college, opportunities for women with advanced scientific degrees lay in expanding high school science departments or in specialized government agencies like the Department of Agriculture or the National Museum. Government jobs seldom afforded ambitious single women the independence that a successful medical career promised as they were dependent upon the good will and support of male administrators. Positions with scientific agencies were entirely out of reach of married women. Columbian's discontinuation of coeducation, therefore, withdrew a valuable career option for single women and made professional work all but impossible for married women with scientific or career interests.[66]

Women who were geographically mobile could have left Washington to study elsewhere. But by 1900 and later, opportunities for female medical education were diminishing throughout the country. Columbian's action in 1892 was not "against the spirit of the times," as women had assumed. Rather, it presaged the beginning of a nationwide reaction against female medical education. In 1902, for example, the medical college of Northwestern University, which had graduated 350 women doctors between 1870 and 1892, abruptly closed its women's division in mid-semester. Tufts University Medical School, the largest in New England, reduced female enrollment from 42 percent of the senior class in 1900 to 7.6 percent by 1907. At the same time, other marginally operating coeducational schools, like National and the Washington Homoeopathic Medical College, closed. Nationally, female enrollment in coeducational medical instutituions dropped by one-third, from 1,419 in 1895 to 921 in 1903—well before the results of the Flexner report. After its publication, the number of regular medical schools—which had risen nationally from 44 to 126 in the second half of the nineteenth century—dropped by almost half, to seventy-six by 1920. Many of the schools that failed had admitted women. Of the twenty-two homeopathic medical schools in 1900, the majority of which were coeducational, only five remained in 1920.[67]

In this post-1900 period when so many medical schools were closing, Columbian managed to survive, although it labored under pressing debts assumed in the late 1890s. In 1892, after the staff excluded women, members of the department had undertaken a campaign to improve the program's image and standing. That autumn, the medical faculty published a much larger and more attractively designed catalog. It reflected the college's aspiration to "rival [the] great seats of learning . . . like those at Cambridge, New Haven, Princeton, and Charlottesville," as the president declared in his annual address three years earlier. At the same time, they extended the curriculum to four years, equipped new chemical and bacteriological laboratories, and invested in a major renovation of physical facilities, including a complete electrification of the medical school building. To accomplish these renovations, they borrowed $5,000 from the university. In addition, they added three more members to the teaching staff, bringing that group to a total of sixteen members compared to nine on the staff just two years earlier. In 1894, the faculty entered into further negotiations with the university to underwrite a fully equipped hospital that opened in 1898.[68]

Male student enrollment did increase between 1892 and 1900, but only by the same rate that it had risen before the school barred women; neither the exclusion of women nor the expansion of the program substantially altered enrollment in the medical department. The added debt that the faculty incurred to make the changes of 1892–94, however, did place an inordinate burden on the medical school as well as on the college itself. Negotiations between the medical staff and the trustees over the mounting debt resulted in the complete integration of the medical school into the university in 1898. The university assumed the unpaid portion of the medical school's debts, and the medical faculty relinquished its authority over finances and appointments and became a teaching faculty only. Members accepted fixed salaries in lieu of their former percentage of student tuition. The university itself now carried the debt of the medical school in addition to its own financial problems. Unable to secure an endowment, the college borrowed $360,000 to pay off prior mortgages and to add needed space. In 1903, the trustees, in special arrangement with the medical faculty of the defunct National University Medical School, accepted that school's male students to offset some of its expenses.

At the same time, in a desperate attempt to win the favor of John D. Rockefeller and the American Association of Baptists, the university revised its charter to increase the number of trustees and to require that two-thirds of them be Baptists. This action placed the school under Baptist control for the first time in its history. The strategy, born of desperation, came to naught, because the Baptists refused to endow the college anyway. Looking back on that period, the college's own historian viewed the times as a struggle between "life and death." [69]

In 1903, university administrators entered into negotiations with the George Washington Memorial Association, a group of women interested in establishing a coeducational graduate school in memory of the first president. Ultimately, the women, in concert with the Columbian trustees, agreed to forsake their initial plan of establishing an independent school and linked their efforts to an existing university. In May 1904, they reached accord with the trustees of Columbian. The association agreed to donate $500,000 to the university if the school's governing body would change Columbian's name to the George Washington University and agree to promote graduate work. The association also insisted that the Columbian trustees drop the sectarian designation that they had adopted in their bid for Baptist patronage. Mrs. Archibold Hopkins, president of the association, and Phoebe Hearst, women who had been active participants in the efforts of the Women's Fund of the Johns Hopkins Medical School, participated in these negotiations. No direct evidence indicates that members of the women's committee pressured the trustees to accept women throughout the departments of the graduate school—including the medical department. Yet considering the lengths to which Columbian's trustees went to curry the favor of the Baptist association, they may well have encouraged the medical faculty to adopt coeducation in order to facilitate the negotiations. [70]

In 1906, the medical school of the George Washington University unofficially admitted one woman; in 1907, two more registered. That same year, 1907–8, the trustees on the finance committee declared the state of the college "most grave" and called for severe retrenchment and salary reductions. It placed the medical and dental departments and the hospital on a self-sustaining basis. The school's prospects had deteriorated so seriously, and tensions had grown so markedly between the women's committee and President Needham of the college, that the association withdrew its grant from the college. Reports from national medical associations cited the school for frequent evasions of minimum entrance requirements. Local doctors claimed that had Columbian's requirements been enforced, the medical school would have closed altogether. It was only by accepting students with substandard preparation that the school maintained enrollments. Evidently, women had more than adequate credentials. One of the female medical students admitted with this change of policy had already earned a Ph.D. In 1910, in the middle of these problems, the medical department quietly restored coeducation, albeit on a restricted basis. Throughout the twentieth century—until recent times—women's registration remained below 5 percent of the class.[71]

The position of women medical students in Washington in the 1890s through the early 1900s thus anticipated the situation that women would confront nationally over the next few decades. Despite their best efforts, women could not establish a strong foothold in any of Washington's medical programs. They rejected an institution that welcomed them—whether because of their own or society's racism or because of inadequate facilities and poor quality—and put their faith in institutions that rejected them. To their dismay, they discovered the inconstancy of their allies and learned how powerless they were to avert the closing off of their opportunities. Neither behind-the-scenes pressure nor public expressions of outrage could alter the decisions of male physicians who opposed the admission of women to the club. In one case, money may have talked—albeit with a whisper. A well-timed and sizeable donation from a women's association, the George Washington Memorial Committee, may have reopened the door—however narrowly—for a few women to enter the medical school in 1906. But such gains were marginal. The golden age that the opening of Washington's elite medical schools in the 1880s presaged faded as women seeking entry into the professional ranks faced renewed barriers in the ensuing decades.

ranz J. Heiberger family. *Front:* Franz Heiberger, his wife Emma, and daughter orence. *Rear:* Ida Heiberger (physician) and her sisters, Lilla and Minnie. Ida eiberger founded the Woman's Clinic in 1890. Her sister Minnie served as easurer. Heiberger practiced for almost fifty years and remained active in the nic during that time. (Courtesy of Mrs. Elizabeth W. Newby, Bethesda, Md.)

Ida Heiberger's diploma, Woman's Medical College of Pennsylvania, 1885. (National Museum of American History, Smithsonian Institution)

Ida Heiberger's medical license granted by the District of Columbia Medical Society, 1887. (National Museum of American History, Smithsonian Institution)

Caroline Still Anderson, Woman's Medical College of Pennsylvania, 1878. Anderson, a widow with a five-year-old daughter and a degree from Oberlin College, entered the Howard University Medical Department, where she completed the first year and then transferred to the Woman's Medical College. She practiced for more than thirty years in Philadelphia after her remarriage. (Library Company of Philadelphia)

ulia P. Hughes, Howard University Medical Department, 1897, was a graduate of Scotia Seminary. She opened a pharmacy in Philadelphia after completing the medical program at Howard. (Moorland-Spingarn Research Center, Howard University)

Sarah M. Loguen, Syracuse Medical College, 1876, interned at the Woman's Hospital in Philadelphia and the New England Hospital for Women before opening her office in Washington in 1880. Frederick Douglass, a family friend, hung her shingle outside her office door. (Moorland-Spingarn Research Center, Howard University)

Graduating class of the Syracuse Medical College, 1876. Sarah Loguen is in the front row, second from left. (Moorland-Spingarn Research Center, Howard University)

Alice M. Waring, Howard University Medical Department, 1900. Waring's father was a prominent Washington businessman. Her brother also graduated from the medical department, and her sister was a principal in the District of Columbia segregated public school system. (Washingtoniana Collection, Martin Luther King Memorial Library)

Anita Newcomb McGee, Columbian University Medical Department, 1892. The U.S. Army recognized McGee's success at establishing a nursing service in the Spanish American War by awarding her the rank of acting assistant surgeon. McGee's father was Simon Newcomb, the astronomer and mathematician; her husband was William J. McGee, acting director of the U.S. Bureau of Anthropology. (National Library of Medicine, Bethesda, Md.)

Mary E. Parsons, Howard University Medical Department, 1874. Pasons was the second woman to graduate from the Howard Medical Department and the first to gain entry into the District of Columbia Medical Society. In 1902, she served as vice-president of that group. (National Library of Medicine, Bethesda, Md.)

Ada R. Thomas, Woman's Medical College of Philadelphia, 1893. Thomas practiced in Washington for thirty years and was one of only two women clinicians with male patronage to be appointed to a facility established by male physicians. (National Library of Medicine, Bethesda, Md.)

Louisa Miller Blake, Columbian 1893, entered medical school after she had been married for several years. Five years after she graduated, her husband, Levi Blake, completed his medical degree at Howard, and they practiced jointly in the city for many years. (Washingtoniana Collection, Martin Luther King Memorial Library)

Phoebe R. Norris, Columbian 1891. Norris, a graduate of Juniata College, worked as a government clerk while she attended medical school and established a practice. (Washingtoniana Collection, Martin Luther King Memorial Library)

Amelia F. Foye, Howard University Medical Department, 1898. Foye, a close friend of Frederick Douglass, practiced in Washington for more than fifty years. Her horse, Charley Fox, was as well known as the doctor, and her patients expressed their decided disapproval when she exchanged him for an electric Raush-Lang. (Washingtoniana Collection, Martin Luther King Memorial Library)

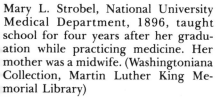

Mary L. Strobel, National University Medical Department, 1896, taught school for four years after her graduation while practicing medicine. Her mother was a midwife. (Washingtoniana Collection, Martin Luther King Memorial Library)

Anna Bartsch-Dunne, Howard University Medical Department, 1902, practiced in Washington for more than fifty years. In 1955, she endowed a scholarship for women medical students at Howard that provided funds for three students per year. (Washingtoniana Collection, Martin Luther King Memorial Library)

Anna Augusta Wilson, Royal College of Physicians and Surgeons, Edinburgh, 1892. After completing the medical program in Edinburgh, Wilson trained at the Woman's Medical College of London, and then opened the Dorothea Dix Dispensary in Washington. (Washingtoniana Collection, Martin Luther King Memorial Library)

Howard University Medical Department faculty, 1869-70. Seated, *left to right,* Alexander Augusta, Gideon S. Palmer, Robert Reyburn, Charles Purvis, and Phineas H. Strong. Standing, *left to right,* Silas L. Loomis, Oliver O. Howard, and Joseph T. Johnson. (Moorland-Spingarn Research Center, Howard University)

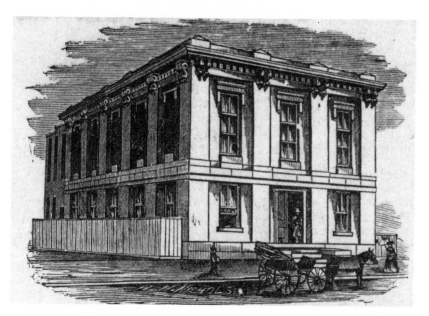

National Medical College of Columbian University, 1880. (Washingtoniana Collection, Martin Luther King Memorial Library)

Medical Department of Howard University, 1870. (Moorland-Spingarn Research Center, Howard University)

Isabel Barrows, New York Medical College and Hospital for Women, 1868. Barrows did postgraduate study in ophthalmology in Vienna and accepted a teaching position at Howard University Medical Department upon her return. She resigned after two years to move with her husband, stenographer to Secretary of State Seward, to Boston, where she practiced. (Moorland-Spingarn Research Center, Howard University)

Isabel Haslup Lamb, Howard University Medical Department, 1897. Haslup married her professor, Daniel S. Lamb, in 1899. Together they contributed their services to the Woman's Clinic for more than thirty years. Lamb, who served as a medical inspector in the public schools, maintained a private practice, and founded the Women's Medical Society of the District of Columbia with Mary Parsons. (Moorland-Spingarn Research Center, Howard University)

5

Women's Dispensaries and Clinics, an Alternative System of Training

"For Women, by Women Doctors"

Late nineteenth-century dispensaries and clinics linked medical school with a successful practice. There, students and newly graduated doctors gained needed experience and made the contacts that promoted success. Established doctors and aspiring specialists perfected their techniques and reinforced their networks of referrals. In Washington as elsewhere, control of the regulars' infirmaries and access to the equivalent of today's internships and residencies rested with the white male elite who ran the medical schools and professional societies. Without exception, until the late 1890s, these men denied women medical students and doctors access to training and staff positions. In response, Washington's regular women doctors of the period established their own medical infirmaries—the Women's Dispensary in 1883, the Woman's Clinic in 1890, and the Dorothea Dix Dispensary in 1894—all run by and for women.

The success of these institutions varied; in large measure their fortunes reflected the obstacles that participating doctors faced themselves. They operated successfully through the mid-1890s when the female medical community was at its height, and then declined after Washington's medical schools closed to women, decimating the ranks of female medical students and doctors available to staff them. One dispensary closed after three years; another became absorbed into the male medical establishment and became a facility operated for the benefit of male students and specialists. Only one, the Woman's Clinic, survived the rigors of Washington's health care politics. It operated for fifty years on the fringe of Washington's respected medical community, testimony to the longevity of its founders and their dedication to the city's needy women.

75

Homeopathic women doctors encountered a different situation. Because Washington's homeopaths had never established a medical school or hospital, women homeopaths did not have to confront pre-existing male-dominated institutions. More important, they experienced greater cooperation from their male colleagues than their counterparts trained in regular medicine. Thus, in 1882, when homeopathic female physicians and supporters organized the Homeopathic Free Dispensary, male and female physicians worked side by side. Black women doctors, barred from every infirmary in the city run by white physicians, lacked the resources and the support of their male colleagues to open their own institutions.

Washington's dispensaries and clinics were part of a national health care movement begun in the early 1800s by social reformers and doctors. Early medical infirmaries were designed to treat the so-called "worthy" poor—those who lived a step above the almshouse—and to prevent the spread of disease. As late as 1877, a District of Columbia Board of Health officer reminded the community that "supplying the destitute with medical attendance and medicine is not only an act of charity, but a measure of protection to the community from the incursion of fatal epidemics . . . and loathesome diseases [that] may be spread through a whole community." The number of these medical facilities increased markedly after the Civil War. By then, however, their medical-training functions began to supersede their humanitarian origins. In 1879, for example, when Georgetown medical faculty members proposed the establishment of a new dispensary, they declared that "Should the public poor incidentally receive any gratuitous benefit at our hand, all sincere and humane men would rejoice." A local newspaper editorial supporting the clinic echoed such sentiments stressing "the reciprocal advantages" that medical colleges and clinics derived. "Without patients with whom to illustrate lectures, the teachers of the healing art labor under great disadvantage," the author proclaimed.[1]

Clinics and dispensaries served the needs of medical practitioners at every level. Students observed their professors demonstrate diagnosis and treatment in their respective specialties. Medical school seniors appointed to the resident or dispensing staffs treated minor ailments, dispensed drugs, and scheduled patients for appropriate clinics. Newly graduated physicians on three-month rotating positions as members of the visiting or dispensing staff received greater responsibilities; in particular, they handled maternity cases to become experienced in the nucleus of any general practice. Established physicians served on the consulting staff, lending their expertise while building their reputations and patient referrals in return. Little wonder that medical students and graduates eagerly competed for available assistant, resident, and externe appointments to perfect their skills, establish their reputations, and integrate themselves into the city's network of respected doctors.

Women doctors recognized that clinical experience was vital to their training as well. Elizabeth Blackwell, America's first trained woman doctor and founder of the Woman's Hospital of the New York Infirmary, acknowledged her concern that women doctors would remain mediocre without the "positive medical knowledge" derived from clinical practice. Her sister, the physician Emily Blackwell, emphasized the broader implications of clinical opportunities. "Almost without exception," she declared, "eminence in any department of medicine, in practice, in surgery, medical teaching or writing, is founded on a wider experience due to [clinical] connections." Leading women doctors of the period echoed such sentiments. In 1891, in her widely read article about women in the profession, physician Mary Putnam Jacobi called hospital study and practice "absolutely indispensable both to obtaining and maintaining a valid place in medical practice and in the medical profession."[2]

In the mid-1880s, when women began to graduate from medical colleges in greater numbers, their professors usually permitted them to observe clinical demonstrations; participation was another matter. Routinely, male doctors denied women coveted senior residencies and clinical appointments. At an 1891 meeting of the Woman's Medical Fund of the Johns Hopkins University, Emily Blackwell underscored the frustration women experienced in attempting to secure clinic or dispensary experience. Women do receive "privileges of undergraduate students," she explained, "but they can go no further. . . . They are ineligible either as residents or attending physicians in any of our public hospitals and dispensaries." "For actual experience," she continued, "they are dependent upon their private practices."[3]

Such was not the case for women homeopaths. Before the 1880s, male homeopaths throughout the country admitted women doctors to their clinics, dispensaries, and hospitals. Washington lacked such institutions until 1882, when homeopaths in the city established the Homoeopathic Free Dispensary. That infirmary actually grew out of a dispute between the city's homeopaths and regulars. The regulars refused to accept the homeopaths' offer to share facilities at a hospital to be established in memory of the slain President James Garfield, a homeopathic supporter himself. Lay women homeopaths on the joint hospital committee realized that the regulars would never support a "grand, unsectarian hospital." Because they feared the recently established homeopathic hospitals would close, they obtained a federal charter in November 1882 to open a dispensary. The Homoeopathic Free Dispensary became the first facility in the city where women could practice side-by-side with their male colleagues.[4]

Several members of the Homoeopathic Free Dispensary Board of Directors were women's rights activists and designed the clinic so that women would play a major role in its operation. Isobel Lenman, president of the board, was also a member of the National Woman Suffrage Association and the Moral Education Society, a group founded to elevate women's rights through the adoption of new social and sexual values. (She later helped to form the National Science Club, a women's organization dedicated to promoting the careers of women in science.) Isabella M. Bittinger, another board member was also an active suffragist and Moral Education Society member. With others on the all-female board of directors, these women supervised the dispensary's budget, appointed and discharged professional and maintenance staff, and established rules regarding patient care—unique responsibilities at a time when men assumed such functions, and "lady managers" raised funds and supervised the housekeeping. The women's concern about possible medical abuse of poor patients prompted strict regulation of surgical practices. By-laws prohibited doctors from performing major surgical procedures without the consent of members of the consulting board and required the presence of other staff members at any operation.[5]

Women homeopathic physicians participated actively in the operation of the dispensary. In the first year, each of the four women homeopaths in the city served on the dispensary's staff, two as attending physicians and two as consultants. Between 1882 and 1893, every woman homeopath who had practiced in the city in those years had assisted at the health center at one time. According to annual reports, they handled all routine cases, cared for obstetrical and gynecological surgery patients, and supervised treatment of the eyes, ears, and throat.

In addition to treating more than two thousand patients a year— the majority women and 60 percent black—the doctors sought ways to extend their services to the needy who lived in the area. Minnie C. T. Love, an 1887 graduate of Howard, treated patients in their homes. Unlike her male counterparts, who were compensated from the city for this service, Love received no fee. Another Howard graduate, Grace Roberts, recognized that "nourishing food [was] as much needed as medicine." She persuaded her roommate, Ernestine Alberti, to donate a $1,000 bond to the dispensary. Interest, placed in trust to Roberts, went into a special fund to purchase food for dispensary patients. Other doctors expressed their concern about working women whose plight was less dire, but serious nonetheless. Mary Hart and Caroline Winslow attempted to open a women's hospital so that "thousands of women that are employed in the government offices might have a retreat when sick [and] skillful medical care . . . from the wise and tender of their own sex." In 1888, the two doctors abandoned the project for lack of support and donated $76.31, which they had raised for the project, to the dispensary's treasury.[6]

The Homoeopathic Free Dispensary lasted approximately ten years. In 1895, the board of managers apparently merged the dispensary with the clinic of the National Homoeopathic Hospital (organized in 1885). Available records offer no clue to why they took this action. But the same year that notices of the dispensary disappeared, the names of women doctors who had been affiliated with the clinic began to appear on the list of the hospital's staff. While not solely responsible for the hospital as they had been for the dispensary, these doctors and female lay advocates assumed major responsibility for the operation of the hospital's clinic. In part, this resulted from a lack of interest on the part of male board members. In 1892, for example, before the two institutions merged, hospital board member Sara Spencer complained about the limited participation of male supporters and attempted, without success, to increase "active male membership as a source of permanent strength." The homeopathic hospital survived well into the twentieth century even though the Superintendent of Charities repeatedly denied requests for funds on the ground that the hospital duplicated services available elsewhere. Throughout the years, homeopathic women doctors enjoyed the same hospital privileges as their male colleagues.[7]

During the 1880s and 1890s, when women homeopaths were working alongside their male colleagues, white women regulars were struggling to obtain comparable courtesies. Professors from Columbian and National did permit female students to observe their clinics: Columbian's 1889 medical catalog emphasized that women received "the same privileges in all respects as are accorded other students." But the faculties denied women students the internship and residency appointments that would have guaranteed them firsthand experience. Columbian's first woman graduate, Clara Bliss Hinds, who had attended the college between 1884 and 1888, recalled that before 1890, doors of "the hospitals and clinics . . . were closèd adamantly to women knockers." In 1872, for one year only, Freedman's Hospital staff had appointed a woman physician, Isabel Barrows, to their clinic; she was also on the Howard faculty. Almost thirty years passed before the hospital engaged another woman physician. For many years, that medical staff similarly bypassed women when assigning the rotating three-month residencies at Freedman's Hospital to students, despite women's objections.[8]

In 1882, women physicians petitioned Congress—without success—for permission to attend clinics and to serve as residents in the Columbia Hospital for Women, an infirmary chartered by the federal government. Congress referred the bill to the Commissioners of the District of Columbia, where it was tabled.[9] Eighteen years later, in 1894, Howard University professors appointed Julia Hall to the gynecology clinic; four years after that, Isabel Haslup, the soon-to-be wife of Howard professor Daniel S. Lamb, received an "externe" appointment in the same specialty. Columbian professors, however, consistently denied female students and graduates resident "studentships" or house staff appointments.[9]

During these decades, some regular women doctors may well have abandoned the profession because they felt inadequte to practice without further training. Others, such as Mary Parsons and Mary Spackman, Howard graduates in the early seventies, entered medical practice with only the experience they had received assisting or observing their preceptors—as was customary. A few women who possessed the means sought clinical training in Europe. Barrows had studied ophthalmology in Vienna before her appointment to the Howard staff in 1871. Ida Heiberger, who graduated from the Woman's Medical College of Pennsylvania in 1885, took postgraduate courses in Freiberg, Germany, and Zurich, and Vienna before returning to Washington to practice. Some doctors exercised another option: Between 1870 and 1885, seven of the twelve white women who took regular training at Howard switched to homeopathic medicine and served the equivalent of residencies at the homeopathic dispensary.[10]

After 1880, regular women doctors in Washington, as elsewhere, adopted a fourth alternative. They began to establish their own dispensaries and clinics. The Women's Dispensary was the first of these in Washington. In 1883, Annie Rice and Jeannette Sumner, recent graduates of the Woman's Medical College of Pennsylvania, a school noted for the training of medical missionaries, established the Women's Dispensary. Rice and Sumner intended to improve the care poor women received through sympathy and appropriate training. They believed that female patients would be more willing to discuss intimate details of medical disorders with them than with male physicians, and they hoped to improve female medical care by discovering such problems at earlier, more treatable stages. Sumner discussed the practical effect of such service by describing a case history of a patient in her care. In a report delivered at an alumnae association meeting in 1882 and later published in the association's proceedings, Sumner told how she had saved the life of a woman whose uterine tumors were badly infected. Before Sumner undertook the case—at the urging of the patient's sister—male doctors had mistakenly treated the woman for malaria, based on her reported symptoms. (The woman had refused to allow male doctors to perform an internal examination.) Close to death, according to Sumner, the woman confessed her true symptoms and permitted Sumner to examine her. The resulting diagnosis and treatment saved the woman's life, the doctor claimed.[11]

The two doctors put their philosophy into practice shortly after their graduation. Upon their return to Washington in the spring of 1883, they wrote to James W. H. Lovejoy, dean of the faculty at Georgetown, where they had studied between 1880 and 1881. They had learned, they said, that the medical faculty planned to close a small dispensary it had operated, and they wished the surplus furnishings. Meager funds prevented them from purchasing anything beyond the most essential medical supplies, they explained. There is no record of the dean's reply. The women opened the dispensary a few weeks later.[12]

To ensure the success of their venture, Rice and Sumner contacted their former professors on the Georgetown staff and invited them to join with several other prominent doctors in the city as staff consultants and as members of the board of managers. Of the eight consultants—all male—who joined the Women's Dispensary staff, three taught at Georgetown. One of these men, Joseph Taber Johnson, a gynecologist, was president of that faculty. Three others were from Columbian. Albert F. A. King, one of those doctors, was also a gynecologist and was dean of Columbian's faculty.

Sumner and Rice had personal as well as professional contacts within the upper echelons of Washington's professional community. As members of professional families themselves, they were able to enlist the support of men and women of their own background. Dispensary incorporators included Augustus Worthington, a Washington lawyer who lived in the same building as the Rice family; John Sherman, a real estate broker; Maud Bascomb Johnson, wife of the physician and herself a member of a prominent Washington family; and Jane C. Hitz, an officer of the Medical Society's Washington Training School for Nurses.[13]

Women physicians were notably absent from the dispensary's medical or managing staffs. The women then practicing in the city, although experienced and qualified, were graduates of Howard University Medical Department. The founders of the dispensary may have shared the emnity and prejudice of their former professors toward Howard medical school graduates, or they may have been unable to circumvent the authority of their mentors. The exclusion of experienced women doctors from the staff of the Women's Dispensary and Rice and Sumner's dependence on prominent male consultants influenced the future of the dispensary.

At first, the Women's Dispensary functioned as a "free dispensary for the medical and surgical treatment of women and children by women only," as the doctors advertised. To bring their services to the greatest number of needy, the women opened the clinic at 10th and E streets, Northwest, the area with the highest mortality rate in the city. The dispensary was open daily from twelve to three. The women doctors conducted early morning and evening hours in their own office across the street. Within the first year, Rice and Sumner saw approximately 1,000 charity patients. The majority were black women, although men also received treatment at the infirmary.[14]

The death of Annie Rice the following year at the age of thirty-four, increased the burden on Sumner's shoulders. She operated the clinic without the aid of another attending physician for the next three years. The frequency with which she changed her own address, moving five times in as many years to different rented rooms in poor neighborhoods, suggests that she managed the dispensary in the face of increasing financial and personal difficulties.[15]

In 1887, Sumner began a series of changes in the operation of the dispensary that radically altered its future development. The appointment of a male doctor to the attending staff represented the first of these changes. Magruder Muncaster, a young physician from a distinguished Maryland family with close ties to Georgetown Medical School, became "outdoor physician" for the dispensary, a position that carried a small remuneration paid by the city. His appointment represented a significant departure from the founders' original goal of providing care "for women by women."

A second change in the dispensary staff that same year had even greater implications. Joseph T. Johnson, one of the infirmary's consulting physicians, began to offer clinics there in gynecology for Georgetown students. Clinical settings were in critically short supply at the time. With enrollments rising in all the city's medical schools, faculty members found themselves hard-pressed to provide opportunities for their students to witness diagnostic, therapeutic, and surgical procedures. In private correspondence just three years before, Johnson had offered Patrick Murphy, surgeon in charge of Columbia Hospital for Women, "half of his chair" at the medical school if Murphy would permit students to witness gynecological procedures at the hospital. Murphy refused, concerned that other medical colleges in the city would "claim equal privileges . . . and . . . impair the usefulness of the Institution for clinical purposes." Sumner was in no position to reject Johnson's offer. Pressed by the workload of the dispensary and dependent upon Johnson and other doctors of the consulting board, she consented. Johnson's introduction of clinic sessions at the Women's Dispensary initiated that infirmary into Washington's system of male-dominated medical education and training and changed its course.[16]

In response to its new function, the Women's Dispensary moved to larger quarters within a few months. Now located at Maryland Avenue and Four and One-Half Street, Southwest, in a building used by the Miner Institute for the Education of Colored Youth, the Women's Dispensary became the first medical facility for the poor in that section of the city. The move went hand-in-hand with increasing male domination of the dispensary. The arrival of another woman doctor did little to slow this trend. The year the clinic moved, Ida Heiberger, an 1885 graduate of Sumner's alma mater, joined the dispensary staff. Although Heiberger cut short her study in Freiberg at Sumner's request, she stayed at the dispensary for little more than a year. She left in 1890 to establish the Woman's Clinic, soon after several more male faculty members of Georgetown, National, and Columbian joined the consulting staff.[17]

During the next five years, 1890–95, the directors of the Women's Dispensary consolidated and expanded upon the changes they had set in motion before Heiberger's departure. The board of managers even changed the name of the institution to the Women's Dispensary and Hospital to reflect the increased scope of its operations. The dispensary, past its modest beginnings, seemed now on the verge of becoming a relatively well-financed medical and surgical institution and a major clinical training facility for doctors.

Immediately following Heiberger's resignation in 1890, four male doctors joined the attending staff. Two of these men, James Kerr, specialist in obstetrics and gynecology, and William Wilner, ophthalmologist, had just moved to Washington to accept positions on the Georgetown medical faculty and were attempting to establish private practices. Kerr, a prominent forty-two-year-old surgeon from Canada with influential relatives in Washington, also directed the surgical clinic at the Central Dispensary. Wilner was a graduate of the University of Virginia.[18]

The other two physicians, William C. Woodward and Thomas N. Vincent, were recent graduates of Georgetown and Jefferson medical schools, respectively. Like other favored graduates, they used the Women's Dispensary to advance their early careers. Between 1890 and 1899, at least a dozen more male physicians joined the attending staff of the Women's Dispensary. These men were members of a select group appointed to one or more of the thirty clinic and dispensary posts available annually in the city. Each of these recent graduates remained for two or three years, making connections and gaining experience while he built his own practice. All but one of them still practiced in Washington twenty years later. Their future activities in the medical societies and specialist organizations attest to their more than average success.[19]

Sumner remained the only female doctor at the dispensary for several years. According to city directories, in 1893, four women graduates of Columbian's medical department joined the staff. With the exception of Phoebe Norris, Columbian '91, who remained for several years, their affiliations were short-lived. Julia Smith and Jessie Kappelar, both 1890 graduates, left to join the Woman's Clinic within the year. Effie Falls, Columbian '92, left the city the same year.

The appointment of these women to the dispensary staff came shortly after Columbian's faculty discontinued coeducation. The timing may have been more than coincidental. Public protests against Columbian's action may well have influenced the decision of the Columbian doctors who served on the Women's Dispensary board. Appointing former female students as attending physicians demonstrated to the public that Columbian's dismissal of women students was not in the spirit of discrimination, as some claimed.

The appointments, however, failed to mark a significant change in the status of women doctors at the dispensary. During the next few years, women doctors remained a minority on the staff. Sumner, who left in 1895, had greatly reduced her activities after 1893 because of ill health. She died in 1896 at the age of fifty. Between 1894 and 1896, Norris was the only woman doctor treating dispensary patients. In 1896, four more women graduates joined the infirmary. Three of them were Columbian graduates: Anita Newcomb McGee had graduated in 1892, and Margaret Potter and Alice Crush in 1894. The fourth, Anne Wilson, a local resident, had graduated in 1892 from the Royal College of Physicians and Surgeons in Belfast. These women and four male graduates of Columbian and Georgetown made up the attending staff for the next few years. Women doctors never served on the dispensary's consulting board.[20]

During this time, the infirmary's financial base also underwent considerable change. Before 1890, the center had been a hand-to-mouth operation; Sumner relied on modest donations to pay for medical supplies and on small federal appropriations for fuel and rent. Beginning in 1890, however, when Kerr and other prominent male doctors joined the staff, the Women's Dispensary began to enjoy the patronage of Washington's best-known residents. The contributors' list in the 1890–91 Women's Dispensary statement resembled a distaff "Who's Who" of prominent Washingtonians. Mrs. Alexander Graham Bell, Kerr's cousin, led the list followed by Mrs. Leland Stanford, Mrs. Gardiner Hubbard, and Mrs. George Lathrop Bradley. Each contributed at least $25, a handsome sum in the 1890s, when $2 represented a generous donation. Less known charity-minded women also contributed substantially, swelling the dispensary's coffers to more than $2,000 in 1891 alone.[21]

The enlarged staff and the increase in available funds enabled affiliated doctors to treat more patients and to change the nature of the services offered. In 1895, doctors saw 1,424 patients, up from 667 in 1887. More important, they performed 241 surgical procedures, compared to 97 eight years earlier. In 1896, the board acquired additional space at the Miner Institute and enlarged the dispensary's surgical operations. Not surprisingly, 40 percent of the operations were gynecological. New surgical techniques and advances in anesthesiology contributed to the rise in the number of operations. But the expanded role of the Women's Dispensary as a teaching facility meant that participating surgeons performed more operations in order to demonstrate techniques for their observing students.[22]

The years 1890 to 1897 represented the high point of the Women's Dispensary services. After 1897, when the medical staffs of Georgetown and Columbian founded their own university hospitals, the fortunes of the dispensary declined dramatically. Tired of appropriating unsatisfactory facilities of existing infirmaries like those of the Women's Dispensary and frustrated over their lack of control over student training in other infirmaries, the faculties of Georgetown and Columbian convinced their respective trustees to aid them in constructing their own hospitals. Both faculties opened university hospitals in 1898.[23]

At the same time, dispensaries throughout the city suffered a decline. Government officials responsible for granting public aid became critical of neighborhood health facilities. In 1898, in keeping with a national trend, the District of Columbia Superintendent of Charities criticized the "inefficiency" of local operations and the duplication of services they fostered. He objected also to the increase in "imposture," the acquisition of free medical services by patients able to pay. Doctors with modest practices devoted to working-class and lower-middle-class patrons joined the protest, convinced that they lost paying clients to the free infirmaries. Concluding that local clinics and dispensaries were "extravagant" and wasteful of taxpayers' money, the superintendent reduced or withdrew their appropriations. In 1900 alone, the Washington Board of Charities eliminated seventeen of thirty-three neighborhood infirmaries while increasing appropriations to the expanding municipal hospitals.[24]

By 1900, conditions at the Women's Dispensary and Hospital had deteriorated considerably. In 1898, the dispensary's board of managers had requested a special $1,000 federal appropriation instead of the $500 supplement they had received the previous year. The board claimed that the cost of medical supplies and food for patients had forced them to close the surgical wards. The superintendent denied that request and subsequent applications for funds to reopen the wards. He maintained that the dispensary's building was unfit for surgical purposes and did not deserve further funding. He also turned down comparable requests from similar facilities, refusing, he claimed, to contribute further to "discreditable makeshifts and monuments of a disconnected patchwork policy." After 1900, the Women's Dispensary continued to function, but on a far more limited scale.[25]

The Women's Dispensary and Hospital thus underwent radical changes from the time it was founded in 1883 until its decline in 1900. Begun as a facility run exclusively by women doctors for the benefit of women patients, it temporarily became an adjunct to Washington's male medical establishment and was then discarded by the elite physicians responsible for its operation. Despite its varied career, the Women's Dispensary did provide numerous benefits for participating women doctors. Even though they assisted only in obstetrics, gynecology, and pediatrics, women physicians gained invaluable experience in those specialties by working with some of the most prominent physicians in the city. Moreover, the presence of even a few women doctors in the obstetrical and gynecological clinics afforded women patients a certain measure of comfort and understanding, a primary goal of the original founders. Women doctor were also able to demonstrate their skills to their male colleagues and earn status and referrals. When male medical doctors transferred their allegiance to the university hospitals, the women who had been affiliated with the Women's Dispensary lost an important opportunity for professional relationships with their male peers. Women's former colleagues barred them from participating in the Georgetown and Columbian hospitals for almost twenty more years.

The Woman's Clinic, founded in 1890 by Ida Heiberger, followed a different course. Heiberger left the Woman's Dispensary partly in response to the plight of Clara Bliss Hinds, Columbian's first woman graduate (1887) and one of the clinic's incorporators, who had been unable to gain postgraduate training at any city infirmary—including the Women's Dispensary. Heiberger was sensitive to the need for first-hand clinical experience because of her European training and took the initiative in founding the Woman's Clinic. Significantly, by-laws stated that the clinic's dual purpose was to "offset discrimination . . . against women physicians" and to "offer relief work among indigent women."[26]

From the outset the operation of the Woman's Clinic rested primarily in women's hands. The original twenty-member board of directors, which consisted of male and female members of the consulting staff, women doctors from the clinical staff, and interested women in the community, was soon augmented by more women. During the first year of the Woman's Clinic's operation, members reduced the number of consulting doctors on the governing board and increased the number of lay women. Doctors, school teachers, newspaper correspondents, government clerks, and housewives—all women—soon dominated that board. This heterogeneous female-led board directed every aspect of the Woman's Clinic, from the election of the professional staff to the purchase of supplies.

From the start, women doctors served in every staff position. Unlike the Women's Dispensary, whose consulting staff lacked female representation, the Woman's Clinic included female doctors among its consulting and assisting staffs. Two of the city's earliest regular women doctors, Mary Spackman and Mary Parsons, served on the clinic's consulting staff. Spackman had been the first woman to graduate from Howard's medical school, and she and Parsons were the first women doctors to be licensed in Washington. While the board of directors appointed several male doctors who taught at Georgetown and Columbian to the consulting staff, they included also white staff members of the Howard Medical Department, refusing to allow medical school rivalries to interfere with the clinic's operation. They did not go so far as to ignore the gulf that separated the races: None of Howard's eminent black physicians served on the consulting staff.

Male physicians also participated in the founding of the clinic, but they played an auxiliary, rather than a leading role. William Lee, professor of physiology at Columbian, and Daniel S. Lamb, professor of pathology at Howard, were among the incorporators. Both doctors staunchly supported female medical education. Lee, who later was the only professor to repudiate Columbian's discontinuation of coeducation, served as vice president of the clinic in 1892, the year of Columbian's action. Lamb was secretary of the clinic that same year. Lamb and his wife, the physician Isabel Haslup Lamb, Howard '97, served the clinic for more than twenty years. Despite the presence of these and other medical school faculty members on the clinic's board, clinical demonstrations never took place at the facility. In its long history, the Woman's Clinic served only as a treatment center for patients, not as a demonstration center for medical students.[27]

Between 1890 and 1899, newly graduated white women doctors formed the backbone of the clinic's attending staff. Almost every regular white woman doctor who graduated from medical school or practiced medicine in Washington in the 1890s worked at the Woman's Clinic, more than twenty doctors in all. Most stayed at the clinic for at least two years. In addition to Heiberger and Lamb, a few such as Julia Smith, Howard '89 and Columbian '91, and Jessie Kappelar, Columbian '90, served for an entire decade and beyond.

The clinic provided the equivalent of internships for the white female doctors. They handled all cases, from general diseases and diseases of the eyes, ears, throat, and skin to minor surgery and dentistry. "I am getting along very nicely at the Woman's Clinic as Dr. Heiberger's assistant," Anita Newcomb McGee wrote her sister. "I examine and treat patients myself. Go twice a week."[28]

During this decade, board members did not invite black physicians, male or female, to serve on the clinic's staff, however. But between 1910 and 1915, at least one black woman doctor worked at the clinic. Sarah Loguen Fraser had practiced for more than twenty years in the Dominican Republic after closing her Washington practice in 1884. In those early years, she had assisted Mary Parsons. (According to Fraser's daughter, some white women doctors expunged the record of her mother's presence and that of other black women from the clinic's case reports concerned, perhaps, that affiliation with a racially integrated professional staff might have damaged their careers.)[29]

Affiliated women doctors received valuable administrative training as well as medical experience at the clinic. By-laws required that each member of the clinical staff serve for one month as general supervisor of the clinic. The supervising doctor managed the medical staff, ordered supplies, and monitored patient care. At the same time she served as ex officio member of the finance committee. Participating women doctors thus acquired supervisory skills and financial experience at the same time that they developed medical expertise.[30]

The founders' intent that the Woman's Clinic be a female-oriented institution determined the clients it served. By-laws limited treatment to indigent women and their children under five—no men were permitted. The clinic also served wage-earning women, a group wholly neglected by other charities. Members of the board of directors, working women themselves, recognized that many of the women employed in Washington needed medical assistance in times of incapacity. When ill through "overwork" or a "lack of proper sanitary conditions," women who were otherwise self-supporting could "find no place for relief," noted the writer of a Woman's Clinic brochure in 1893. Such women could not afford the one to three dollars that most physicians charged, an amount that represented 10 to 20 percent of their weekly salaries. Yet they were ineligible for conventional medical charity, or they regarded it as demeaning and refused it.[31]

Founders devised several means to attract wage-earning women. By setting a small fee of 10 cents per visit, which included the cost of a prescription, female clients who refused to call on the clinic unless they paid something avoided the "disgrace of charity." Founders located the clinic near the boardinghouse district where most government clerks lived, yet close enough to poor neighborhoods so that it was still convenient for indigent women. They also added evening hours to morning and afternoon sessions so that working women could visit the clinic at the end of the work day. Because of these accommodations, the clinic reached many patients who might otherwise have gone untreated. In the first year of its operation, 1890–91, doctors treated almost 1,000 patients. By the mid-1890s, approximately three to four thousand women and infants received treatment annually. Only the dispensaries of the larger hospitals exceeded that case load.[32]

The clinic was able to maintain its financial independence without government assistance, a factor that contributed to its longevity. The board of trustees derived its income from several sources. As was customary, charitable donations accounted for the bulk of the clinic's receipts. Washington residents of modest means contributed 25 cents to $2 annually; a few wealthy individuals gave larger donations. Phoebe Hearst, for example, paid two months' rent for the clinic in 1892. Members of the clinic's medical staff and female medical students interested in the clinic's work contributed $5 each to the sustaining fund. The 10 cent patient fee covered more than one-fourth of the clinic's expenses.[33]

One goal of the clinic's directors remained unmet. Consistent with the trend toward hospital service, women doctors and trustees planned to establish a hospital and "sanitorium" for women and children "as soon as practical." In 1893, a pamphlet soliciting funds presented the case for a hospital—run and staffed exclusively by women. Founders envisioned a facility to serve the entire female community. Women doctors, denied privileges at all local hospitals, were to benefit most directly. They would be able to develop surgical skills and expertise in handling critical cases. In addition, they would no longer lose patients to male physicians who could provide comprehensive medical service. Women patients would also benefit from such a hospital, members of the clinic explained in a brochure soliciting funds. Without a woman's hospital, women in critical situations who preferred being treated by a woman doctor were denied that service. The participants of the Woman's Clinic also recognized that a woman's hospital would create new jobs and training for women as administrators, nurses, and pharmacists. Despite regular appeals, a woman's hospital never did become a reality.[34]

Some Washington hospitals did provide hospital training for women doctors, but on a limited basis and only under extraordinary circumstances. For a few months in 1893, William Johnson, gynecologist at the Central Dispensary and Emergency Hospital, allowed Anita Newcomb McGee to train with him. McGee, who came from a family distinguished in Washington scientific circles and who graduated with honors from Columbian in 1892, wrote her sister that this was "[a rare favor]." No other women worked at that hospital for the next four years. Then, in 1896, when Swan Burnett, chief of the ophthalmology clinic at Central, was negotiating with Phoebe Hearst for funds to equip two new hospital buildings, he appointed two women to the staff of thirty-seven: Adeline Portman, an 1887 graduate of the University of Iowa, and Ada Thomas, an 1893 graduate of the Woman's Medical College of Pennsylvania. Two years later, when Hearst donated money for buildings and a new laboratory (in memory of Burnett's son), two more women doctors joined the staff. At least one woman doctor served on Central's attending staff over the next ten years. In 1896, Burnett also secured the appointment of a woman to the staff of the Episcopal Eye, Ear, and Throat Hospital after Hearst offered a liberal donation. No other women joined that staff.[35]

A fourth women's infirmary, the Dorothea Dix Dispensary, also operated in Washington during this period. Founded in 1894 by Clara Bliss Hinds and Anne Wilson, the Dix Dispensary resembled the Woman's Clinic in several respects: It restricted staff appointments to women doctors and limited service to women and young children. The staffs of the Woman's Clinic and the Dix Dispensary overlapped; several of Washington's women doctors served at both centers. Florence Spofford, daughter of Ainsworth Spofford, librarian of Congress, served as the dispensary's treasurer from its founding. Despite members' connections with Washington's affluent professional community, the dispensary closed in 1897 because of inadequate funds.[36]

Unlike many of the city's health care facilities that closed during this period, the Woman's Clinic survived. Because it was largely self-supporting, it withstood sharp cutbacks in government funds that eliminated small dispensaries and clinics around 1900. After 1910, however, the clinic's importance to women doctors and the range of its services diminished. Two major factors contributed to its decline. First, the number of women doctors graduating from area medical schools dropped sharply, reducing the need for training facilities for women. Based on hand counts, in 1896, at the height of the women's clinics and dispensaries, twenty-four white women regulars practiced in the city; more than 60 percent of them (fifteen) had graduated during the previous five years. Almost ten years later, according to city directory listings, in 1905, only two of twenty-four women then practicing in the city were recent medical graduates. Once the women doctors of the 1890s had established their own practices, they distanced themselves from the health facility that had provided their initial training.

The inability of the women's clinics to provide women physicians with up-to-date surgical facilities was the second major factor that reduced its value to the female medical community. Women doctors affiliated with the Woman's Clinic never were able to build their own hospital. They did pressure administrators of other local hospitals to admit women, however. Eventually, their efforts succeeded. In 1914, members of the Woman's Clinic, along with the local women's medical society, persuaded the medical staff of Garfield Hospital to open their competitive internship exam to women. Kate Karpeles, a graduate of Johns Hopkins, won the position. That same year, supporters of women doctors endowed a bed at Sibley Hospital for the use of the Woman's Clinic. The following year, for the first time in a Washington hospital, a visiting woman surgeon performed a major operation. That same year, 1915, affiliates of the Woman's Clinic performed seventeen operations at Sibley Hospital. In almost every operation the surgical team—operators, assistants, and anesthetists—was composed entirely of women.[37]

Once women were accepted into the city's hospitals on a regular, albeit limited, basis after 1915, the influence of the Woman's Clinic in the female medical community declined further. Newly graduated women doctors chose to affiliate with the more prestigious and up-to-date clinics and dispensaries that now admitted them rather than train at the Woman's Clinic. Their mentors cautioned them to "stay away" from the Woman's Clinic because affiliation could tarnish their reputations.[38]

The mid-1890s, the years in which women assisted at the Homoeopathic Free Dispensary, the Women's Dispensary, the Woman's Clinic, and the Dorothea Dix Dispensary, marked the zenith of women's health care centers in Washington. During their short periods of existence, these women's infirmaries enabled several thousand indigent and poor working women to receive competent medical care from women doctors. Their decline left a serious gap in the services that the city provided. An anonymous woman doctor interviewed at the Woman's Clinic in 1902 commented on the inadequacy of existing institutions. "When I think of all the poor and suffering women that are there in Washington, then think of how small a proportion of them we are able to relieve, I find it hard not to get discouraged," she told an enquiring journalist.[39]

The women's facilities also provided a necessary training ground for women doctors in the 1890s. Newly graduated women physicians received the firsthand clinical and surgical training essential to their success. Contacts gained there led to consultations and referrals. These medical centers also provided a supportive environment for women doctors, enabling them to share information and relieve the social and professional isolation many experienced. If these women's institutions failed to set women doctors on career paths that led to prominence and marked success, they did succeed in fostering a network of women physicians that aided women doctors' professional growth and development.

In 1895, Dr. Francis White, professor of medicine at the Woman's Medical College of Pennsylvania, discussed the role of such facilities throughout the country. White compared the founders of these institutions to the "advanced guard of an invading army, compelled to build their own roads and create their own facilities in advance." Ironically, White's analogy was all too apt. When replacements failed to arrive, the advance collapsed, and the facilities all but closed. Restrictions on women's medical education, over which they had no control,

not only diminished their numbers, but also eliminated their supporting institutions.[40]

White's analogy bears further scrutiny. It may be more correct to
observe that the "advanced guard" of Washington's dispensaries invaded territory that enemy forces were already abandoning. By the
1890s, dispensaries and clinics in American cities were becoming
anachronistic, even as they were multiplying. The field of operations
was shifting to new terrain—the scientifically equipped, up-to-date
university hospitals and the large metropolitan hospitals—a no-man's-
land for women, or more correctly, another "no-woman's-land." After
the turn of the century, these hospital complexes came to signify the
apex of professional medical power. Women lacked both the financial
resources to move their institutions into this new arena and the influence to alter policies that limited their participation. Women's autono-
mous clinics that had shown such vitality during the 1890s became
second-class institutions after 1900. They operated on the periphery
of the male medical establishment—an apt commentary on the status
of their female participants.

6

The Entry of Women into Professional Medical Associations

"All Medical and Chirurgical Persons Qualified"

Status in Washington's regular medical community depended upon membership in the city's medical associations—the District of Columbia Medical Society and the District of Columbia Medical Association. These white male groups controlled access to licensing privileges and consultation courtesies, vital components of a successful practice after the 1860s. Until the 1880s, members of these associations refused to admit women or to grant them the courtesies commonly extended fellow physicians. Mary Parsons and Mary Spackman, Howard's first women medical graduates, strove for three years for the right to be licensed and for six years for consultation courtesies; they struggled longest—for sixteen years—to gain entry into the Medical Society itself. In some respects, admission into the medical fraternity proved a bittersweet victory. As much as they had desired integration, women doctors subsequently found it wanting.

Throughout these years of struggle, white female and black male doctors shared many of the same problems. Although their causes were frequently linked, the outcome of each influencing the other, each group fought its battles alone, and experienced different degrees of success. In terms of licensing and consultation privileges, black men received concessions before white women. In terms of Medical Society membership, however, race proved to be more obdurate than sex: Women gained admission long before black men. As reluctant as male doctors were to admit women to their "club," they resisted even more extending such courtesies to black men. Ultimately, white female physicians and black male doctors formed their own associations. Black women, triply disadvantaged—discriminated against by the city's medical elite, by white women doctors, and by men

94

of their own race—remained isolated in the practice of medicine in the city.

Washington's Medical Society and Medical Association, the groups that held the keys to the required prerogatives, were two of the oldest medical organizations in the United States. Founders of the premier group, the District of Columbia Medical Society, sought a federal charter in 1819. Their purpose, as one of the founders recalled, was to "secure a law that would prevent any but competent physicians from practicing" at a time when "almost anyone could practice." Although these doctors failed to win all the concessions they desired, Congress did grant them the sole right to license all trained practitioners in the city, regular and irregular—or, more accurately, to certify "all medical and chirurgical gentlemen qualified to practice," a phrase that would haunt women doctors some sixty years later. The bill required all practitioners new to the city to obtain a license within six months of their arrival or risk severe penalty. The charter specifically forbade the society from setting fees or restricting the services of physicians previously licensed elsewhere.[1]

In 1833, a group of society members, along with some physicians new to the city, incorporated the city's other regular group, the District of Columbia Medical Association. Their intent was to establish a schedule of fees and a code of medical ethics, prerogatives denied the society by law. Frustrated by their inability to control the practice of medicine with a licensing law that proved difficult to apply, the elite physicians who formed the group sought other means to control what they called "the contentious elements" in the profession. In 1850, largely in response to the growing crossover between homeopaths and regulars, association members added the nefarious Clause Sixteen to their code of ethics, the prohibition against consulting professionally with nonmembers.[2]

As these two organizations evolved, they took on different social and profesional functions. The society represented the more exclusive body of doctors. Membership in that group required a two-thirds vote of approval. Doctors who participated were among the most successful in the city. They held offices in both medical groups and in the city's network of specialist societies. They also taught in local medical schools and were instrumental in founding and staffing Washington's hospitals. At meetings held four times a year, members presented papers, investigated medical topics of interest, and met for social and economic gain. The Medical Association, on the other hand, represented the inclusive body of the city's regular doctors. Membership in that group was available to any licensed physician and required only one-half of the votes cast for admission. Association members turned few prospects away who could provide passable credentials and the entry fee.

After the Civil War, as Washington's medical corps expanded and these two associations grew in size, leaders were able to influence the practice of medicine in the city to a greater extent. The society's licensing function and the association's ability to withhold consulting privileges constituted the principal weapons in their arsenal. Before the war, only a minority of doctors practicing in Washington bothered to acquire licenses; after the war, however, more than half the practioners in the city sought that credential. Doctors intent on winning the patronage of urban white-collar workers and middle-class residents felt compelled to prove to a doubting public that they were duly qualified by a body of their peers. As regularly trained physicians, they wanted to distinguish themselves from the quacks, herbists, and other irregulars who called themselves "doctor."

In a city with a population as mobile as Washington's, few physicians had local connections on which to build a practice. The stamp of legitimacy conferred by an authorized body seemed essential. By 1867, the District of Columbia Medical Society's Board of Examiners, true to its charter, had certified every doctor who could show proof of proper training. Its list of 160 certified physicians included all of the 118 doctors whose names appeared in the city directory, plus numerous others employed as pension examiners, physicians in the armed forces, or white-collar clerks. At the time, the contribution that the $10 fee made to the society's coffers outweighed concerns about limiting the nature or the size of the medical corps in the city. In fact, contrary to the wording of its own charter, the board even licensed several women doctors, a number of homeopaths, and, according to a contemporary, numerous irregulars who lacked appropriate credentials—the last year the board was willing to act so inclusively. In the years to follow, as concerns about the increasing number of women physicians grew and disputes among the various sects intensified, board members refused to license women and hesitated to certify men who had trained at nonregular medical colleges.[3]

The regulars' second weapon, the withholding of consultation courtesies from nonmember doctors, similarly grew in importance during the third quarter of the century. By the 1870s and 1880s, physicians began to join the Medical Association for this privilege alone. The ban was originally adopted to deprive homeopaths of the services of regular specialists in the hope of minimizing the crossover between regulars and homeopaths; when enacted, it worked with particular severity against those regulars unaffiliated with the medical groups. Given the uncertain state of the healing arts in the last half of the nineteenth century, doctors who wanted to establish reputations needed to be able to consult with colleagues to verify their own diagnoses and treatment before a doubting public. Indeed, patients often forced that action upon their attending physicians, insisting they call in colleagues to support their recommendations, and often even calling other physicians to the case themselves.

The consultation clause prohibited members from consulting with nonmembers "in any professional way." With its finely tuned unwritten code of behavior—the consultant, for example, always followed the physician into the sick room and never followed him out—it provided a measure of protection against the raiding of patients by specialists and other doctors, and thus gave cooperating physicians a sense of security. After the 1870s, as specialties increased and patients demanded consultations with presumed experts, particularly those in surgery and gynecology, that courtesy became all the more important to the average practitioner. An unaffiliated doctor unable to call in a consultant or a specialist risked losing patients to doctors who could rely on professional courtesies. Occasionally, specialists would refuse to render aid to a patient whose physician did not belong to the association, forcing the family to discharge the nonmember and hire a member of the club. Without consultation privileges, a doctor also had to forego municipal sinecures and work in charitable agencies, thereby reducing potential income and connections.[4]

Between 1869 and 1888, members of three medical groups who operated at the periphery of the regulars' circle—regularly trained black male physicians, male and female homeopaths, and white female regulars—attempted to force white male regulars to share their exclusive entitlements. Black physicians fired the opening salvo, but registered only partial gains in their struggle for professional recognition between 1869 and 1872; homeopaths won some concessions in 1870, largely in the wake of the furor over black rights. Attempts by supporters of women doctors to use the unrest created by black physicians failed altogether at this time. Women's efforts succeeded more than a decade later, largely a result of their increasing numbers in the city's elite medical schools.

At least six black male physicians practiced in the city after the Civil War. Licensing presented no obstacle to them; those who applied, obtained licenses to practice from the board of examiners. Because these doctors were able to present the qualification of regular training defined by the Medical Society's charter, the board of examiners had no official grounds on which to reject them. Several had graduated from recognized medical schools, and had served as surgeons and physicians among the Union troops. Alexander Augusta, for example, graduated from the Medical College of Toronto and served as surgeon of the Seventh United States Colored Troops. Immediately after the war, he managed the government hospital in Savannah, and then moved to Washington, where he affiliated with Howard University and Freedmen's Hospital. Charles Purvis, another black licentiate of the 1860s, graduated from the Western Reserve School of Medicine before joining the armed services and settling in the capital. Society members, however, resisted when black physicians attempted to join the Medical Society and when they demanded consulting privileges. The battle lines were drawn in March 1869, when a group of society members, which included Robert Reyburn, D. Willard Bliss, and Joseph Taber Johnson (instructors in Howard or Georgetown medical schools who were noted for their abolitionist sentiments) proposed Augusta and Purvis, their black colleagues from Freedmen's Hospital, for membership along with another black physician, A. S. Tucker.[5]

The society, composed of numerous former Confederate soldiers and sympathizers, decisively rejected that application and others that black supporters presented in the following months. Frustrated by the response of the largely southern—and Democratic—Medical Society, proponents of integration brought their case to Republican Senator Charles Sumner of Massachusetts. Sumner took up the cause with a vengeance, and in December 1869, proposed to the Congress that the Senate revoke the Medical Society's charter. By denying nonmembers consultation privileges and access to scientific discussions that would benefit the general public, he claimed, the society forsook its public charter and operated instead as an illegal monopoly or private club.

Sumner reported that the consultation ban placed black physicians in double jeopardy: White physicians denied them consulting courtesies because they were not society members but then refused to admit them to their organization. Even worse, on several occasions— under the pretext of the consultation clause—society members stole black doctors' patients. Testifying before Sumner's committee, Augusta and Purvis told of repeated instances when doctors affiliated with the Medical Society refused to examine their patients unless the families dismissed the black physicians from the case and hired a society affiliate instead. In only one instance, said Augusta, did a family refuse to bow to the pressure of the society specialist and insist on retaining him in the case. The black physician then sent for D. Willard Bliss, "well known," according to Augusta, "for his liberal nature."

Bliss agreed to consult with Augusta at the risk of society censure. Sumner noted in his report that there were a few other members of the society who, like Bliss, "bravely challenged the censure of the Society" and willingly consulted with the black physicians.[6]

The ostracized physicians further complained that exclusion from the society brought them professional harm, because it prevented them from participating in discusssions of "peculiar and interesting cases with their appropriate treatment" and "shut [them] out" from the opportunity of submitting their own cases for discussion. Although the excluded doctors may have attributed more significance to the educational benefits of membership than was warranted, their plea reflected a legitimate desire to share in the recognition, professional camaraderie, and contacts to which they were entitled by training and ability.[7]

While Sumner's investigation was under way, Reyburn submitted a resolution at the January meeting of the Medical Society that would have eliminated the principal cause of contention. His proposal that the consulation clause be modified to read "that no physician [who is otherwise eligible] shall be excluded from membership in this Society on account of race or color" failed by a wide margin. However, his challenge to the society and the unfavorable publicity the issue aroused did force Medical Society members to publish a defense of their actions. In "An Appeal to Congress," the members attempted to circumvent the issue of the consultation ban by claiming that the law had not been violated because enforcement of the consultation clause fell to the Medical Association rather than to the Medical Society, a position most professionals knew to be a ruse. Members also claimed that, despite the name of the organization, the society represented a club, or a "privilege of association and social reunion," rather than a professional society that endowed its members with special economic and professional benefits.[8]

The same week that this defense appeared, blacks and their supporters took action on another front. Anticipating the success of Sumner's effort to repeal the society's charter, the doctors who taught at Howard and worked at Freedmen's Hospital organized the National Medical Society, the first biracial medical group in the country. They presented a memorial to the Congress, requesting a charter for the "new Society which [would] give all rights and privileges and immunities to all physicians, making only the presentation of a diploma from some college recognized by the American Medical Association and good standing in the profession, the qualifications necessary for membership." Once the Medical Society's charter was revoked—as members of the new group felt assured it would be—the NMS would assume official status as the only medical group chartered by the federal government in the District of Columbia, and its doctors could turn the tables on their recalcitrant opponents. Events were to prove NMS members wrong, however. In February 1870, Sumner presented Senate Bill No. 511. The Senate, unwilling to become embroiled in the local debate, refused four times to consider the measure. Disappointed by the setback, black physicians and their supporters moved their cause to another front, the floor of the American Medical Association convention, scheduled that May in Washington.[9]

While these events were taking place, the city's homeopaths used the ensuing publicity for their own ends. The same month that Reyburn and others established the NMS, Tullio Verdi, self-appointed dean of Washington's homeopathic physicians, requested that Congress charter a national homeopathic society. Under the existing Medical Society charter, Verdi claimed, homeopaths had no recourse by which they could collect their fees; that privilege was reserved for regulars alone. Moreover, he claimed, homeopaths faced a peculiar "dilemma" when applying to the regular's board of examiners for licensure. Because they possessed diplomas from nonregular medical schools, they were vulnerable to "being declared by this inimical board incompetent to practice medicine, thus ruining all their prospects of success in the city." Others, he claimed—himself among them—refused to pay "that august body $10, the fee required by the society, for putting their names to a lie." Either way, he pointed out, homeopaths were exposed to a $200 fine under the law for practicing without a license. Obviously capitalizing on the Medical Society's predicament, Verdi's proposed charter welcomed all physicians "without exception on account of color."[10]

Although the charter failed to mention sex specifically, it did imply that women would be admitted equally with men. Verdi and others openly criticized Washington's regular medical association for "berating the intelligence of women" and for "proscribing eminent medical men on account of their color." Relying on a powerful lobby that had the support of Radical Republicans, the homeopaths' bill passed both houses in April 1870. At that time, at least two women homeopaths—Caroline Winslow and Susan Edson—practiced in the city; both, ironically, had been licensed by the Medical Society's board of examiners in 1867.[11]

While medical society members experienced consternation over Verdi's coup, they dared not dwell on its implications as they prepared for the confrontation looming at the Washington AMA meeting the following month. Fearful that the existence of their organization was at stake, Medical Society doctors came well prepared to defend themselves against the charges of the opposing physicians. Reyburn, Bliss, and a dozen other Medical Society physicians had formed several medical groups—at least two were biracial—for which they demanded recognition and seating in place of the Medical Society's delegation. The fight on the AMA floor was bitter and often raucous. Never openly mentioning the real issue, that of the race of the contending groups, the AMA committee on ethics rejected the claims of the challengers, accusing them of unprofessional behavior.[12]

The minority committee report, signed by Alfred Stille, soon-to-be president of the AMA, found them "qualified practitioners of medicine, who have complied with all the conditions of membership" and recommended that they be seated. (Significantly, the following year, the liberal-minded Stille recommended against seating women doctors with equivalent credentials.) At the conclusion of the session, Robert Storer introduced a resolution that had the practical effect of deleting any racial overtones from the record of the hearings. Passed by the assembled body, the resolution declared that the "consideration of race and color had had nothing whatsoever to do with the decision of the question of the reception of the Washington delegates."[13]

During the following year, 1872, blacks made no headway in their attempt to integrate the Medical Society or the AMA. Once more, Sumner sought to repeal the society's charter, but Congress again refused to act in the medical dispute. Reyburn, Bliss, and others repeatedly offered their colleagues' names in membership at Medical Society meetings, also without success. Attendees of the AMA convention in May once again refused to seat delegations that included black physicians.

The cause of women physicians also surfaced at the 1872 meeting. Stille, the AMA president, was unable to use his influence to seat the biracial association delegates, but he did set the tone toward women applicants that prevailed during the sessions. In his presidential address, Stille castigated women physicians as "monstrous productions . . . unfitted by nature" for medical practice. "Woman," he said "is characterized by uncertainty of rational judgement, capriciousness of sentiment, fickleness of purpose, and indecision of action which totally unfit her for professional pursuits." Not surprisingly, when confreres later refused to seat the integrated Howard Medical Department and Freedmen's Hospital delegations, they justified their action, by a vote of eighty-three to twenty-six, on the fact that a woman doctor was affiliated with Freedmen's Hospital and with the Howard

Medical School—sidestepping the issue of race entirely. At the time of the meetings, Isabel Barrows served as attending physician of ophthalmology and otology at Freedmen's and taught in the medical school; seven women were then enrolled in Howard's medical department. Opponents of integration, mindful of the support blacks could garner, recognized that it was safer politically to discriminate openly against women doctors than against black male physicians.[14]

Immediately after the national convention, blacks' supporters tackled a related issue, that of consultation privileges. Here too, blacks' and women's fortunes were joined. Unlike San Francisco, however, in this instance black physicians scored an important victory. Women doctors, on the other hand, experienced the first of numerous defeats. The debate over the consulation clause began in early spring, when Bliss deliberately set out "to test the power of the Association," as his opponents claimed. One of the most successful practitioners in the city (the vice-president of the United States was one of his patients), Bliss believed himself above censure and sought to expose the hyprocisy of members who adhered to the letter of the consultation clause when it came to black doctors, but ignored its proscriptions when their white male colleagues were concerned. In a letter to the organization, Bliss announced that contrary to the rules of the Medical Association, he had consulted with Christopher C. Cox, a white physician whose application the group had just rejected for his participation in the fight to seat black delegates at the AMA. Bliss also boasted that he had intentionally "violated" the association's rules and met with Augusta, "an educated and reputable colored physician who has equally fallen under your proscriptive and unwarrantable ban."[15]

To Bliss's astonishment, members promptly expelled him; the first time in its history that it took such action. Reyburn cast the only dissenting vote. Despite the near unanimity of the action, Bliss regarded his expulsion lightly. Even the then-Senator James Garfield congratulated him on being "decorated" by the association. "I have no doubt it will do you good," the senator wrote. However, to Bliss's consternation, his case load dropped precipitously, and his Georgetown colleagues forced him to resign from the faculty. Within a few years, from an income estimated at upwards of $10,000 a year, Bliss's practice dwindled so that he could no longer support his family. Five years later, "contrite and repentant," according to a contemporary who recorded these events, Bliss apologized to the association, applied for readmission, and rejoined.[16]

Bliss's precipitous action, damaging though it was to his own career, secured the desired result for black doctors. In November 1871, a few months after members expelled the popular doctor, they adopted a resolution that amended Clause Sixteen to permit consultation "with any regular physician of African descent." The notoriety caused by Bliss's action and the lingering threat of Senator Sumner's challenge to the existence of the Medical Society forced members to acknowledge that they had to give black doctors some concession or risk dissolution. In addition, black doctors appeared to be gaining supporters within the Medical Society. Confederate sympathizers feared that a majority of society members would admit blacks at the next showdown. Given the choice of being "compelled to meet with colored physicians socially at the debates and entertainments of the Society," as one observer phrased it, or consulting with them on a professional basis, members granted the concession, convinced that consultation was a lesser evil than fraternization.[17]

During this time, the issue of women's status in the medical organizations began to assume greater importance. At the October 1871 meeting, just a few weeks before members voted to modify the consultation clause, Reyburn raised the issue of the status of women doctors. An outspoken advocate of women's rights, he engaged the society in debate when he moved to amend the constitution to admit "all graduates of regular medical colleges who are licentiates of the Medical Society." Such an amendment would have had the practical effect of admitting both blacks and women to the club. Reyburn might well have been prompted to this inclusive wording by his concern for his female students at Howard. He recognized that some, like first- and second-year medical students Mary Parsons and Mary Spackman, would have been excluded from the society even though they met all the criteria for membership—but one. In addition, as a professor at Howard, Reyburn consulted regularly with Isabel Barrows, who practiced medicine next door to him.[18]

Reyburn's relationship with Barrows placed his own society membership in jeopardy. Indeed, the society had already formally "rebuked" him for his activities on behalf of blacks. Some members might well have relished the opportunity to use his professional association with the nonmember woman doctor as the pretext to punish him for his participation in the events of the preceding two years. Reyburn's attempt to pave the way for women and blacks failed. Association members rejected his inclusive amendment by a large majority. In the words of one participant, animosity expressed toward women physicians at the meeting was "quite as vehement and far more general" than resentment against blacks.

Despite their victory in terms of the consultation clause, blacks were unable to wrest further concessions from the professional white male community. In December 1872, Sumner attempted for the last time to repeal the society's charter; again, his colleagues refused to report it out of committee. The National Medical Society, formed to take advantage of Sumner's anticipated success in revoking the medical society charter, itself disbanded. In 1884, black and white male physicians once more attemptd to create a racially integrated association and organized the Medico-Chirurgical Society. Although women doctors, both black and white, practiced in Washington at the time, none held membership in that group. Within a few years that society ceased to function as well. In 1895, however, after several promising attempts to integrate the medical associations failed, black male physicians revived the Medico-Chirurgical Society. It ultimately became one of the leading professional organizations in the black community.[19]

Women's struggle to integrate the organized ranks of Washington's medical professionals followed a different course; time was on their side. Although initially these pioneers faced considerable opposition, bonds of race and class eventually prevailed over distinctions of sex. In the spring of 1872, following the resolution of the consultation controversy in favor of black male doctors, regularly trained women doctors began their drive for professional certification in earnest. In March, Mary D. Spackman, Howard's first woman medical graduate, applied for a license to practice medicine. During the next fifteen years, she and Washington's other pioneer women doctors waged their struggle on all three fronts—licensing, consultation, and membership. With their male allies, women used numerous tactics to dismantle the prohibitions against them. Only when it served society members' interests, however, or when forced by law did they grant women the privileges to which they were entitled.

Even more than their male colleagues, pioneer women doctors required the legitimacy that a license bestowed. In addition to contending with the competition of irregular male practitioners, they had to distinguish themselves from Washington's female abortionists, herbists, quacks, and midwives, who boldly called themselves "doctress" and "doctor." Even as late as 1889, abortionists such as "Mrs. Dr. Renner" were advertising in local newspapers in the euphemistic code that promised a "safe and sure relief in all female trouble." Landlords often refused even to rent quarters to women doctors, fearing the taint of questionable practice. Acquiring the license from the Medical Society's examining board would have alleviated such suspicions, but it hung on the wording of the 1819 charter that specified certification for "medical and chirurgical gentlemen" only.[20]

A few days after her graduation, Spackman applied to the society for certification. The secretary of that group, William Lee, reluctantly rejected her appeal. He informed her that the organization's charter prevented him from fulfilling her request. In actuality, ignoring the letter of the law, the board had licensed at least four women who had applied in 1867. Two were graduates of irregular colleges, while the background of the other two is not known. Spackman had to open her practice without the coveted license and wait for a more propitious opportunity.[21]

Washington's medical men may have hoped that the issue of women's licensing, if left alone, would just go away. But two years later, in June 1874, Howard's next woman graduate, Mary Almera Parsons, applied for her license to practice. Parsons's applicaton led to a protracted discussion on consultation rights for women as well as for other members of the Washington medical community, such as sundown doctors and military physicians. James W. Lovejoy, the physician who had presided over the Medical Society in 1872, when the organization had rejected Spackman's application, spoke on the justice of awarding consultation rights to women. Although he was not an "advocate" of women doctors or of female medical education, he said, events had forced him to concede that women did have a right to practice medicine—and the Medical Association had no right to deny the patients of qualified nonmembers the benefits of consultation. "Consultations were for the benefit of and belonged to the patients," he argued. "No local society has a right to restrict [them]."[22]

Lovejoy chastized those doctors who wanted to deny women such privileges in order to force them out of the profession. He urged the group to consider the matter at length. At Lovejoy's request, Flodoardo Howard, president of the Medical Association, appointed a committee to investigate the possibility of granting women consultation rights. He charged the group to report their findings at the fall meeting. Howard's choice of committee members reflected his own bias against women and seemingly prejudiced the outcome of the committee report. Samuel Claggett Busey, future president of the society and a supporter of Parsons's application, refused to serve on the committee. He was convinced that the outcome was foregone because its members fundamentally opposed women doctors. Busey's suspicions were confirmed; at the next meeting, in October 1874, the committee did, indeed, recommend against further modification of the consultation clause to include women. Busey and Reyburn submitted amendments to remove all restrictions against women, but members rejected them overwhelmingly as well.

Unable to move such unyielding opposition, women sought redress from another quarter. J. Ford Thompson, a doctor with a valued reputation in the city and a participant in the effort to seat black physicians, encouraged them to appeal to the federal government, adopting the tactic that he and other physicians had used five years earlier on behalf of blacks. Because Congress had incorporated the Medical Society, he argued, it had the authority to change the wording of the original charter that denied women the opportunity to be licensed. Following Thompson's advice, on January 14, 1875, Parsons and Spackman petitioned Congress to amend the society's charter by striking the word "gentlemen" and replacing it with the word "persons." At congressional hearings, the women physicians claimed that without licenses, they were "denied the privileges of consultation," that they "could not legally collect [their] fees," and that they could not receive "proper recognition as physicians." After several readings and delays, both the House, on January 23, 1875, and the Senate, on March 3, 1875, approved the bill. The revised charter, empowering the society to license "such medical and chirurgical persons as they may . . . judge qualified to practice," forced the board of examiners to grant qualified women the coveted license to practice medicine.[23]

Although women won the right to be licensed, they still required consultation privileges and membership in order to enjoy equal professional rights. Between 1875 and 1878, Parsons and Spackman applied annually for membership in both the Medical Society and the Medical Association, hoping their success in winning membership would resolve the consultation issue as well. But both groups consistently rejected the women's applications.

Support for women doctors was growing, however. Some doctors even quietly disregarded the ban against consultations by volunteering their services at the Women's Christian Association where Spackman treated women residents. Unofficial acceptance took concrete form in the spring of 1878. At their annual meeting, association doctors adopted the amendment changing the by-laws of the organization that had prohibited consultations with women doctors. Busey and Thompson, the latter newly appointed to the Columbian faculty where the admission of women to the medical school was being debated, took the initiative. They argued that women who were being trained side by side with men deserved the same privileges.

Their colleagues, however, may have had more practical reasons for reconsidering their previous position. With women gaining support in the society, opponents hoped to undermine their demand for full membership by granting consultation privileges, a tactic that had successfully prevented blacks from joining the medical organization six years earlier. At the same time, the rising number of homeopathic women doctors entering practice in Washington provided a source of concern for regular male doctors. Women homeopaths were highly respected in the city and could rely upon consultations with their male colleagues, conceivably winning female patients away from regulars. Susan Edson, for example, was family physician for President Garfield, and her activities received regular press coverage as did those of women's rights activist Caroline Winslow. During the 1870s, five more women doctors had entered the practice of medicine in the District— all in the homeopathic camp. Two of them, Caroline Burghardt and Grace Roberts, had graduated from the regular medical department at Howard and then adopted homeopathy. Many male doctors viewed the granting of consultation rights to women regulars as a means of keeping female graduates in the regular ranks, thereby drawing additional clients into the fold rather than forcing them away. Thus, instead of viewing women doctors as liabilities as they had in the past, regular medical men began to regard them instead as potential assets.

In addition, Washington doctors were well aware that women physicians were gaining acceptance elsewhere. By 1878, several state and local medical societies had relaxed consultation restrictions against women doctors, and some had even opened membership to women physicians. In addition, influential specialists saw little to gain in turning away possible referrals. Thus, while some doctors sincerely argued for the justice of granting the very women they were training consulting privileges, others supported the proposal for more pragmatic reasons. Women, grateful for the opportunity on whatever terms, regarded their success as the opening wedge to membership, hardly suspecting that that privilege would take almost another ten years to achieve.[24]

In 1879, with licensing and consultation victories behind them, women doctors sought membership in the two medical organizations. That year, Parsons reapplied for membership in both the Medical Society and the Medical Association. As Busey later recalled, "there was no power either in argument or legislation by which men could be persuaded or made to vote for [women's] admission to full membership." For the third year in a row, members of both groups denied her application. Dismayed by continued rejection, neither Parsons nor Spackman applied to either medical body for the next six years.[25]

Then in 1885, confident she had a chance, Parsons renewed her efforts and applied for admission to the Medical Association (the more inclusive medical body). This time she applied with Jeannette

Sumner, a doctor who had been practicing in Washington for two years. Times had changed since Parsons and Spackman had first applied for membership thirteen years earlier, and the status of women doctors in the community had improved. The first women doctors had practiced on the fringe of the respectable medical establishment. Early students of Howard's program, they suffered the double stigma of graduating from that upstart school and of being women at a time when most male physicians either refused to acknowledge them as colleagues or feared their rivalry. Sumner, on the other hand, had close ties to leaders of Washington's medical community who possessed sufficient influence to guarantee her admission. She had attended Georgetown Medical School in 1880 and, following her graduation from the Woman's Medical College of Pennsylvania in 1883, she had opened the Women's Dispensary with the aid of physicians from the faculties of Columbian and Georgetown, among them the president of Georgetown Medical School and the dean of the Columbian faculty.

Moreover, the number of regular women doctors practicing in the city had increased in the intervening years. In 1885, six women regulars practiced in Washington who qualified for membership in that organization. Even more significantly, the prospect of more well-trained women doctors loomed on the horizon with the opening a few months earlier of Columbian's medical program to women. To have denied women doctors admission to the medical organization when they were already attending the most prestigious of Washington's medical schools appeared absurd, even to women's detractors.

But pragmatic considerations also influenced the outcome. Medical Association members realized that unless they included the growing numbers of women regulars in their professional societies, they would have no means of regulating the women's professional conduct and fee-setting policies. Because women already had consultation privileges, there was no way to discourage or prevent them from advertising in the newspaper, setting lower fees, or stealing patients. The association's only weapons in such cases—chastisement or expulsion— were of no avail if women were not in the club. Thus, association doctors finally realized what their former president had declared thirteen years earlier—if women doctors were an "evil, [they] were such an evil that neither this organization nor the entire medical profession of the country could abate." It was, therefore, as Lovejoy had stated earlier, "the part of wisdom" to admit them—at least to membership in the Medical Association.[26]

Admission to the Medical Society was another matter. If Medical Association doctors had acted out of self-interest when they admitted women into their group in 1885, members of the Medical Society had no such compulsion. Doctors in that group had long viewed their organization as an exclusive club with regular meetings devoted in part to scientific discussions, but also to social pleasures. The changing realities of Washington's professional social life forced them to reevaluate their position. In the mid-1880s, other professional and quasi-professional organizations such as the Anthropological Society of Washington and the Cosmos Club among numerous others, began to compete for the loyalty of successful practitioners. As a result, attendance at society meetings dropped, and membership declined. In 1887, in an attempt to halt the decline and to increase membership, society members relaxed their regulations and opened their meetings to all regulars licensed to practice. Women's admission to the society was the next logical step. In October 1888, when Parsons again applied, members of the Medical Society approved her application.[27]

Samuel Busey, a chronicler of these events, credited women's eventual success to their willingnes to "accept the conditions as they found them and wait in patience" for their eventual admission. In a sarcastic reference to the tactics blacks had used in 1870, Busey applauded women who "did not array themselves into a cabal with hostile intent and flaunt their accusations and grievances in the arena of popular indignation." The refusal of the society to admit blacks for almost seventy-five more years, however, proved the inefficacy of patience as a strategy. In actuality, women won entry into both professional organizations, not because they waited in traditionally ladylike patience, as Busey wished to believe, but because the time had come when voting members recognized it was in their own best interest to change that policy.[28]

Following the society's change in policy, women's applications received the same consideration as did those of their male colleagues in both the Medical Association and the Medical Society. Even more than male doctors, women valued the prestige that membership in these groups conferred. In 1896, one year for which there are records, 77 percent of eligible female doctors, compared to 30 percent of the city's eligible male doctors, joined the District of Columbia Medical Association. Between 1888 and 1900, almost 90 percent of that group's female members affiliated also with the Medical Society; only 66 percent of the male doctors held joint memberships.[29]

Women doctors in Washington found that membership in the society and the association provided them with the social and professional contacts that men had long taken for granted. Although they may have felt somewhat uncomfortable at medical social events where doctors' wives previously had been the only females present, medical women found that having their names linked in the newspapers with Washington's foremost specialists constituted a valuable form of indirect advertising. Society membership also boosted careers through contacts. Rosalie Slaughter, noted surgeon, remarked in her memoirs that Medical Society members made her feel welcome when she attended a meeting the day after she passed the District medical exam in 1902. Referrals from a male physician she met there who knew her prominent family and from women doctors present at the meeting enabled her to recover office expenses within her first year of surgery practice, she claimed.[30]

Women took advantage of their new status and participated actively in scientific discussions. During the 1890s, published minutes of society meetings indicate that they contributed papers and commented on topics raised by colleagues and that male members responded to their contributions without apparent condescension. The range of subjects discussed by the women shows that their interests extended beyond traditional female medical areas. Parsons, considered by her female colleagues to be one of the most brilliant physicians in the city, was most outspoken. The first doctor in the city to do fluoroscopy, she discussed its use, developments in blood and kidney diseases, the incidence of neurasthenia in men as well as women, the necessity for higher medical standards, and increased physician responsiveness to patient needs. (Parsons's collection of pathological specimens laid the foundation for the collection of the International Pathological Society. Unbeknown to patients' families, she would perform an autopsy and carry off the specimen in her bustle.)[31]

Women doctors adopted the standard practices of the day. Parsons, for instance, approved the use of ovariotomies in the treatment of epilepsy. But these doctors also provided a unique perspective as women. Sofie Nordhoff-Jung, for instance, insisted on greater conservatism with regard to surgery in diseases of women. She urged her colleagues to become experienced with alternatives to ovariotomies and described the Thure-Brandt technique she had learned during postgraduate study in Germany. Her colleagues, however, rejected that method because of the extensive training required. Other women doctors tried to dispel their male colleagues' belief that education damaged the health of adolescent girls. Women members also urged colleagues to support child labor laws.[32]

Women also contributed to the organization by volunteering for various committees. In 1894, Ida Heiberger, founder of the Woman's Clinic, represented the Medical Society at the AMA convention in San

Francisco and sat on the national body's judicial council from 1894 to 1897. In 1896, she served on the Medical Society's board of censors. Amelia Erbach joined the committee on public health that same year. The election of Mary Parsons to the vice-presidency of the society in 1901 signified the capstone of women's participation in that group. Parsons publicly expressed her appreciation and "surprise," calling the year she held the office the "happiest of my professional life." As the Medical Society's first female member, she confessed that the "honor . . . meant more to me than it could possibly have meant to any man, and perhaps more than to any other woman."[33]

However, one must be cautious in attributing too much significance to Parsons's election and to the nominal acceptance women received as participants and contributors to the society. By the time women gained their foothold in the two medical organizations in the 1890s, these groups no longer represented the pinnacle of institutional power in the medical community. By then, influence and prestige had shifted to such specialist societies as the Obstetrical and Gynecological Society and the Medical and Surgical Society, and more notably to the university hospital complexes emerging in the city—areas from which women were totally excluded. Thus, women's advantage seemed to lay in groups whose power was being eclipsed by other medical institutions in the city.[34]

Although women became part of the male professional establishment, they nonetheless recognized a need for their own organization. They may well have shared the view of a New York female physician on the need for separate women's medical societies. Dr. M. Stark, a charter member of the Blackwell Medical Society in Rochester, observed in 1899 that "the medical societies are under [male] control; we have been admitted to these after the persistent knocking of the pioneer women of the profession but we are not at home there as in our own circles." These integrated societies have a vital place in women's professional lives, she continued. "We need the general societies to broaden our minds and give us lines of thought." But women also needed their own groups, she maintained. "Our work and growth should be free where we are without embarrassment or restraint," she concluded.[35]

There were differences of opinion about establishing separate medical societies for women. An article in the *Woman's Medical Journal* in 1908 pointed out that some women doctors believed that "men and women of the profession should have no separate medical organizations" because "united action on the part of medical women would create a feeling of exclusion" and change "existing pleasant relations."

The majority of Washington's women doctors held a different view. In 1909, eighteen of thirty women who practiced in the city established the Women's Medical Society of Washington. Significantly, this group included all but one of the remaining pioneer and post-pioneer women doctors still in active practice. Its purpose was to meet, first, for "scientific purposes" and then for "mutual benefit" and "sympathetic understanding." Mary Parsons, the leading force behind this group, served as its first president.[36]

Activities varied. By-laws called for papers to be delivered at the eight regular meetings in members' homes throughout the year. Parsons's presidential address concerned the problematic increase in Caesarian sections; Emma Lootz Erving, a Howard graduate, later reviewed developments in orthopedics. Members established scholarships for local female medical students. Through petitions, letters, and personal appeals, they worked for the admission of women into the city's hospitals both as interns and as practitioners. Concerned with health standards in the community, they formed a speakers' bureau of medical lecturers for lay groups. In one year, 1912, members delivered forty-six lectures in the city.

As a group, these women concerned themselves with almost every issue relevant to the woman physician, but one—the problems of black women doctors. A few of the Women's Medical Society's members, such as Mary Parsons, Ida Heiberger, and Isabel Lamb, enjoyed professional relations with black women doctors; the majority of their peers avoided such association. Black women doctors, too few in number to create the professional networks that white women doctors found so helpful, faced exclusion from organizations that black male doctors formed. In 1895, when black physicians revived the Medico-Chirurgical Society, no black women's names appeared on its membership list. One of the prominent male doctors who revived that society, Daniel Hale Williams, saw no discriminatory intent in suggesting that opportunities for "colored young women and colored doctors" be improved. By "women," he meant nurses, and by "doctors," men. A dozen years later, when sixteen black physicians opened the 19th Street Baptist Dispensary, not one woman's name appeared on that list of participating physicians. At the time, at least three of the city's twenty-five full-time black doctors were women. Even in the 1930s, only one black medical society of four in the city listed a woman on its roster.[37]

White women doctors may have justifiably complained about the problems of being women in a men's professional world. They had to struggle for sixteen years to gain acceptance into the city's professional societies, for more than forty years to practice in male-dominated hospitals, and for a century to secure a firm foothold in the prestigious white medical schools. If white women believed they bore a stigma for being women, then black women undoubtedly shared the views of Julia Pearl Hughes, Howard '97, who complained that she "labored under two disadvantages at least: First, being a negro . . . ; second, being a woman." Those disadvantages made integration into emerging professional institutions even more problematic for black women than for their white colleagues in the late nineteenth century—and beyond.[38]

7

Career Patterns of Women Doctors

"I Can Stand the Work and I *Will* Stand It."

In order to establish successful practices, Washington's pioneer and post-pioneer women doctors surmounted personal and professional barriers unique to their sex. From the outset, women's training and career paths differed from those of their male counterparts: Limited resources compelled them to extend the time it took to complete their medical education; lower wages forced them to supplement the income they earned while attending medical school; and domestic obligations intensified the many demands already made on their time. Women transcended these difficulties but encountered others. They withstood the active discrimination of male colleagues and won the patronage of a devoted group drawn from a wary public. The extent of their success varied. Most of the white women doctors who practiced or trained in Washington before 1900 were able to establish longlasting practices. The majority practiced full-time, but several maintained part-time practices for years while holding other salaried jobs. Overcoming obstacles of an even higher order, an impressive proportion of black female medical graduates similarly established lifelong medical practices—as well as hospitals and clinics that served their communities for decades into the twentieth century. A few black women physicians never opened private practices, but used their medical training to promote distinguished careers in other fields.

White women's career paths took slightly different forms from those of black women medical graduates and are worth examining separately. From the outset, white women appeared more determined to earn their credentials than their male classmates. Fifty percent of Columbian women graduated (22 of 44), 25 percent with high honors, compared to 41 percent of Columbian male students enrolled during the same years (155 of 375). It took women longer to finish the pro-

gram, however. Between 1884 and 1896, Columbian's female graduates required an average of 3.6 years to complete the three-year program; less than one of every two women (12 of 22) graduated in the
expected time. Of the rest, half required four years to graduate; the
remainder needed five years or more. By comparison, two out of
three, (100 of 155) of Columbian male graduates enrolled during
those same years finished within the expected three years.[1]

Demanding jobs and limited financial resources resulted in white
women's lengthened course of study. In 1892–93, for instance, when
female enrollment peaked at Columbian, almost half of the women
students held full-time jobs (8 of 18 known), six of these in government offices; two others taught school. National University women
students presented a comparable picture. In 1894, officials at that
school estimated that 50 percent of their women students were employed, the majority as clerks or teachers. One of the most resourceful
of National's students worked for the government during the day, attended evening medical classes, and managed a thirteen-room boarding house. Attending school while working full-time was a common
practice. At least half of National's male students followed a similar
pattern; almost every one of them clerked in a federal department.
Based on employment reported in city directories, 61 percent of the
men enrolled in 1892–93 in Columbian's medical program held government posts (47 of 77). The rest listed no occupation.[2]

Male students were able to earn considerably more than their female classmates, a factor that enabled them to afford the medical program more easily. Federal regulations in effect through the 1860s set
women's *maximum* salary at $900 a year and men's *minimum* at $1,200.
Such differentials multiplied with years of experience. When legislators removed this discriminatory differential, custom perpetuated
the ratio. In the 1890s, women clerks earned an average of $900 per
year. Men in the same grade levels—and frequently in the same
jobs—received $1,500. Moreover, women were most often hired to fill
entry-level, low-salaried positions such as counter in the Treasury Department or census taker. These positions were most vulnerable to
reductions-in-force. Government officials frequently rehired capable
women discharged during such reductions, but at entry-level wages
once again. In this way a woman's annual income would have been reduced not only because she experienced weeks or months without pay,
but also because she remained for years at an entry-level salary.[3]

The work history of Alice Harvey, a widow who came to Washington
after her husband died, illustrates the wage marginality that she and
other women medical students experienced. Harvey joined the Cen-

sus Bureau in 1890 at a salary of $720, a few months after entering Columbian's medical program. She worked in that office for eighteen months before she lost her job as part of a reduction in force. During that time, she had received an increase to $900 per year and a subsequent reduction so that her salary was again $720 at the time of her dismissal. The bureau chief reinstated Harvey five months later at a salary of $600 per year, but dropped her from the rolls once more in 1893. Harvey left Columbian at that time. Women who taught school in the Washington metropolitan area had somewhat greater job security, but experienced similarly low earnings. School teacher salaries in the District of Columbia averaged $450 to $720 a year. A few women, with extremely high status and more than ten years of service, earned $1,000 or more.[4]

Such salaries provided little discretionary income. The situation of Fannie Brewer, Columbian '95, an honor medical student, is illustrative. Brewer came to Washington in 1890 after having taught for three years in Annapolis. Like Harvey, she secured a temporary appointment in the Census Bureau at a salary of $600 annually. The following year, Brewer transferred to the Treasury Department and at the same time enrolled in the Columbian medical program. At her new job, where she earned $780 a year, Brewer sorted and numbered money orders. Given Washington's high cost of living, a thrifty woman could have lived respectably on $780 but have had little remaining for education-related expenses. Adelaide Johnson, a contemporary of Brewer's who also worked in a government office, kept a diary of her daily expenses. It reveals that her room, board, carfare, and miscellaneous expenses totaled $55 a month. (The room she shared in a private home cost $21 a month; board, which she took elsewhere, cost another $18 dollars a month.) According to Frank Carpenter, a contemporary Washington journalist, that was a bargain. He estimated that "very shabby" accommodations in the city ranged from $15 to $40 a month, depending upon the number of women who shared a room and the floor on which it was located. Board, he claimed, averaged another $20 a month.[5]

With comparable expenses, Brewer would have had only $10 remaining each month, or $120 a year, that she could have applied toward medical school. When she attended Columbian, direct educational costs for the three-year course of study ranged between $200 and $250 per year. Tuition alone averaged $125 a year. Anatomy, examination, laboratory, and tutorial fees ran as high as $100. Books and carfare were additional. In order to have been able to afford medical school on her income, Brewer could have attended part-time

116

and paid for individual course tickets at $15 each instead of registering for a full course load at $125. That would have enabled her to spread the cost of medical school over four or five years instead of three. Brewer apparently did just that and graduated, fourth in her class, four years after enrolling.

In 1891, Mary Putnam Jacobi noted that women medical students often resorted to "innumerable devices" to pay for their schooling because their jobs paid so little. While working as teachers or editors, she claimed, women earned extra money nursing the sick and giving massages. Louease Lenman, an 1895 graduate of the Washington Homoeopathic Medical College, found even more creative ways to supplement her meager resources. While working as a seamstress and selling women's clothes, she operated a "perfumery" and acted as sales representative for what she listed as "Dr. Sanche's Electropoise 'Victory' System." Jacobi also commented on women's tendency to follow a discontinuous pattern of study that similarly lengthened the course of study. Women worked "till they could scrape a few dollars together," she observed, "expended that in study—then stepped aside for a while to earn more."[6]

Women who bore principal wage-earning responsibilities for their families found it even more difficult to accumulate the funds needed to complete the course of study on time. With the $720 she earned as a Treasury Department clerk, Mary Hart supported both of her parents (aged sixty-nine and seventy) and a younger sister. Her mother contributed to the family income by taking in boarders; her father worked occasionally as a janitor. Hart graduated from Howard's two-year program in 1880 in three years. Adeline Rochefort, a pharmacy student at Howard in 1887, maintained her father until his death and contributed to the support of her widowed sister's children. She held temporary appointments as a copyist, a skilled laborer, and a census taker. Her salary rose from $600 to $720 and fell again to $620 during the period. Rochefort withdrew before she completed the medical program.[7]

Not all of Washington's white female medical students delayed their graduation because of financial difficulties. Six of the ten Columbian medical students of 1892 for whom no employment information could be found listed themselves as being married. These women required an average of 3.8 years to graduate. Like May Baker, they may well have had small children to care for. Baker withdrew from Columbian after one year's study because her infant child was ill. Five years later, she completed the course at Howard.[8]

After Baker earned her degree, she trained at the Woman's Clinic and sought additional postgraduate study at Johns Hopkins. During the 1870s and 1880s, postgraduate training such as Baker pursued was optional; it consisted primarily of assisting an established physician in the office and accompanying the doctor on rounds. But by the 1890s, such study was fast becoming the rule rather than the exception. In the 1884 Columbian Medical School catalogs, for instance, 63 percent of the students listed preceptors (forty-nine of seventy-eight). By 1886 (the last year the school provided such information), that proportion had dropped to 45 percent (forty-eight of one hundred six). Five years later, in 1891, William Osler, physician at Johns Hopkins, estimated that only 5 percent of all medical students contracted with preceptors. The rest, he claimed sought formal postgraduate clinical training.[9]

Washington's white women also sought such training in larger numbers as the end of the century approached. Approximately 90 percent of the post-1885 female white medical graduates secured postgraduate training, the majority at local clinics established by the women themselves. One-third of these physicians received additional training elsewhere. European hospitals provided the best training, problematic though it was. In order to attend those clinics and hospitals, women had to overcome financial, social, and language barriers and then face rigorous admissions criteria—nor did their acceptance signify that their mentors were free of prejudice. Alice Hamilton, a contemporary of Washington women doctors, graduated from the University of Michigan and then took advanced study in Leipzig and Munich. She found conditions in Germany "exasperating," she reported in her autobiography. Her teachers and fellow students held her in contempt on two counts: because she was American, and because she was a woman. In their view, that combination made her "uneducated and incapable of real study."[10]

At least eight white women of the Washington group overcame these difficulties and studied abroad. Three of them, Isabel Barrows, Ida Heiberger, and Elizabeth Sargent, graduated before 1885. Barrows and Sargent studied ophthalmology in Zurich; Heiberger trained in general medicine in Zurich and Vienna and then studied gynecology at the Frauen Klinik in Freiberg, Germany. The rest of Washington's white women doctors who studied in Europe trained in the 1890s. Among them, Anne Augusta Wilson took her medical training in Edinburgh at the Royal Academy of Physicians and Surgeons and then served an internship in Glasgow. Sofie Nordhoff, Columbian '93, studied in Munich and Paris. Anna Bartsch, Howard 1900, studied in Vienna, London, and Paris.[11]

Women fared less well in American hospitals run by male administrators. Those who served internships or residencies won them in hospitals that permitted women to sit for competitive examinations. Before settling in Washington, Ada Thomas, a graduate of the Woman's Medical College of Pennsylvania in 1893, interned at Blockley Hospital in Philadelphia; Mabel Cornish, a Washington native who graduated from the Woman's Medical College of the New York Infirmary in 1892, interned at Babies Hospital in New York City; and Carrie Davis, Howard '97, at the Lying-In Hospital in Philadelphia.[12]

American hospitals run by female physicians provided women with somewhat greater training opportunities, but these were still quite limited. In 1896, a year in which more than one thousand women graduated from medical schools throughout the country, the seven leading women's hospitals granted only twenty internships, two residencies, and thirteen "externe" or "visiting doctor" positions. A few of Washington's early white women doctors were able to take advantage of these opportunites. Celia Low, a graduate of the New England Female Medical College, interned at the New England Hospital for Women before she entered Howard for postgraduate study in 1872. Anne McCormick, a Howard graduate in 1883, interned at the New York Hospital for Women; and Alice Burritt, a graduate of the New York Medical College of Women, at Fabiola Hospital in California.[13]

Conditions at these clinics were far from ideal. In the early years, staffing and funds were inadequate, and clinicians themselves often had little or no previous training. Shortages of food and supplies were common. In 1877, shortly after her appointment to the Philadelphia clinic, Sarah Marinda Loguen wrote to her sister describing the hardships that she endured. "Two of us have the work of four," she lamented. "In fact for a week or so I have done the work of one in the house and all of the work outside." The pace was debilitating. "You know," she continued, "when you are going all day and are called up and out two and three times in the night, one is apt to feel tired." Her discomfort was compounded by insufficient food. "I am always as hungry as can be," she complained. Occasionally, she said, she would walk long distances back to the clinic and use the carfare she received from patients to buy "three cents worth of crackers and eat them on the street." Demonstrating the determination necessary for success, Loguen assured her sister, "I can stand the work and I *will* stand it."[14]

Later, as the number of graduating physicians increased, clinicians at the few women's hospitals suffered from overstaffing. Hamilton, who served as an intern in the dispensary out-practice at the New England Hospital before going abroad in the mid-1890s, left that position after a few months because she received little direct clinical experience. When she first arrived, she complained to her cousin that it was a "very strange novelty to me to be in a place where I actually have not enough to do to keep me busy." Her impatience grew, and she bemoaned the waste of precious time. "I am simply losing a year which I cannot spare sitting around and reading textbooks, when I need practical work." [15]

By far the most available and the most intense training opportunities for later Washington white women doctors were those provided by clinics that they had established themselves. Of forty-five white women who graduated from local medical schools between 1889 and 1899, thirty-five, or 77.7 percent, assisted at one or more of these infirmaries. Although the clinics were limited in the range of cases they provided and in the opportunities they offered, they were vital nonetheless to the eventual success of the doctors who participated.

With or without clinical training, the vast majority of the city's pioneer and post-pioneer white female medical graduates whose careers could be traced entered the practice of medicine: Forty-two of sixty-one (68.8 percent) established longlasting medical practices. Only four of these white female graduates never practiced at all. Two remained at their government jobs. One of these, Fannie Brewer, continued "assorting and numbering money orders" for fifteen years at the Treasury Department even though she graduated with honors from Columbian in 1895. Two other medical graduates never practiced because they married. Augusta Pettigrew, another promising student from Columbian, remained at her job as a clerk in the auditor's office of the Post Office Department while she took postgraduate courses in German and psychology at Columbian's graduate school. She married her former medical professor, Dr. Kerfoote Shute, and continued working in a government office. [16]

At least two white medical graduates practiced part-time for many years while working as government clerks. Margaret Potter graduated from Columbian University Medical School in 1894 and remained at her post in the War Department for the next twenty-five years, practicing medicine all the while. Kate Lozier, an 1895 Columbian graduate and a clerk in the Patent Office, followed a similar pattern for at least ten years. These women joined a cadre of male physicians contemptuously referred to as "sundowners" by their full-time colleagues who tried on numerous occasions, without success, to limit their professional activities and to drive them from medical practice. [17]

These practice rates compared more than favorably with those of men. An irate practitioner placed male rates as low as 30 percent.

Writing to the editor of a local newspaper in 1889, he complained that desperately needed cadavers were wasted on medical students, only 30 percent of whom ever used that knowledge. Practicing physicians like himself, he declared, needed cadavers to refresh their anatomical skills in preparation for surgery, but were unable to obtain them because of the medical schools. More direct evidence indicates that 40 to 60 percent of Howard, Columbian, and Georgetown male medical school graduates ever attempted to practice—proportionately less than their female classmates. Only twenty-four of the forty-six male graduates in Columbian's class of 1892–93 (52.1 percent), for example, entered practice, four of them part time; nine (19.5 percent) continued to work at their pregraduation clerical jobs without a change in status. Another thirteen left Washington (28.2 percent), a few possibly in government employ as pension examiners. Their names never appeared in the standard national directories of practicing physicians.[18]

Opportunties to acquire promotions and better-paying jobs in government because of their medical degrees militated against male graduates establishing full-time practices. The Pension Bureau, for example, annually hired dozens of the city's newly graduated male physicians to examine petitioners. Pension doctors' salaries ranged from $1,200 to $1,800 a year, the equivalent of earnings from an average practice. In 1892, the government employed 3,795 examining surgeons nationwide. Other male graduates never practiced because they harbored second thoughts about leaving the security of their relatively well-paying posts for the uncertainties of a beginning practice. A local gossip columnist commented on this tendency and warned her female readers not to expect the promising medical students they married to actually become doctors. Once the men graduate, she said, they "never resign"; they "hold on like grim death." [19]

Women lacked comparable opportunities in government service. For many, a medical career offered the best—and often, the only— opportunity for a successful career. Like their male colleagues, however, women doctors needed patience and resourcefulness to persevere during the early lean years of practice. A popular doctors' manual, Daniel W. Cathell's *The Physician Himself and What He Should Add to His Scientific Requirements* claimed it took two to three years to develop a moderately successful practice that yielded an annual income of $1,500 to $2,000. Cathell may have been accurate in terms of men's experience, but not in terms of women's. A survey of 430 women who graduated from American medical schools between 1870 and 1890 showed that only half could support themselves after three years in practice. The early years were particularly bleak. Dr. Lilian Welsh, an 1889 graduate of the Woman's Medical College of Pennsylvania, compared her first year of practice in Baltimore to "solitary confinement." "The proverbial wolf howled loudly at [the] door," she wrote in her autobiography. "Patients were few and far between."[20]

Welsh's Washington neighbors might have commiserated with her about those early years, but by the third year, they, too, began to feel established. Anita McGee earned only $280 during her second year in practice, 1894. Her practice was growing, however, and earnings projected from incomplete records of her third year suggest that she might have earned $800, a far cry from Cathell's $1,500, but a marked improvement. Clara Bliss Hinds, an 1887 graduate of Columbian and a friend of McGee's had a better experience. Years later she recalled that she had become "firmly established" after the third year. Record books of Julia Green, an 1898 Boston University homeopathic graduate who trained at the Memorial Hospital for Women and Children in New York before settling in Washington, put her somewhere in between. Green earned between $800 and $1,000 in her fourth year of practice.[21]

Based upon the fee structures of the medical societies to which these women subscribed, they probably charged 50 cents to $1 for office visits and $1 to $3 for home visits. These fees varied with the distance traveled. Mary Parsons, an early graduate of Howard who practiced in Washington for more than fifty years, charged a flat rate of $5 for a confinement, delivery, and one year of infant care at the turn of the century—and likely after as well. That represented far less than male specialists earned for their services. In 1894, Hunter Robb, a Cleveland gynecologist referred a patient of his who was visiting in Washington to Anita McGee for treatment. "Charge her *$5 EACH TIME YOU TREAT HER*," he instructed McGee, to maintain his own fee structure.[22]

Male doctors, especially if they were well connected, could more easily withstand the difficulties of the early lean years by supplementing their incomes with medical school teaching jobs and charity appointments, positions denied women. During the 1892 school year, men who had graduated from Columbian in the three prior years filled the lower ranks of that medical school's faculty. They were employed as clinical assistants and demonstrators of anatomy, histology, and minor surgery. Favored males also worked as almshouse, police station, and visiting physicians. In 1892, for example, ten physicians to the poor—"young men and men of good standing,"—each received $40 per month for their services; in 1900 the visiting physician for the Washington Asylum earned $1,080. That same year, the city paid a total of $7,891, at 50 cents per visit, to male doctors authorized to treat destitute patients. Doctors also received $1 a day for being on call. Although seasoned physicians discouraged their proteges from accepting government charity work, newly graduated doctors competed for these jobs in preference to financial distress. During the late 1890s, representatives of the District of Columbia Federation of Women's Clubs repeatedly petitioned the city government to appoint women to such posts to no avail.[23]

The old saw that women did not really need the income was contradicted by the numbers who had to support themselves—and others—on their slim earnings. A national survey performed in 1892 revealed that at least 32 percent of the nation's practicing women physicians supported themselves and contributed to the support of others. Washington's women doctors were no exception. Ida Heiberger made a home for her two sisters, who lived with her for their adult lives. Amelia Erbach similarly supported two unmarried sisters, one of whom was severely handicapped. Mary Strobel, Margaret Potter, and Louise Hartman, also single women, maintained homes for their widowed mothers. Married women who had been divorced, separated, or widowed similarly needed a secure income for dependent children. Mary Spackman and Jessie Kappelar were both widows with young children; Clara Bliss Hinds, a divorcee, had a young daughter. Caroline Winslow, whose husband was a carpenter, considered herself the principal wage earner. She supported not only her husband and herself, but also her orphaned niece.[24]

Such women had to find ways of supplementing their income when earnings were inadequate. Winslow, a homeopath, ran a pharmacy for some years. During 1890, Clara Bliss Hinds served as medical director of a women's gymnasium. There, she said, women "could escape for a few hours from the torturing and disfiguring stays then in fashion, the unhealthy layering of petticoats, and cramping, tightly laced boots. . . . [and] under proper medical supervision . . . take the invigorating exercises which so many needed." In 1894, Alice Harvey and Louise Hartman listed themselves as "Masseurs" in the classified section of the city directory.[25]

What began as a temporary expedient became a life's work for many including Julia Erlania Smith, an 1889 Howard graduate who studied at Columbian between 1890 and 1891. Smith served as house physician and physiology instructor at the exclusive Mt. Vernon Seminary. Lilian Welsh had less freedom at Baltimore's Goucher College, although she held a similar post. There, administrators reassured concerned parents that the "lady doctor" who taught hygiene would not treat the female students. Abbie Tyler and Mary Bland took in boarders, a common strategy that women doctors and wives of male doctors employed. In some cases, boarders served another function. According to the 1900 census, Laura Reville, an 1890 graduate of the Woman's Medical College, listed six nurses, all white and ranging in age from twenty-eight to thirty-five, as boarders. Alice Burritt listed two. Reville and Burritt probably ran nurses' registries. They provided homes for the nurses between their assignments and referred them to patients and physicians.[26]

Not all of Washington's white women doctors had to resort to such methods of self-support. Almost one-third of the women doctors who began practicing before 1900 were married and living with their husbands. Such women had to overcome problems different from, but no less formidable than, those their colleagues faced. Child care and family obligations were primary. Anita McGee, for instance, demonstrated as much determination to transcend domestic difficulties as a woman in her circumstances could have. During her pregnancy with her first child and after her daughter's birth, McGee attended private sessions with a preceptor. She enrolled in classes at Columbian when her daughter was only eight months old. Reliable domestic help was a constant source of concern. At one point McGee was able to hire a trained nurse—a "veritable treasure," she wrote to a friend—to take care of her two-year-old daughter. This proved temporary. She next enrolled her youngster in a nursery school—"the baby of the school"—the child's grandmother noted. McGee carefully coordinated her childbearing and child care responsibilities with her practice and often called upon her mother to baby-sit. But, ultimately, she forsook her career because of family problems.[27]

Other married women proved more successful than McGee at integrating their careers and family lives. Undoubtedly, they endured considerable strain. Martha Burritt, an 1896 graduate of Howard who took postgraduate courses at Johns Hopkins and at the Southern Homoeopathic Medical College in Baltimore, had to be more resourceful than most. Between 1894 and 1900, she attended medical school and undertook advanced training, taught in Baltimore, ran the children's clinic at the National Homoeopathic Hospital in Washington, and maintained an active medical practice—all with five young children. Another physician, May Baker, Howard '96, took several years off from active practice because of familial demands. Before reentering practice, she studied pediatrics and thoracic medicine at Johns Hopkins.[28]

Doctors with large families like Burritt's were in the minority. Most of Washington's married white women doctors had few children. As physicians, these women were familiar with birth control techniques and used that knowledge to limit the size of their families. Of the married women for whom such information is known, 90 percent had two children or less: 50 percent of these (twenty-two of forty-four) had two; 20 percent (nine) had one; and another 20 percent (nine), none at all. Only four women doctors, or 9 percent, had three or four children, nearer the national average.[29]

McGee's private papers provide indirect evidence that she, and no doubt her colleagues, used birth-control devices to manage their childbearing so they could integrate their careers with their family responsibilities. While on vacation in London with her mother in the early 1890s, McGee wrote her husband that she planned to visit a shop where she had seen "Malthusian appliances" advertised. The notice probably referred to Mensinga diaphragms, then available in England but not sold in the United States until the 1920s.[30]

On another occasion, in 1891, she outlined her plan for integrating her career with childbearing. Her "Plan for future work—proposed summer, 1891," detailed her expected schedule of pregnancies, practice, and scholarship:

92 Sum.   Prepare for practice-move
    Win.   Start practice & read coms.
             [likely material about religious communities, a
             particular interest of hers]
93 Sum.   Visit coms
    Win.   Prac. Write coms
94 Sum.   Rest   Fall. Start Donald
    Win.   Practice. Finish coms book—
95 Donald
    Win.   Prac. Start Sex book.
When sex book is done; Donald 2; then start Newcomb.[31]

The first of these scheduled children—a son named Donald—was born within the time period McGee had predicted. Tragically, he died suddenly and inexplicably when he was four months old. McGee re-entered her practice shortly thereafter but lacked the enthusiasm to continue. She closed her office, temporarily, she believed, but never did practice again, although she continued to devote her energies to the concerns of professional women in medicine.

A few of Washington's married women doctors (ten of thirty-three) discontinued their practices between the tenth and fifteenth years, points in their careers when male colleagues would have considered themselves well established. Husbands who had encouraged their wives' careers when both of the couple were young and struggling may have later resented the strain their wives' practices placed upon domestic arrangements. The absence of economic necessity may have discouraged some women from struggling to combine careers and family life. Mary Morrison, valedictorian of Howard's 1886 graduating class, taught at the National University and at the Howard Training School for Nurses in 1893, appointments denoting special ability. She retired in 1897, however, after eleven years of practice in order to, as she said, "devote herself fully to social and economic questions." By that time, her husband, who had attended Howard's school of pharmacy, was earning $1,500 per year in the Bureau of Pensions.[32]

Like McGee and Morrison, other married women who withdrew from practice transferred their energies to civic or social reform. Isabel Barrows forsook her medical career of more than fifteen years when her husband became editor of the *Christian Register* in Boston. During the next twenty years, she assisted him at the newspaper and served as editor for the *Proceedings of the National Conference of Charities and Conventions,* assistant secretary of the National and International Prison Congresses, and editor of the Lake Mohonk conferences on the Indian, the Negro, and International Arbitration. At the same time, she helped to organize and run the Association of Superintendents of Institituions for the Feeble Minded.[33]

Despite the personal, professional, and social obstacles they encountered, the majority of white women doctors maintained longlasting practices. At least 68.8 percent of local graduates who could be traced, (forty-two of sixty-one) practiced five years or more. No distinctions emerged between the pioneers and the post-pioneers. The true proportion may be even slightly higher, because this figure does not include women who may have married and practiced under their married names elsewhere in the country. Twenty-five of the seventy doctors who studied or settled in Washington whose lives could be traced (36 percent) practiced for twenty-five years or more; eight practiced for fifty years.

These figures compare more than favorably to those for male graduates. At Columbian graduation exercises in 1892, Dr. Daniel W. Prentiss referred to a survey of male alumni that revealed that only twenty-nine of one hundred Columbian male graduates, 30 percent, were practicing ten years after graduation. An analysis of the career patterns of Columbian's class of 1887–88 (the first class that included women) also shows that only one-third of the male graduates in the class practiced in Washington five years after graduation, although almost all remained in the city.[34]

Fragmentary evidence suggests that women's general practices consisted primarily of women and children. During 1894–95, for instance, McGee saw twenty-one different patients. The majority were widowed matrons living in fashionable boarding houses in her neighborhood; the remainder were children and servants. Only one man appeared in her record book in three years of practice. "Mr._____, 1207 Conn. Ave." either neglected to leave his name or else McGee chose to protect his anonymity in her records. Recollections of relatives and acquaintances of pioneer and post-pioneer white physicians Mary Parsons, Ida Heiberger, Amelia Erbach, Isabel Haslup Lamb, and Julia Green confirm that male patients comprised a small proportion of their case loads. The fears of male physicians that women doctors would win female patients and through them monopolize family medicine appear exaggerated in view of these doctors' practices.[35]

A few women, however, chose to specialize in obstetrics and gynecology. Sofie Nordhoff-Jung was the most distinguished of these. After she graduated from Columbian, Nordhoff-Jung studied at the Pasteur Institute in Paris and at the Universities of Berlin and Munich. She practiced for more than thirty years before being invited to join the Georgetown University medical faculty—where her husband was affiliated—at the rank of instructor of clinical gynecology. Six years later, when she was seventy-two, she was awarded emeritus status.[36]

Several of Washington's women doctors specialized in the treatment of women and children in joint practices with their husbands. In a manner reminiscent of the petty bourgeoisie family shop, women doctors shared offices with their husbands, complementing the men's general practices with their own specialization. Others conducted daytime office hours while their physician husbands, who held government jobs during the day, practiced medicine in the evenings. Daniel Smith Lamb, a professor of medicine at Howard, referred to such dual practices in his remarks to the graduating class of 1885. "Several of our graduates" he said, "hunt in couples in order to bring down the game with greater precision." Although Lamb was then referring to three black couples, at least eleven white couples also practiced together in these years. They included Seneca and Rosalind Moore Bain (who met at the National University and later married); Levi and Louisa Miller Blake (who attended medical school after they had been married for several years—she first at Columbian, he later at Howard); and Joseph and Hannah Ellis (she attended the National Homoeopathic Medical College to join him in his practice.)[37]

Among the specialists, at least one woman was a dermatologist. Daisy Orleman studied at the Universities of Zurich, Berne, and Paris following her graduation from Columbian with an M.D. in 1890, a B.A. in 1893, and a B.S. in 1896. She established her practice in New York City and lectured at the New York Polyclinic Medical School. During World War I, Orleman served as a surgeon in French military hospitals and later established an international reputation in the care of venereal diseases, winning high commendation from the French government.[38]

Two ophthalmology specialists had the support of a male sponsor. In 1896, Dr. Swan Burnett, a prominent ophthalmologist who benefitted from Phoebe Hearst's patronage, appointed Adeline E. Portman, a University of Iowa graduate and London postgraduate, and Ada R. Thomas, an alumna of the Woman's Medical College of Pennsylvania and a former Blockley Hospital intern, to clinical assistantships in ophthalmology at the Central Dispensary and Emergency Hospital. At the time, Burnett was negotiating with Hearst for a donation to build new hospital quarters and to equip a scientific laboratory in memory of his son (made famous as Little Lord Fauntleroy by his wife, the novelist Frances Hodgson Burnett). There is no evidence that Hearst specifically requested that Burnett appoint women to these posts, but circumstances suggest that the male specialist considered it prudent to curry the favor of a woman who had but recently led the Washington effort to guarantee women's admission to the Johns Hopkins Medical School and who was a staunch supporter of professional women.[39]

Portman and Thomas eventually became associate clinicians, the only women in the city to hold such posts in a male-run hospital. Although they never directed clinics themselves or became consulting physicians as did the men with whom they entered Central, they remained affiliated with that hospital for at least ten years. Thomas, reputedly one of the more promising doctors in the city, died in 1925 at the height of her career. Portman maintained an office in the city and lived in the exclusive suburbs of Washington.[40]

Women physicians also did their share of uncompensated charity work. Julia Green's daily records suggest that one-fourth of her patients paid no fee. She also volunteered at the local clinic and cared for residents of a home for the elderly. Some doctors maintained such affiliations for many years. Heiberger directed the Woman's Clinic for more than thirty years, served as physician to St. Rose Industrial Home for twenty-eight years, physician to the Women's Christian Association and the Young Woman's Christian Home for as many decades, and even took patients from the clinic to live in her home when they were destitute. Mary Parsons treated Washington's impoverished

Chinese women and children over several decades. A contemporary recalled Parsons's stories of threading her way through "dark and gloomy" opium dens to reach her patients' living quarters. Parsons also cared for the women in a camp of gypsies in nearby Virginia.[41]

By any standard, Washington's early white women doctors could boast a measure of success. Although none of them achieved the wealth and prominence of Washington's male medical elite, a few could boast better-than-average practices. None practiced in the Farragut-Lafayette Square area where the most well-to-do male doctors had their offices, for instance, but the majority did work in the same districts as ambitious and successful men. Three women were even elected vice-president of the District of Columbia Medical Society. Single women such as Mary Alice Brosius, Amelia Erbach, and Ada Thomas left handsome legacies of jewelry, furniture, cash, and property to relatives and friends. After her retirement, Anna Bartsch-Dunne transferred $40,000 worth of stock to Howard University and designated the interest for annual scholarships for women.[42]

Washington's black women doctors forged different career paths. Primarily single, self-supporting women—often the primary support of others—they confronted similar obstacles as their white counterparts, and more. Their early education and training patterns resembled those of their white counterparts, however. Female black medical students had a rate of medical school completion even higher than white women—71.4 percent of those who enrolled in Howard graduated (twenty of twenty-eight identified as black) compared to 50.9 percent of Howard women identified as white (twenty-seven of fifty-three) and 50 percent of Columbian women. Because Howard's program was less costly, the majority of women there graduated within the allotted time as did the men. The few black women students who listed paid employment taught in Howard's preparatory school or in the District of Columbia public schools.[43]

Black women's medical training experiences began to diverge from those of their white counterparts when it came to post-medical school training. Only 10 to 15 percent of black female medical graduates, compared to the majority of Washington's white medical women, served the equivalent of clinical internships. Two of the city's black women doctors studied abroad. Nanette Stafford, an early graduate of the Howard program, studied in Germany and then in Zurich, where she settled permanently. Among the later graduates, only Mary Louise Brown acquired European training. She studied in Edinburgh for a year after graduating from Howard in 1898. American hospitals run by men excluded black women entirely. Freedmen's Hospital denied women residency or intern appointments until 1894—despite student and alumnae protests. In that year, doctors appointed Julia Hall, Howard '92, to the attending staff in gynecology.[44]

Black women fared somewhat better in female-operated American hospitals, but opportunties there were inconstant. Pioneer medical graduates had a better chance at appointments. Rebecca Cole, Woman's Medical College of Pennsylvania '67, was a "sanitary visitor" at Elizabeth Blackwell's hospital in New York City; Caroline Still, an 1878 graduate of the Woman's Medical College of Pennsylvania, who had previously attended Howard, worked at the New England Hospital for Women; and Sarah Marinda Loguen, Syracuse '76, interned first at the Woman's Hospital in Philadelphia and then at the New England Hospital for Women.[45]

The first few days of Loguen's internship at the Philadelphia clinic proved disconcerting for unexpected reasons. Upon her arrival, she met a fellow physican-intern, Dr. Loughune, a white woman from Nashville, Tennessee (sixteen miles from Loguen's father's birthplace), who was her shocking look-alike. "Thee might be twin sisters," commented the clinic superintendent. Both Loguen and her equally astonished white colleague realized that they were related. For the next few days, the white physician ate alone in her room; she resigned a few days later.[46]

Post-pioneer graduates could not rely on the courtesies their predecessors had received. As the post-Civil War reform spirit waned and the number of white female medical graduates increased—enlarging the pool of potential interns—administrators at women's hospitals sharply reduced the number of black appointees. Not one of Washington's post-pioneer black physicians trained at an American clinic run by women or men. Clinics run by Washington's white women doctors similarly excluded them. None of the black Howard graduates served there, although white female classmates did. (Reportedly, in 1911, upon her return to the United States from the Dominican Republic, where she had practiced for twenty years, Loguen, then Sara Loguen Fraser, assisted at the Woman's Clinic.)[47]

Just as with their training opportunities, black women's career paths differed sharply from those of the white women who had studied medicine during the same years. Black female medical graduates who wanted to enter private practice faced an uphill struggle. Middle-class blacks, upon whom their paying practices depended, refused to patronize black physicians—no less black female physicians. An 1882 survey of the black community in nearby Baltimore showed that only 1 percent of insurance holders consulted black doctors; the remainder sought paid-for medical advice from the white regular medical community or from irregulars. In 1892, a slight increase in the number of trained black doctors raised that proportion to 10 percent. In 1898, a writer in the widely distributed newspaper, the *Colored American*, criticized his readers for patronizing physicians of their own race "only when we wish to run a bill we do not intend to pay."[48]

Nor were black male colleagues necessarily supportive. Every one of Washington's black pharmacists rejected Julia Pearl Hughes's application for the apprenticeship she needed to complete the requirements for her pharmacy degree. "Being a woman," she complained, "caused proprietors . . . to doubt even my ability to learn the profession, and as they had never employed a woman druggist as an apprentice, of course, I was not made an exception to their rules." The pharmacist at Freedmen's Hospital finally allowed her to assist him in the hospital pharmacy. "I heartily endorse the idea of our young women becoming pharmacists," Hughes wrote to Daniel S. Lamb, her former medical school professor. She added, "I feel that our fewness in number doesn't arrive from our inability but from a lack of opportunity and encouragement." Hughes also mentioned that Leonard Medical School in Raleigh, an institution for black students, earlier had rejected her application because she was a woman.[49]

Given their limited opportunities for medical and postgraduate training, their relatively low wages, and their lack of acceptance as professionals within the black community, it is a wonder that more than half of the twenty-six black women who graduated or practiced in Washington between 1870 and 1900, who had careers that could be traced, practiced at all. The early women doctors fared somewhat better than their successors. Four of the nine pioneer women physicians established lifelong medical practices. Rebecca Cole, for example, graduated from the Woman's Medical College in 1867 and practiced more than fifty years in Washington, in South Carolina, and finally in Philadelphia. Caroline Still entered medical school at Howard in 1874 when she was widowed, later remarried, and maintained an active practice in Philadelphia for more than thirty years after her graduation from the Woman's Medical College of Pennsylvania.[50]

Proportionately fewer post-pioneer black women doctors established practices that lasted as long as the pioneers. Only four of seventeen whose careers could be traced, or less than 25 percent, had full-time medical careers. Artishia Gilbert, a graduate of the Louisville Medical College in 1893, also graduated from Howard in 1897. She and Sarah Garland Jones, Howard '93, returned to their native states, Kentucky and Virginia, respectively, where they distinguished themselves in medicine. Gilbert taught at the medical college, and Jones established a Richmond hospital, later renamed for her. Julia Hall, Howard '92, practiced for many years in Washington and served as matron and medical adviser for girls in the Howard University dormitories. She was the first woman appointed to the Board of Children's Guardians in Washington. A fourth black doctor, Ionia Whipper, Howard '03, became resident physician at the Collegiate Institute in West Virginia and then physician of girls at Tuskegee Institute. In 1920, she returned to Washington, where she established a home for unwed mothers and practiced until her retirement.[51]

Some post-pioneer black women supplemented the full-time jobs that they had held while going to medical school with part-time practices. Three Howard graduates, Carrie Thomas '90, Mary Louise Brown '98, and Sara Winifred Brown '03, taught for many years in the District of Columbia public schools during the day and practiced medicine in the evenings. Mary Brown took a year of postgraduate training in Edinburgh, and Sara Brown, who had earned a B.S. from Cornell before entering Howard, registered for additional courses in pathology and physiology at Howard. She also taught obstetrics at that school in 1907 while practicing and teaching high school biology.[52]

A medical degree paid dividends that made medical study attractive to black women despite its hardships. Expertise in a scientific subject, for instance, led to promotions, salary increases, and higher status in the segregated Washington school system. Competition for teaching positions and promotions was keen in the 1890s. To be appointed, one had to rank among the top normal school graduates and pass implicit tests of breeding and light skin color. Once appointed, teachers confronted sharp distinctions in rank. Salaries in the lower grades averaged $600 per year, compared to $1,000 and more for the high school. Equally important, appointments in the upper grades carried greater prestige in the community. Under such circumstances, ambitious teachers sought additional education to enhance their teaching credentials in order to secure raises and promotions to higher grade levels. Thomas and Brown, for example, received promotions to more interesting and financially rewarding jobs after graduating from medical school. Thomas, who had been a first grade teacher, became the "physical culture" instructor for upper-grade children and received a 70 percent increase in pay (from $500 to $850). After her graduation, Brown, an English teacher, left her high school position for one in the science department of the normal school. She too received a substantial raise, 54 percent, from $650 to $1,000.[53]

For these reasons, a number of black women attended medical

school in order to earn a medical diploma rather than to practice medicine. The honorable title, "Doctor," and the income and status it conveyed, provided sufficient incentive for three to four years of study. In the prestigious black District of Columbia segregated school system, which boasted Harvard Ph.D.s, a Howard medical or law degree represented the only advanced post-normal school training a local professional woman could acquire. Harriet Riggs, for example, referred to by her contemporaries as "class personified," had already advanced from teaching first grade to teaching high school English with a salary of $1,000 a year when she enrolled in the Howard Medical Department in 1897. She was thirty-three at the time. Four years later, when Riggs became head of the English department, it little mattered that her title referred to a medical degree rather than to the academic Ph.D. Lucy Moten, principal of the District of Columbia segregated normal school and at the peak of her profession when she entered the medical program, began the study of medicine at the age of thirty-seven, completing four years later. She, too, used the title bestowed by the medical degree. Mildred Gibbs was another principal who entered Howard after she had established herself in education administration. The same year as her promotion to principal, 1896, Gibbs enrolled in the medical school. She graduated five years later. Like Riggs and Moten, Gibbs never attempted to practice, although she used her title throughout her career.[54]

These black women eductors demonstrated a desire for professional and community status evident in the lives of their female medical contemporaries. Along with the black and white women physicians who established practices in Washington, they demonstrated that despite personal, professional, and social obstacles, women could establish a niche for themselves in the city's emerging professional class. What they could not anticipate was how difficult it would be for women to maintain this foothold in an increasingly institutionalized professional society.

8

Women Doctors' Organizations and the Consolidation of Washington's Professional Elite

"When Science Shall Regard the Work Only— Not the Worker"

In the last decades of the nineteenth century, Washington's women doctors joined more than twenty organizations—the majority between 1885 and 1895—that defined and reinforced their professional middle-class status. Over the years, the nature of these groups changed as the backgrounds and perspectives of the participating women physicians themselves changed. In the 1870s and 1880s, pioneer physicians established women's rights organizations that championed the solidarity of their sex and sought to improve women's social, economic, and legal status. Their successors, the post-pioneers of the 1890s, displayed a different sensibility. They rejected the feminist, cross-class perspective their predecessors had displayed. More concerned with their identities as professionals than with the supposed disadvantages they suffered as women, post-pioneers sought to integrate themselves into the emerging professional, middle-class, male culture. When excluded from the men's groups to which they aspired, post-pioneers established organizations that imitated the very societies from which they were barred—societies to which their fathers, brothers, husbands, and male colleagues belonged. The associations that both pioneers and post-pioneers formed enhanced their lives in important respects. But these groups had the paradoxical effect of reinforcing the segregationist practices that many of these women were attempting to overcome.[1]

Pioneer homeopaths who settled in Washington shortly after the Civil War played a major role in founding the city's first postwar white women's associations. In particular, they helped to establish the National Woman Suffrage Association and the Moral Education Society, groups that demanded redress for women's social and economic disabilities through public awareness and legislative reform. Nurtured on abolition, temperance, and women's rights, doctors who lent their support to such groups viewed themselves—and all women—as members of an embattled class, and they drew their strength from their confrontational roles.

Women's rights groups and homeopathy shared constituencies. Some pioneer female homeopaths had participated in women's rights activities even before they began to study medicine. Through their feminist associations, they met with reformers devoted to improving female medical care. These reformers and their supporters protested the invasive and harsh procedures practiced by the regulars. Through public meetings and published literature, they encouraged women to undertake medical study, particularly among those sects—homeopathy for example—that practiced gentler therapies than the regulars. Elizabeth Cady Stanton and Susan B. Anthony, for example, patronized women homeopaths and actively promoted their cause. These leaders found the moderate and holistic tenets of homeopathic practice congruent with their own views, and equally important, they valued the opportunties that homeopaths offered to women. In addition to women who had been activists before they entered medicine were those pioneer homeopaths who joined the women's rights movement after they had embarked on their careers. The opposition that some of these doctors encountered when they studied and practiced medicine radicalized them to the feminist cause.[2]

The career of Caroline Brown Winslow, Washington's first trained woman physician, illustrates the link between women's rights and homeopathy. It also demonstrates the role that female homeopaths played in the formation of Washington's post-Civil War women's organizations. Winslow, a native of Utica, New York, an area in which numerous reform movements took shape, began the study of medicine after a lengthy stay in 1849 at the Glen Haven Water Cure Resort. There, under the guidance of eclectic physicians Rachel and R. D. Gleason, she studied physiology and attended lectures given by the women's rights activists who toured such spas. She soon decided to become a doctor. Her parents objected strenuously to her decision and withdrew all financial support, hoping to dissuade her. Winslow, then twenty-seven years old, defied her parents and enrolled in the Cincinnati Eclectic College. Her parents never relented, and she suffered "particularly severe" economic hardships—she later recalled—while earning medical diplomas from both eclectic and homeopathic schools. During the course of her studies, Winslow also endured physical threats and verbal abuse from fellow male students and townspeople. Such experiences merely intensified her commitment to women's rights. By the time she moved to Washington to nurse the wounded during the war, Winslow was thoroughly dedicated to the women's rights movement.[3]

Soon after her arrival in the capital, Winslow joined the Universal Franchise Association, an organization composed of men and women dedicated to extending suffrage to all disenfranchised groups. Stung by the decision of the association's male members to support the Fourteenth Amendment—enfranchising black males at the expense of women—Winslow thereafter devoted herself to women's causes exclusively. In 1869, she helped to organize the National Woman Suffrage Association, and in 1873, while serving as that group's vice-president, she established the Moral Education Society (MES), an organization to which the majority of Washington's pioneer women homeopaths ultimately belonged.[4]

Initially founding that group to combat the distribution of pornographic literature to school-age children, Winslow and fellow members soon broadened their mission. The women lawyers, journalists, government clerks, and wives of civil servants and tradesmen who belonged believed that women's childbearing functions lay at the root of their oppression. They promoted "voluntary parenthood" or "Alphaism," by which they meant sexual union for procreation only. The ideological underpinning of "Alphaism" played a dual role. It enabled Moral Education Society members to celebrate the maternal role and, by extension, women's sphere. But at the same time, it provided the rationale—and the means—by which participants could liberate themselves from the restrictions imposed by that traditional role.

At regular meetings and in the *Alpha*, the journal that Winslow edited, members advanced social and economic reforms to benefit women. Extending their critique of women's status beyond the marital relationship, they defined prostitution as a consequence of economic and sexual oppression and encouraged supporters to visit imprisoned prostitutes and speak out in their behalf. Using the same rationale, they denounced abortion and feticide as consequences of women's victimization rather than as crimes deserving punishment. In concert with the NWSA, members promoted suffrage, divorce, temperance, and dress reform, and gave moral and financial assistance to striking women workers. Articles in every issue of the *Alpha* also highlighted the accomplishments of a growing number of professional and career women.[5]

Subscriptions to the *Alpha* and memberships in the organization rose steadily during the society's first few years. By the early 1880s, however, the association began to decline. Members' preoccupation with moral regeneration through sexual abstinence, their bold emphasis on the sexual oppression of women, and their insistence on comprehensive social change to improve women's status held less appeal for career- and reform-minded women of the 1880s. After the mid-1880s, Winslow repeatedly solicited funds from subscribers to continue publication of the journal. Her pleas unanswered, she bore the cost of printing and distributing the *Alpha* herself for several more months. Bereft of resources, she published the last issue in April 1888, and the association disbanded.

The demise of the Moral Education Society signalled a shift in the orientation and strategies of women's organizations, but not an abandonment of women's causes. In part, this shift reflected a greater conservatism in American society and an increase in class consciousness. The violent labor and civil disorders of the 1870s and 1880s, culminating in the Haymarket riot in 1886, tempered the outlook of many Americans who had advocated comprehensive social change—including the women in groups such as the NWSA and the Moral Education Society. At the same time, a new generation of career women was emerging who viewed themselves differently from their predecessors. Although such women were well aware of the economic and legal disabilities they faced, they believed that women's opportunties were improving. No longer considering themselves martyrs or members of an oppressed group as did the pioneers a decade earlier, they forsook their forbears' critique of American society and their confrontational stance. More pragmatic, they focused on specific measures to remove barriers to women's advancement. Although committed to programs to improve women's status, career clubwomen also used their organizations to consolidate their own advances into the professional, middle-class ranks.

The indefatigable Winslow played a leading role in establishing several of the groups formed in the late 1880s. In particular, she helped to organize the District Woman Suffrage Association, the Washington chapter of the Women's Educational and Industrial Union, and the Wimodaughsis (an acronymn for *wi*ves, *mo*thers, *daugh*ters, *sis*ters)— all groups begun within a year of the disbanding of the earlier group. The prominent role Winslow played, however, did not guarantee that her views regarding female solidarity would prevail. More than once, Winslow and her women's rights colleagues found themselves out of step with career women and other converts to women's causes who supported programs that were as self-serving as they were woman-serving.

The District Woman Suffrage Association, founded in 1888, most closely resembled the feminist groups of the 1870s. As the local chapter of the NWSA, it recruited suffrage supporters who belonged to the national organization. The fifteen to twenty women who regularly attended meetings included three physicians—Flora Stanford, Ella Marble, and Clara McNaughton. Journalists, government clerks, and lawyers attended as well. Participants arranged for annual NWSA conventions in Washington and supported a multifaceted program to accomplish their goal, "the enlargement of women's sphere." Among other activities, they researched and wrote legislation to relieve the civil disabilities of married women, to provide equal parental rights of guardianship, and to ensure women's ability to own property free of their husbands' control. Members also lobbied the District of Columbia government to appoint women physicians to care for women in prison, almshouses, and public hospitals. In addition, they pressured public officials to place women matrons in police stations, and they attempted to secure a girls' reform school staffed only by women. All of these projects aided less-advantaged women and, at the same time, expanded employment opportunities for middle-class professional and working women like themselves. For professional members, idealism and self-interest often went hand-in-hand.[6]

Despite the various strategies they employed—mass meetings, behind-the-scenes lobbying, and published appeals—District Woman Suffrage Association members attained few of their goals. President Mary Lockwood visited National Museum officials to "demand" the reinstatement of women employees at the National Museum or "risk a mass meeting of women's club members"—without effect. In 1899, Congress reversed legislation revising the married women's property acts, which the organization had persuaded the Senate to pass in 1891 and the House in 1896. According to committee chair McNaughton, "no amount of influence" could alter the government's refusal to include women doctors when appointing physicians to the poor. The government similarly denied the group's request to allow women to serve as attending physicians in the Columbia Hospital and Lying-In Infirmary for Women. A girls' reform school, one of the group's priorities, did become a reality, but to members' dismay, city administrators appointed only men to its board of directors. One woman physician, Anne Wilson, a graduate of the Medical College of Edinburgh in Scotland, served as physician to the girls during 1894. Members also succeeded in securing the appointment of women as matrons for three of the city's nine jails—a number inadequate to serve the female population, they felt—but they received no concession in their demand for the appointment of female police officers.[7]

Social opposition may have limited the success of some programs, but it did not prevent participants from deriving important benefits from affiliation. Often dismissed by their contemporaries as "strong minded," women doctors and their female colleagues provided one another with essential moral support while they used their organization to expand their prescribed roles and challenge institutional practices that restricted their progress. The District Woman Suffrage Association, which also connected members to the growing network of women's organizations, lasted for more than twenty years.[8]

Two other organizations that Winslow and her colleagues established in the late 1880s—the Washington branch of the Women's Educational and Industrial Union and Wimodaughsis—differed from the suffrage group in goals and organization. Rather than focusing on political and legal change to aid women, these groups offered educational and social programs for middle- and working-class women similar to those offered by YWCAs and settlement houses in other cities. The Washington chapter was the local branch of a national organization established in 1877 in Boston by Harriet Clisby, a homeopath and NWSA member. At meetings of the annual congress of the Association for the Advancement of Women held in 1888 in Washington, Winslow heard favorable reports about other chapters and decided to establish a Washington branch. She succeeded in attracting both regulars and homeopaths to her cause. Besides Winslow, its president, officers included homeopaths Flora Stanton and Ellen Sheldon, and regular physician Clara Bliss Hinds, a recent graduate of Columbian's medical school. The noted Washington resident Clara Barton also served on the board. Less ambitious in its undertakings than its parent organization, the Washington chapter of the Women's Educational and Industrial Union strove, like that group, to cultivate "fraternity and cooperation of sympathy among women" and to "elevate labor [of all women] to the proper dignity in the estimation of the world."[9]

The group's rhetoric took tangible form in the offering of courses in literature, art, and science by the "Department of Education" and of lessons in hygiene, fancy needlework, and food preparation by the "Department of Industry." The club also sponsored a "protective agency" to collect the wages of working women withheld unfairly by their employers. With middle-class women invariably providing such services and poorer women receiving the benefits of their aid, largesse was usually one-sided. We are "not a charity in any sense, nor a reformatory," Winslow felt compelled to state, "but a help for all women in all stations of life." "All women have needs," she added parenthetically. Apparently, not everyone shared Winslow's equalitarian view. Her goal that "uncharitable criticism and discrimination between high and low . . . will be swallowed up by the desire to help all and instruct all" suggests that beneath the rhetoric of sex-solidarity, relations among women of different stations were less than harmonious. The president's appeal to members to "remember that we are women in the bonds of fraternity and usefulness" hinted at underlying tensions. The chapter may not have survived its first few years. No indication remains of its existence beyond 1890.[10]

Wimodaughsis, the third group of the late 1880s to which pioneer doctors gave their support, similarly demonstrated a decline in sisterhood even while it extolled its virtues. The most ambitious of the women's organizations of that decade, Wimodaughsis was primarily concerned with establishing national headquarters for NWSA in Washington. Through ads placed in the *Woman's Journal* and in newspapers throughout the country, the group sold stock worth $5 a share to finance the venture. Within two years, members were able to purchase a fifteen-room house at Thirteenth and I Streets, NW, a fashionable neighborhood convenient to the Capitol and other major points of interest. The Women's Christian Temperance Union, the Red Cross, the *Woman's Tribune*, and the Women's National Press Club rented office space from the club, which also provided transient and long-term lodging for NWSA members. The president of Wimodaughsis in 1891, Anna Howard Shaw, a homeopathic physician herself and later leader of the National American Women Suffrage Association, maintained a residence there for several years.[11]

In keeping with one of their primary goals, "to furnish educational advantages in practical, industrial, and educational work" for women "of limited means," club leaders offered courses in stenography, typing, dressmaking, and arithmetic. To provide "intellectual and ethical opportunities such as the YMCA provides for men," they said, they presented lessons in French, Spanish, elocution, physical culture, and dancing. "Mothers' clubs" that focused on the "care and moral training" of children were another regular feature. Each year at club headquarters hundreds of women—the vast majority government clerks—registered for courses that fellow members taught at nominal cost.[12]

The clubhouse also served other purposes. In 1891, for example,

Wimodaughsis hosted a 500-guest reception to honor anthropologist Alice Cunningham Fletcher's appointment as a Fellow of Harvard University. The following year, the District Woman Suffrage Association organized a meeting of representatives from twelve different women's clubs in the city to plan a "mass meeting to arouse public sentiment" in favor of the girls' reform school. According to a report in the *Woman's Journal,* government officials, women's club members, police matrons, businessmen, and ministers attended the meeting to compose a bill that representatives later presented to the Congress. Wimodaughsis's "small social . . . opportunites," noted even by contemporaries in other cities, attracted members as well. Entertainments, receptions for visiting women celebrities, lectures, and regularly scheduled teas enabled the club's many single women who lived alone to enjoy social activities away from their cramped boardinghouse quarters. The opportunity for women to entertain male guests in a socially respectable setting proved vitally important in a fluid, urban society like Washington's.[13]

Indeed, for some, the social life Wimodaughsis afforded provided its chief attraction. When that feature was threatened, scores of women forsook their commitment to sorority and abandoned the association; sisterhood could cross class boundaries, but the color line was inviolable. In the fall of 1890, a black elementary school principal registered for a Wimodaughsis course. Enrollment automatically entitled her to attend evening receptions. Upon learning that the new student "had some colored blood in her veins," a group of Wimodaughsis's most influential members led by journalist Mary Desha demanded her withdrawal. They argued that "colored women" would inevitably invite "colored men [to] the entertainments" and destroy the club's major social benefit.[14]

Board members—who included physicians Caroline Winslow and Anna Howard Shaw (as well as attorneys Ruth G. D. Havens and Emma Gillette)—refused to cancel the registration. They reaffirmed the club's commitment to all women, regardless of race. Hearing this, the protesters resigned en masse. Desha, one of the founders of Wimodaughsis, challenged the board's interpretation of the club's mandate, citing the group's preeminent social function. Wimodaughsis is a "social organization," not a "business corporation," she argued in her letter of withdrawal. "It was by presenting this social feature that I was able to induce my friends, a large number of them being Southern ladies, to subscribe for stock in the organization." Furious that board members took the rhetoric of the association at face value, Desha concluded that "the trouble all lies with the woman-suffragists,

[who] to be true to their doctrine of equality must advocate the admission of negroes."[15]

Wimodaughsis suffered serious financial problems after the mass resignation. Leaders acknowledged that the club was "in trouble because we stood for right and justice." The organization weathered the storm with the "self-sacrificing generosity of women of limited means" and continued to offer programs for the next twenty years. But the pioneer doctors who lent their support to Wimodaughsis and to the Women's Educational and Industrial Union, expecting that cross-class female solidarity—the ideal to which they had long been committed—would mitigate class and race distinctions, were disappointed. Career women of the 1880s and the 1890s were as susceptible to divisive social currents as their male counterparts; self-interest, rather than sisterly communion, often dictated their commitment to women's organizations. Instead of alleviating class and race disparities as their founders had hoped, Washington's cross-class societies of the late 1880s occasionally heightened them instead.[16]

The conflict between the Wimodaughsis leaders, who remained committed to the values of feminism, and their successors, who sacrificed sisterhood for social ambitions, highlights the changing perspective of many of Washington's post-pioneer professional women. These changes became even more apparent in the decade of the 1890s, when career women and college graduates established organizations whose ideologies differed markedly from those that had motivated the pioneers' societies only a decade or two earlier. In large part, the differences in such groups reflected a changed outlook in the career women of the early 1890s. In 1892, physician Ella Marble, an active NWSA member and a graduate of the National University Medical School, noted the change in attitude of the younger generation. She criticized the female medical students who spoke disparagingly of the early women activists. "Did these young women not realize," she said, that "but for the woman suffragists who had knocked long and persistently . . . and suffered ridicule and insult by being the first to brave public opinion . . . [their successors] could not be where they are today?"[17]

The changed focus of women's groups in the 1890s also mirrored the vastly altered professional milieu in which women doctors and other female professionals found themselves. Instead of the handful of loosely organized groups and institutions that characterized the professional community in the immediate postwar years, Washington's turn-of-the-century professional middle-class boasted a large and complex network of institutions—invariably male dominated. Participation in this network was vital to membership in the professional elite. Inevitably, male members refused to admit women doctors and other female professionals to their associations. Most post-pioneer career women avoided challenging these sex-segregated policies directly, and instead created parallel women's groups, some of which duplicated in structure and function the men's societies from which they were barred.

Women doctors actively contributed to the foundation of these organizations. In the late 1880s and the 1890s they helped to establish the Business Woman's Club, the Association for Collegiate Alumnae, the Women's Anthropological Society, the Daughters of the American Revolution, and the Washington Club. Unlike their predecessors who espoused the ideology of sex-segregation, founders of the later groups regarded some same-sex organizations as temporary expedients, essential only until they could achieve their ultimate goal: integration as equals into the emerging middle-class professional structure. Anna Garlin Spencer, social activist in the 1870s and 1880s, underscored this different focus when, in 1892, she called for a "needed corrective." The "ideal" is no longer separate women's institutions, she claimed, but groups that would allow men and women to "meet together on equal footing." Physician Sarah H. Stevenson, addressing a conference of women doctors in Washington the following year, echoed Spencer's sentiments. "The time has passed," she said, "when it is necessary to have much if anything for women. Women have shown their ability to work successfully with men, now let them stand with men . . . rather than alone."[18]

Few women professionals could be so bold. They recognized women's changing status but preferred to meet in their own groups. Members of the Business Women's Club, the most modest in size of the post-pioneer groups, attempted to combine earlier views of female sex-solidarity with the professional viewpoint of the new career woman. The stated purpose of the group, organized in late 1893 at the height of the depression, was to "promote friendly relations" among self-supporting women of different economic and social ranks. Doctors, lawyers, dentists, and teachers—some, popular Washington debutantes—joined the club along with manicurists, milliners, dressmakers, and typists. While the membership of the group was diverse, it was the professional women who assumed leadership roles. Three of Columbian's graduate physicians—Clara Bliss Hinds, Edith Jewell, and Phoebe Norris—served on the club's six-member board of governors the year that it was founded.[19]

Business Women's Club members supported a varied agenda. They sponsored reading groups at club headquarters on Tuesday afternoons, social receptions on alternate Fridays, and monthly "Gentlemen's Evenings." Occasionally, club members organized special events. In 1894, for example, member Frances Benjamin Johnston, a professional photographer and government clerk, organized an exhibit, "A Mart for Women's Work," at the club's headquarters. The exhibit's purpose was to demonstrate to the public that "breadwinners" could be "womanly and domestic." Members displayed breads they had baked and items they had embroidered alongside their legal documents and medical instruments. In this way, they used their association to disarm criticism of their lifestyles. Whereas pioneers had drawn strength from their collective unorthodoxy, publicly challenging social and political mores, post-pioneers sought integration into the professional male middle-class community through public acceptance.[20]

Other groups of the 1890s to which women doctors belonged fostered professional women's ambitions more directly. The Washington branch of the Association for Collegiate Alumnae (later known as the American Association of University Women), a more socially elite group, attracted several women doctors. Washington physicians Ada Thomas and Isabel Lamb, both regulars, and homeopaths Alice Brosius and Julia Green joined that group in the 1890s. Like their colleagues in other cities, women physicians in the Washington branch investigated job opportunties and pay scales for local women college graduates and offered scholarships to young women of every economic class. In 1893, the same year that Columbian closed its doors to women, members joined with other women's groups in the city to petition Congress to establish a national university which would admit women equally with men in every department—including the university's medical school. Members also worked for the appointment of women to the District of Columbia school board and as public school inspectors.[21]

The programs of the collegiate organization enjoyed varying degrees of success; most notably, women won District of Columbia school board representation (Mary Church Terrell received one appointment) and school inspector positions. The scholarship program also afforded numerous opportunties for young women. Other projects failed of immediate results—wage scales remain problematic to this day. But physicians who joined the Association for Collegiate Alumnae received benefits that made affiliation worth more than the group's collective accomplishments. In addition to having a publicly recognized platform from which to pursue the projects they deemed worthwhile, doctors made contacts that contributed to their success and consolidated their claims to membership in the professional middle-class elite.

The DAR, another group of this period that appealed to post-pioneer women doctors, originated in Washington in 1890, when women were excluded from the newly formed Sons of the American Revolution. Washington journalist and District Woman Suffrage Association member, Mary Lockwood, protested the "discrimination against her sex." "Were there no mothers of the Revolution? Were these sires without dams?" she demanded in a *Washington Post* article. Her annoyance struck a responsive chord, and within a few weeks, career women and local socialites joined with her to form the Society of the Daughters of the American Revolution. Cofounder, journalist Ellen Hardin Walworth, later recalled that initially, the public regarded members with "suspicion." Some critics maintained that the DAR would bring women into "public work" and "demoralize all who had escaped the suffrage fever." Others, she said, regarded DAR leaders as "advocates of a foolish and disloyal aristocracy."[22]

Founders disarmed public criticism by linking women's patriotism to the maternal role and by cultivating the support of "carefully selected" prominent women; Caroline Harrison, the wife of the president, represented their major coup. Career women and socialites comprised a significant proportion of the club's early membership. Anita Newcomb McGee, then a student in Columbian's medical school, joined the DAR soon after its establishment. Other physicians such as Alice Burritt, Julia C. Harrison, and Mary Alice Brosius (all homeopaths) and Kate Waller Barrett and Isabel Lamb (both regulars) joined as well.

As Caroline Brown Winslow had promoted the interests of pioneer women physicians of her generation through the associations to which she belonged, so Anita Newcomb McGee represented the post-pioneer professionals in her activities. Serving on the DAR's board of trustees, on numerous DAR committees, and as first Librarian General of that organization, McGee worked to elevate the status of her peers. As head of the library, she established the priorities that enabled it to grow into a valuable repository of materials highlighting women's role in the Revolution. She also organized a comprehensive directory of the associations' two thousand chapters and fourteen thousand members, and she edited the group's national journal.[23]

At the end of the decade, McGee focused her efforts on enhancing the status of trained nurses and increasing women's opportunities for graduate and professional education. In 1898, immediately after the outbreak of the Spanish American War, McGee organized a committee of DAR members to establish a professional female nurses corps. The wife of Geoge Sternberg, Surgeon General of the Armed Forces, was among them. Using rigorous criteria, the committee selected one thousand nurses from five thousand applicants. In appreciation of McGee's efforts, Sternberg appointed her acting assistant surgeon of the U.S. Army. The first woman to receive such a commission, McGee worked to gain professional status for women in the corps. She adamantly opposed Sternberg's decision to use women nurses in kitchen duty only. She demanded instead that they perform the same tasks for which they had been trained as their male counterparts, even in war zones. Sternberg relented when raging typhoid fever in the camps and mounting casualties exhausted his reserves.[24]

McGee kept in close contact with the women in the corps, even with those assigned to duty in the Pacific. She investigated their complaints that supervising male physicians treated them badly and brought these problems to Sternberg's attention. She also traveled throughout the country organizing DAR relief efforts and visiting army camps and hospitals where she distributed clothing, bandages, hospital sheets, nurses' aprons, and reading material collected by chapter members. In 1900, McGee successfully lobbied Congress to create a permanent nurses corps. Legislators rejected her proposal to establish a federal teaching force of one hundred women nurses and a war reserve of two thousand trained women.

While she was active in behalf of the nurses corps, McGee used the forum of the DAR to expand women's opportunities in other ways. As a member and sometime leader of the DAR's standing committee on the National University, she worked with representatives of the Association for Collegiate Alumnae, the National Science Club, and the George Washington Memorial Committee (all composed entirely of women) to establish a national coeducational graduate school in Washington. That project had been among the earliest goals of DAR founders who considered it "imperative" that women receive an education that would enable them to take their place alongside men in government, professional, and academic life. Washington women doctors such as Alice Burritt and Julia Harrison served on that committee with McGee along with other DAR activists such as Lucia Eames Blount, president of ProReNata, Jane Spofford, treasurer of the Dorothea Dix Dispensary, and Jane Stanford, founder of the coeducational Stanford University.[25]

At annual national conventions between 1893 and 1904, the committee recommended support of the graduate school. In 1897, the general membership did authorize pursuit of an appropriation from Congress for the project, but soon withdrew that commitment. Members feared that the proposal would divert congressional attention from the DAR's request for federal land on which to build a library and national headquarters. McGee and others on the committee continued without success to urge Congress to support the graduate school proposal. The committee disbanded in 1904, when the George Washington Memorial Committee, which had raised the bulk of the money for the new school, awarded its share of the funds to Columbian University. At that time, the DAR committee recommended that the association endow a chair in American history at the George Washington University.[26]

The DAR's potential for "demoralizing" members to challenge women's status was ultimately subsumed by its aristocratic, institution-building tendencies. Yet like the Business Woman's Club and the Association for Collegiate Alumnae, the DAR played an important role in affirming the social status of women doctors who chose to join. Whereas the cross-class working women's group enhanced members' identities as career women, and the Association for Collegiate Alumnae consolidated their status as members of an educated elite, the DAR certified their standing in a new aristocracy based on family lineage. These groups also infused the activities of professional women with greater significance and provided them with platforms from which they could exercise leadership on issues of concern. But they proved inadequate substitutes for the stimulation, recognition, and colleagueship that membership in the segregated, quasi-professional male organizations multiplying in the city would have provided. Women doctors and their peers established different kinds of associations for those benefits.

During the 1880s and 1890s, Washington's male professionals had been creating organizations that reinforced their professional middle-class identities and strengthened their institutional ties. Local groups such as the Anthropological Society of Washington, the Biological Society, the Chemical and Entymological Societies, and the Geological Society of Washington (all founded between 1879 and 1893) comprised heterogeneous groups of scientists and professionals—all male. In these groups, men found the camaraderie and contacts that advanced their careers. The connections they made and the heightened public esteem they earned through fellowship in such groups encouraged ambitious professionals to join not one, but several organizations at one time.[27]

Ambitious women physicians and their colleagues in other fields recognized the tangible and symbolic benefits affiliation provided. But no matter how excellent women's professional credentials or ardent their interest in scientific subjects, they were disqualified from membership in every one of these groups because of their sex. Rather than confront existing practices head on, professional and scientifically motivated women established compensatory organizations, identical in many respects to the men's groups emerging in the city. Women doctors were active in two of these, the Women's Anthropological Society, founded in 1884, and the Washington Club, established in 1890.

Matilda Coxe Stevenson, an anthropologist whose research among the Zuni Indians was earning grudging respect from her male colleagues, organized the Women's Anthropological Society. Stevenson had been encouraged in her efforts by the renowned British anthropologist, Edward B. Tylor. Impressed by her field research among the Zunis, Tylor advised the members of the Anthropological Society of Washington not "to sound the 'bullroarer' and warn the ladies off from their proceedings," but, instead, "to avail themselves thankfully of their help." Buoyed by Tylor's support, Stevenson sought unsuccessfully to join the men's group to which her husband belonged.[28]

Undaunted, she issued a call for "intellectual women" to join her in the study of science. Despite the certainty of her husband and his colleagues that the "project would fail" because "not a half-dozen ladies could be found deeply enough interested in science to form the nucleus," Stevenson soon assembled a group of ten supporters. They included such well-educated and "cultivated women . . . of social position" as Eliza Nelson Blair, wife of Senator Henry Blair, and Jane Lawrence Childs, wife of the Reverend Thomas Spencer Childs, first archdeacon of Washington. By the end of the year, founders incorporated the society with thirty-four members in active status and more than a dozen prominent women in corresponding status, including Ellen H. Richards, Vida Scudder, Marion Talbott, and Maria Mitchell. Approximately fifteen women attended meetings regularly. "No direct encouragement or aid has ever been received from other societies of scientific men, and none has ever been sought," members later declared with satisfaction. On the group's third anniversary, pointing to a membership of almost one hundred women, officers boasted that "in spite of prophecies to the contrary, the society has slowly but steadily grown—all without a single unfriendly disagreement or any presage of dissolution."[29]

Medical women were among the key participants in this organization, that satisfied their scientific interests and their claims to elite professional standing. Sarah Scull and Ellen Weir Cathcart, two of the group's founders, were in their first year of medical school—members of Columbian University's first coeducational class—when they joined. Both taught school at the time, Scull in an exclusive female seminary in Washington and Cathcart in the public schools of Washington. Within the year, Clara Bliss Hinds, their classmate at the Columbian Medical School, joined them as well. Anita Newcomb McGee entered three years later, in 1888, the year before she enrolled in medical school. (Her association with Hinds, Scull, and Cathcart may have contributed to her sudden decision to study medicine after she had made scholarly contributions to the field of sociology.) Within a few years, when physicians Sofie Nordhoff-Jung, Isabel Haslup Lamb, Margaret Magnon York, and Ida Heiberger had joined the Women's Anthropological Society, that society boasted the largest membership of women doctors in the city in a nonmedical association since the disbanding of the Moral Education Society.

In addition to physicians, the Women's Anthropological Society attracted women whose education, training, and experience varied from professional researcher to amateur observer. Specialists included Alice Cunningham Fletcher, scholar of the Omaha Indians, and Zelia Nuttall and Margaret Kalapothakes, Mexican and Greek ethnographers, respectively. Amateurs who had accompanied their husbands on expeditions to exotic locations joined as well. Sybil Augusta Carter, wife of H. A. P. Carter, envoy-extraordinary and minister plenipotentiary to Hawaii, and Emma Louise Hitchcock whose husband, chemist and curator of the national museum, had taught in the Imperial College in Japan for two years, reported on their observations in those lands. Emma Dean Powell and Emma Howard Ward, wives of men affiliated with the Bureau of Ethnology (John Wesley Powell was bureau chief and Lester Frank Ward was a researcher) had themselves participated in ethnographic and geological studies in remote areas of the continent. By a contemporary's account, Powell deserved a "dower-rite" in her husband's "scientific eminence" for her unheralded assistance on his expeditions. The club also boasted such professional luminaries as Rachel Bodley, dean of the Woman's Medical College of Pennsylvania, astronomer Maria Mitchell, archeologist Sophie Schliemann, and mathematician Christine Ladd Franklin among its corresponding members.[30]

Founders structured the group as closely as possible to the men's society that they wished to emulate. They adapted almost without change that group's constitution, defined their purpose strictly in scientific and intellectual terms, and carefully screened potential members—as did the men's group. The Standing Committee on Communications previewed all papers to be sure that they warranted presentation and that they could be delivered in the stipulated thirty minutes. Scrupulous avoidance of refreshments and the decision to hold meetings in rooms provided by Columbian University rather than in members' homes testifies also to the professional spirit that pervaded their activities. Hinds's declaration that a "great wave of knowledge [is] sweeping over the world. . . . Are we women to sit idle and wondering while men work and reap such rich rewards?" captures the enthusiasm with which the professional members, at least, looked forward to conducting research and earning recognition for their contributions.[31]

As their "guide" of work, the women adapted an outline titled, "What is Anthropology?" prepared by Otis P. Mason, past president of the Anthropological Society of Washington. Expanding upon Mason's presentation—which they printed—leaders maintained that their members, unschooled by outmoded theories, could make significant contributions to numerous fields, among them ethnology, psychology, physiology, archeology, art, linguistics, sociology, and mythology. "Factors of great anthropological value must remain *unknown* unless developed through the opportunities, tact, enthusiasm and scholarship of women," they declared in a published report.[32]

As much as some participants welcomed the challenge of such an endeavor, others feared that their lack of training and credentials would expose them to ridicule. Anita McGee, recording secretary in 1891, recalled that several founders considered the undertaking "hazardous" because "only one of the original participants had ever done scientific work." Lacking what they viewed as the requisite education "fitting us to enter the race for intellectual attainment without handicap," these members preferred to participate in a separate women's organization, at least until they could prove they were worthy to join the men's group. "We have no desire to perpetuate a distinction of sex in science," they said, "but under existing conditions we are satisfied to work out our own problems."[33]

Concerned also about being branded "strong minded," such members defended as "legitimate" their desire "to open to women new fields for systematic investigation." Whether they were sensitive to public opinion or concerned themselves about the proprieties of engaging in masculine pursuits, society leaders carefully placed the activities of their organization within the context of the traditional womanly role. Participants' research, they maintained, was as "sacred" as tasks performed by "heroic laborers in benevolent and Christian enterprises." "May we not lift on high the lamp of research, since we seek only for the precious hieroglyphics of human experience?" they asked.

Activites of the Women's Anthropological Society did not threaten the social order, they assured their audience, but supported it. "Women are not exhorted to *leave* present life-conditions, but to *master* them in the interest of science." As mothers, teachers, and physicians, women could provide special insights into anthropological research. Child study could be enriched, for "who can collect so valuable material" as mothers? Sociology, they said, would benefit because women exerted a "controlling influence at home" and thus better understood the "great principles of association." The understanding of mythology would be enhanced because of women's "highly organized religious nature," a brochure further explained. Even physicians could play an important role, because they could contribute facts of "thrilling interest drawn from the workings of human nature in its normal and abnormal conditions."[34]

In the projects they undertook, women physicians in the group demonstrated the tension between activities deemed appropriate for men and those prescribed for women. Hinds, who later told a reporter that it was important to "keep feminine when doing a masculine job," urged members to employ their talents and skills in the domestic realm they knew best. In 1886, for example, she organized a study section called "Anthropometry" or "Child Growth." Her interest drew on the research of G. Stanley Hall of Clarke University and others who believed that a careful study of children's growth patterns would explain adult behavior and aid in curing disease.[35]

Hinds corresponded with Hall, who replied that "women can obtain material of the difficult and precious sort with a facility far superior to that of men." "Shall we neglect such precious knowledge?" Hinds asked, inviting women to "join to science the wondrous power and richness of the mother life." "There is no need to leave our homes, families [or] schools [to study] the laws governing the growth of body and mind," she wrote in the instructions to the study which she designed. With the help of several other members, Hinds distributed hundreds of these forms to mothers and school teachers—both black and white—urging them to assess their childrens' physical and psychological growth patterns and return the questionnaires to her for evaluation.[36]

Hinds's project reflected her need to stay within the bounds of women's prescribed role while employing strategies to expand that role. The group provided a perfect vehicle for her purposes. Anita McGee viewed her options from a different perspective and used the society to pursue different objectives. She saw no reason for women to be limited by their maternal role. In the projects she undertook,

McGee demonstrated her conviction that women, fully equal to men, had the right to engage in any endeavor. In this, she reflected the point of view of another segment of the organization. By 1889, when McGee became secretary, membership had increased almost three-fold. Journalists, teachers, scientists, and other working women had joined the group along with the anthropologists and society matrons who had founded the association. These newcomers elected a new board of trustees and revised the club's statement of purpose. Instead of "opening to women new fields for investigation," they sought "to promote Anthropology, by encouraging its study and facilitating the interchange of thought among those interested in anthropological research." The revised statement, which omitted any reference to the sex of the participants, reflected the attitude of many of the new members. They agreed with McGee that "advertising work as 'woman's,' and anything making sex in work is a great disadvantage as it makes the very distinction which ought to be obliterated." Like her, they looked forward to the day "when science shall regard the work only—not the worker."[37]

McGee undertook activities to advance women's status in ways different from Hinds. In 1889 she helped to organize a library of anthropological and sociological works that featured monographs and articles by and about professional women and arranged with Powell of the Bureau of Ethnology to make the collection available in the bureau's offices. Authors included Clara de Graffenreid, who was a statistical analyst for the Labor Department; anthropologists Matilda Stevenson, Alice Cunningham Fletcher, and Zelia Nuttall; and astronomer Maria Mitchell—all society members. McGee also used her influence within the men's society—both her father and husband were officers—to arrange joint meetings at which women anthropologists delivered scholarly papers. In 1893, Nuttall spoke on the "Mexican Calendar System," following addresses by McGee and WAS member Caroline Dall. Fletcher gave a series of lectures on folklore in the spring of 1895.[38]

As a member of the Committee on the Investigation of Directive Forces in Society (to which her Columbian classmate, physician Margaret Magnon York, also belonged), McGee designed and distributed surveys to administrators in dozens of cities to determine whether they employed women as superintendents of schools, members of boards of education, college professors, and sanitation and medical inspectors. Although the wording of some of the questions hinted that women did have special attributes for such jobs, the authors urged public administrators and school officials to use "individual fitness" rather than sex as the "criterion of choice" when selecting appointees for "directive and executive work." No record remains of the committee's summary report.[39]

Throughout the 1890s, McGee and others were negotiating a merger with the men's group, which had admitted women in 1891. (Stevenson was accepted that year, by a bare majority and after heated debate. Only two other women were admitted—as honorary members—between 1891 and 1899.) As far as McGee was concerned, by 1899 women had demonstrated their worthiness; there was no longer a need for two anthropological societies in Washington, as many felt there had been earlier. The merger was finalized in 1899, during her husband's presidency of the anthropological society, and when Daniel Smith Lamb served on the board (he was the husband of Women's Anthropological Society member, Dr. Isabel Lamb). Daniel Lamb, the longtime supporter of women's causes, served as first president of the combined group; Alice C. Fletcher held that position four years later.[40]

Undoubtedly, female members were elated with their newly won status. But male acceptance of women into their society represented less an acknowledgement of women's abilities than an admission of their own group's decline. In just one decade, the Anthropological Society of Washington fell from one of the city's most prestigious organizations of professional men to one of lesser importance. In the 1880s, anthropologists and prominent Washington scientists had crowded meetings, considering membership in that society "the best means in the country of making public the results of their work." But by the mid-1890s, they seldom attended. President Lamb felt compelled to point to the "successive establishment of other societies"—all of which actually or virtually barred women—to account for the society's shrinking membership. Such groups "drew away" members, he noted in an annual report. Nationally, the group was also in decline; influence was shifting away from Washington and the Bureau of Ethnology to specialized university-centered anthropology departments, diminishing further the group's status.[41]

Thus, by 1900, when women merged with the men's group, once-coveted membership failed to convey the distinction that it had earlier. The group could not bestow on women'professionals the intangible benefits of prestige and recognition that it had once granted their male peers; power and influence had shifted to arenas where women were unwelcome. Similarly, the women's group had fallen short of meeting members' needs for professional recognition—although it did meet many of their personal needs. Physicians who belonged enjoyed affiliating with like-minded women, and they made contacts that aided their practices. But they could not translate membership in the segregated society to status and rewards in the larger professional community. Limited access to the scientific and intellectual topics discussed in the men's groups—and to the leaders of Washington's male professional elite—combined with the reluctance of some of the society's female members to expand their activities beyond women's traditional sphere hampered career members' professional growth and kept them at the periphery of the emerging scientific establishment.

At the apex of the male professional establishment sat the Cosmos Club, the headquarters of the city's professional elite. The Cosmos included the city's most renowned physicians, surgeons, scientists, and educators as well as its leading artists and men of letters. Membership in the Cosmos was entirely out of reach for professional women, no matter how lofty their accomplishments. Cosmos members fiercely guarded their ranks from the incursion of women—even on special occasions. A temporary relaxation of the prohibition against female guests at the celebration of member James Garfield's presidential inauguration in March 1881 represented a rare concession and resulted in a tightening of the club's rules regarding women's attendance. One of the club's founders, John Wesley Powell, director of the Bureau of Ethnology and a supporter of women, attempted repeatedly throughout the 1880s to have those rules relaxed, but club members resisted adamantly. Most shared physician John Shaw Billings's view that "we may, in the spirit of scientific investigation, secure good seats to inspect the latest patterns of skirt-dancing and high-kicking in the places where these are something of a specialty, but we don't want them at home."[42]

In 1890, a group of the city's most prominent and distinguished women who coveted the benefits that the Cosmos bestowed on male relatives and colleagues, founded the exclusive Washington Club. It courted native-born, white, Anglo-Saxon, Protestant women of well-regarded families who boasted scientific, scholarly, or civic distinction. Hearst, for example, a member from the early years, was the wealthy widow of Senator William Hearst. She won admission by virtue of her civic and philanthropic enterprises, not her wealth and status alone. Hearst had organized or was benefactor of such national groups with Washington headquarters as the Columbia Kindergarten Association and the National Congress of Mothers. She also supported numerous local philanthropies like the Woman's Clinic and the Central Dispensary. Other members enjoyed successful professional careers. Physicians Anita McGee and Sofie Nordhoff-Jung, anthropologist Alice C.

Fletcher, and statistician Clara de Graffenried—all Women's Anthropological Society members—joined the Washington Club at its founding.

In their elegant headquarters a block from the Cosmos Club, members created an ambience to match their self-defined elite status. They enforced strict rules to ensure the proper atmosphere for reading, playing whist, and enjoying lectures by members and guests. Their stated goals, to meet for "literary purposes, mutual improvement and the promotion of social intercourse," were easily met. But, unlike the Cosmos, the Washington Club was unable to provide its members with the benefits that the men's group bestowed: contacts and information that promoted a professional career and ensured status in the community. Women simply lacked influence and control over resources and institutions that facilitated advancement into public life. Limited in their ability to translate their competence and skills into the larger community, club women turned inward. By exaggerating their own exclusiveness—even gaining a reputation among their contemporaries for a "contemptible snobbishness"—they assured themselves at least of their standing among Washington's professional elite.[43]

Like other women's organizations that grew to prominence in the 1890s, the Washington Club could not advance women of promise to substantial career success the way that comparable male institutions promoted worthy young men. Discrimination and occupational segregation, enforced by male professionals and reinforced by career women themselves ambivalent about their traditional female sphere, sustained male dominance in the professional community. Nonetheless, such groups did play a vital role in the personal lives of participants. Diaries of physician Julia Green and anthropologist Alice Cunningham Fletcher reveal that those women frequently attended the meetings of their associations and maintained close ties with other members. In one two-week period in the winter of 1895, for instance, Fletcher attended six different women's club meetings and lectured at three, including the Washington Club. During the same period she dined with Annie Hawes Barus (head of child-life study of the Women's Anthropological Society, Association of Collegiate Alumnae president, member of the National University committee, and president of the Vassar Alumni Association); Sarah Scull (anthropological society member, former medical student, archeologist, and professor of history at the Mount Venon Seminary); Caroline Dall (another anthropological society member and women's rights activist); and Mrs. Henry Pellew (contributor to the Women's Fund for Johns Hopkins University, member of the DAR, and participant in the Literary Society).

In addition, Fletcher also visited Caroline Winslow to seek medical advice.[44]

Perhaps the most important role these organizations played was to enable the women doctors, lawyers, anthropologists, teachers, and others who participated to develop an appreciation of their own self-worth. If male anthropologists at the Bureau of American Ethnology regarded Matilda Stevenson as overbearing and officious, and questioned the value of her work when she demanded a larger share of the bureau's expedition funds, at least her associates at the Women's Anthropological Society appreciated her merits. Secretary of that group McGee publicly praised Stevenson's "energy, ability, and fostering care" and credited her with the "success and harmony" of that organization. Sofie Nordhoff-Jung, another anthropological society member and Washington Club colleague, wrote Stevenson that she was "particularly proud" to show the German gynecology professors with whom she studied in Munich "how thoroughly done" was Stevenson's work on the Zuni and that it "was done by a woman."[45]

Turn-of-the-century black women doctors and their professional contemporaries also sought intellectual stimulation and status affirmation from a society that was loath to offer such recognition to women, no less black women. Like their contemporaries—white and black, male and female—black professional women turned to organizational affiliation, or to what some in the black community referred to as the "mania for club life" to meet those needs. Because founders valued ultimate integration into the white community, they often modeled their associations after white women's groups, just as white women had modeled their groups after men's associations. But societies in the female black community exhibited other characteristics that reflected members' special circumstances and the economic vulnerablility they faced.[46]

The Colored Women's Professional Franchise Association, a club established by black career women in the 1870s (likely in 1878) resembled white woman's rights organizations that were founded at the same time. Mary Ann Shadd Cary, the sister of Eunice Shadd, Howard Medical School graduate in 1875, organized this short-lived association that reflected the outlook of women who had been active in abolition and women's rights. The group's president, she was an outspoken suffragist and member of NWSA. When the group was formed, she had just graduated from the Howard law program and was teaching school in Washington; her sister had just graduated from the medical department. Club minutes reveal that Cary and her associates formed the group because they resented male colleagues' domination of mixed societies. "Very few" members of those organizations were "permitted to know what is done," the women stated. "Our leaders do not take the women into consideration" when deliberating vital issues; "the women want light," they declared.[47]

Association members encouraged women to take the initiative in improving their economic and legal status. Women had to begin by taking an "aggressive stand," members declared, against the assumption that "men only may begin and conduct industrial and other things." The association's twenty-point manifesto called for the opening of cooperative food and clothing stores for and by women, and the establishment of manufacturing businesses owned and operated by women that would employ women. Funds for a joint stock company, formed by quarterly dollar contributions and monthly dues, would be loaned to petitioners to help them start their own businesses. In formulating these plans, members insisted that control remain in women's hands. "While no invidious distinctions may be made," their minutes stated, "women, having the greatest interest at stake, must be the controlling official power." Through such means members sought to expand limited job opportunities for women of their race. "Thirty to forty occupations for white women" exist, their minutes declared, compared to only "half a dozen for colored ones."[48]

The group also worked toward dispelling black women's political inertia through a lecture bureau and a newspaper "unbiased by sex restrictions and jealousies." Suffrage was a high priority. They noted that only two women of their race had attended a NWSA convention the previous week that had attracted more than two thousand white women. Proudly, Cary and her co-members soon wrote to NWSA officers on behalf of ninety-four black women requesting that their names be listed in the centennial publication supporting woman suffrage. There is no evidence regarding their other activities. The association disappeared, leaving no other records.[49]

In the 1880s, instead of relying on suffrage or women's rights organizations, black women doctors and their contemporaries sought redress for economic disabilities in self-help and mutual aid associations. Such groups—segregated by sex—were common in the black community and reflected workers' economic vulnerability. Men's and women's clubs collected and invested funds for members to use in emergencies. A modest initiation fee of $1 to $5 and small monthly dues—generally 25 cents—provided unemployment and death benefits. Male physicians joined such fraternal societies as a matter of course and sought leadership roles. Those chosen to examine applicants for insurance earned several dollars for each examination and benefitted from the prestige associated with this service.[50]

In 1900, more than three thousand black women in the city participated in almost fifty women's self-help societies. Members were usually single, widowed, or divorced working women who were self-supporting and who supported others. They included federal clerks, school teachers, principals, dressmakers, and other regularly employed women. Women doctors participated in these groups, but there is no indication that insurance companies used them as examiners as they did their male colleagues. Carrie Thomas, Howard medical graduate in 1890, a teacher and part-time physician, served as secretary to the O. P. Morton Women's Relief Corps. organized in 1883. Laura E. Wilkes, a Howard medical student and teacher in the public schools, held the post of recording secretary for the Ladies Mutual Relief Organization, founded in 1890.[51]

Other black women's groups organized near the turn of the century satisfied career women's needs for mutual assistance in groups that emphasized sex solidarity, like the Wimodaughsis and the Women's Educational and Industrial Union. These groups provided services to women of different social and economic status. The Sojourner Truth Association for Working Women and the Colored Women's League were both organized in 1892 by school teachers and other interested women in the community. They maintained residences for single women, established employment bureaus, and offered courses in domestic economy, sewing, and other job-related skills. The Colored Women's League used initiation and other dues to establish a women's handicraft market and a kindergarten teacher training school. Because so many women with young children worked outside the home, league members also maintained seven day nurseries. Phoebe Hearst provided some financial support and the group solicited more than $2,000 in contributions from blacks of every social status. This project later led to the introduction of kindergarten classes into the District of Columbia public schools.[52]

The black community also had its share of associations that reinforced members' newfound elite status. One group founded in 1910, the Collegiate Alumnae Club, epitomized clubs of this type and was important for the way in which it mirrored white women's attempts to create a professional middle-class identity. The group resembled its white counterpart, the Association of Collegiate Alumnae. Mary Church Terrell, a graduate of Oberlin and the first woman trustee of the District of Columbia Board of Education, formed this group with several professional women. Physicians were prominent among them; they included Sara W. Brown and N. Fairfax Brown (both Howard Medical School graduates) and Jane Eleanor Datcher (a public school teacher and one-time Howard medical student). Although founders of this group, graduates of Cornell University and Oberlin College, were eligible for membership in the predominately white association because of the institutions from which they had graduated, they chose to form their own society so that graduates of Howard and other "colored colleges," denied membership in the other group, could enjoy the benefits of affiliation. Opposed to segregation "on general principles," members maintained that a segregated institution "was the less of two evils." Within a month of its founding, the alumnae association reportedly included every eligible black woman in the Washington community.[53]

The ostensible purpose of the organization was to "promote a closer union" among female college graduates, to encourage their development, and to "enhance [their] usefulness" in the community. In the club's first few years, however, outreach activities were limited: a few individuals formed a drama and reading group; others collected data on high school students' postgraduation progress. The club's principal activities were self-promotional and consisted largely of hosting receptions for female graduates of the city's segregated high schools. This activity served to encourage young female proteges, but it also provided important opportunties for members to "present" themselves "to the community as a club of organized college women." During the first year, members hosted an impressive community celebration of the one-hundredth anniversary of Harriet Beecher Stowe's birth. The guest list of prominent white politicians and their wives brought members of the group added distinction.[54]

Outspoken members of Washington's black community regarded the apparent pretensions of such groups as the Collegiate Alumnae Club and other women's clubs, like the Literary Society, the Book Lovers' Club, and the Treble Clef, offensive, especially to the degree that members counted a light complexion, sharp features, and elite family background more essential for membership than community mindedness and ability. (Of course critics did not limit their censure to women's groups; social stratification based on color, bearing, and ancestry pervaded urban black society.) Educator Nannie Burroughs was but one of these critics who regarded such "secular clubs" merely as "agencies to bring together certain classes at the exclusion of the poor." Mary Shadd Cary, another local critic, condemned the "builders of rings within rings . . . committed to caste heresy" whom, she believed, practiced a form of intraracial discrimination as virulent as that enforced by the white community. Physician-educator Lucy Moten, a graduate of Howard's medical school and principal of the city's black normal school, drew fire for the "discriminations" she practiced "on account of complexion, social standing and personalities" when selecting and training teacher candidates. Such practices barred many women from vital access to middle-class society and job security.[55]

As much as such elitism appeared to reflect a problem unique to the black community, it differed only in kind from attitudes expressed by the white professional elite towards lower-status members of their own race. Influential segments of both female communities were guilty of sacrificing sex solidarity for social class distinctions. Whether they used criteria of national origin and religion or of complexion and lineage, numbers of professional women of the late nineteenth century—like their male contemporaries—were contributing to the development of a new social order that was as class conscious, sexually segregated, and racially divided as the old. Some women doctors and their colleagues fought those distinctions; others cultivated them.

But their most important goal eluded them. Whether they were activist feminists or conservative change agents, professional women proved unable to integrate themselves into America's emerging professional middle-class culture. They possessed the will but lacked the means to overcome the sexist—and racist—nature of American society. The image of the "new woman" that they epitomized turned out to be a fleeting illusion. Whether pioneer or post-pioneer professionals in the vanguard of this new elite, they shared disappointment. Those whose careers began in the 1870s watched as increasing conservatism and racism during the 1880s and 1890s eroded the limited gains they had achieved. Professionals at the turn of the century, who forsook the feminist activism of the pioneers in their desire for acceptance on terms equal to men, fared little better. Exclusion from men's groups limited their professional contacts and restricted their opportunities to evaluate their own work in light of the theories and practices of their disciplines. Moreover, the highly diverse makeup of their groups, disparaged as unprogressive by men who belonged to increasingly specialized groups, brought women professionals little status outside the female community. Even limited acceptance into male-segregated societies represented a mixed blessing; it often signified the diminished status of the men's groups rather than the recognition of women's merits. And in both black and white communities, integration often meant that women enjoyed the rights—but not the full benefits—of active club membership, restricted as they were to a limited role in the organization's deliberations.

Ultimately, instead of easing women into the mainstream of their professional communities, female associations contributed further to their isolation at the periphery of a highly stratified, male-dominated, white professional middle class. The institutionalization of segregation in the professional realm reinforced women's powerlessness to penetrate the all-male networks of influence and prestige. With a taste of bitter irony, their successors discovered that the networks of associations their forbears had established consolidated the very distinctions they had attempted to erase.

Conclusion

The Gilded Age was a time of promise and disillusionment for Washington's career women. For the first time, they believed, women had a chance for success in the public arena. "The new era with its larger richer life for women is already here," exulted one of its members, Sara Spencer, the owner of a successful business academy. "We cannot, if we would, set back the wheels of time." All signs pointed to the advent of this new age. The rapidly growing federal bureaucracy and the concomitant growth of services in the city demanded more professionals—from administrators and lawyers, to scientists and journalists. Although not accepted as the equals of men, Washington women were gaining entrance into these occupations. Their inroads as well as the gains that women were making in the city's undergraduate, graduate, and professional schools betokened a future bright with promise.[1]

But these hopes were never fully realized. The experience of professional women in medicine epitomizes the reversal of career women's fortunes at the close of the century. Washington's medical schools, gatekeepers to the profession, provided both the entree and the barrier to women's medical careers. During the 1870s and 1880s, when financial insolvency threatened highly competitive medical schools, their faculties agreed to experiment with coeducation—usually as a measure of last resort. When financial conditions improved, however, even those faculty members who had supported women's cause joined ranks with coeducation's opponents to oust women from their midst. No less than male students, male faculty feared the loss of status that might ensue should too many women gain a foothold in the department. Local schools that remained steadfast in their commitment to women either operated on the fringe of the respected medical community or closed, unable to meet the competitive challenge of modernization.

The apparent promise of the age deceived women in other respects. When the Columbian Medical Department barred female students, medical women and those who supported them rejected a plan to establish a coordinate female medical college. They doubted that such a school could provide the rigorous training women needed for professional legitimacy. Instead, women aspired to a coeducational college of the first rank, like Johns Hopkins, which was about to open in neighboring Baltimore. They were convinced that Hopkins, not Columbian, represented the wave of the future.

Postmedical school training presented another barrier that women overcame only temporarily. When discriminatory practices of the male medical elite made it next to impossible to secure postgraduate training or hospital appointments, women doctors established their own training institutions. These required little capital or experience to open, and they received a measure of community support. Yet the growth of these institutions soon created a dilemma. In order to sustain them, participating women physicians had to decide whether to integrate their clinics into the male medical establishment or maintain them autonomously. The physicians who chose integration lost influence over their infirmary's operation. The men who set that clinic's course favored male proteges over female graduates when appointing staff members. Ultimately, this training center initiated only a select few of Washington's women doctors into the professional medical community.

Those women who retained control of their clinics faced different problems. Inadequate funding forced one group to close its infirmary. Another operated its clinic at the periphery of the medical community for many decades—understaffed and underequipped. Its independence, which initially worked in women's behalf, providing the city's white female medical school graduates with critical experience and the support of female mentors, ultimately acted to women physicians' detriment. Later generations of women doctors avoided affiliating because they needed high-caliber, well-regarded postgraduate training, and they feared that association would tarnish their reputations in the medical community. Women doctors who founded this clinic also attempted, without success, to establish a hospital so that women physicians could enjoy the same privileges their male colleagues received at area hospitals. It was not until the 1920s that women doctors regularly were able to admit their own patients to city hospitals, supervise their care, and perform surgery.

Once trained, women were dependent upon the male medical community for legitimation through professional societies. There, too, disappointment followed initial success. At first, male doctors barred women from affiliation because they feared female competition and the feminization of the profession. But their concern about the homeopaths' ability to attract trained women and their realization that women regulars had a competitive advantage unregulated by the professional code of ethics and the fee schedule prompted male physicians to lower the barriers to membership. Even as women gained entry to these societies, however, they faced more formidable barriers. The emerging specialist groups and the medical school-hospital complexes that bestowed higher status, and where the "old boy" network worked even more effectively, refused to grant them membership. Limited access to fellow practitioners in such informal collegial settings limited women's access to useful contacts and their access to new developments in their fields. Where women did gain entry, they frequently felt like outsiders. Eventually, to satisfy professional and personal needs unmet in the inclusive professional groups, they formed their own medical society.

While Washington's women doctors were developing strategies to surmount barriers within the profession, they confronted a growing bulwark of sex-segregated professional and quasi-professional associations in the larger community. In response, along with other career and activist women, they created numerous sex- and race-segregated associations. Several compensated directly for exclusion from male societies. In some cases, women preferred to meet in single-sex organizations, unhampered by male criticism. Sensitive to what they perceived as their own inadequacies, members of such groups conceded men's right to exclude them, at least for the time being.

The sex-segregated women's groups catered to a broad segment of Washington's black and white middle-class female communities. As a result, they adopted diverse goals and approaches. Generational differences were compelling: Early postwar groups challenged prevailing stereotypes of women's place—in the profession as elsewhere; later groups avoided confrontational strategies and chose to bide their time in anticipation of ultimate integration. All, however, adopted agendas to advance women's status.

The wide-ranging memberships of these groups and their diverse goals gave women doctors platforms from which to press for reforms—some in their own behalf. Yet coming at a time when male professionals were creating a maze of highly specialized organizations, the diversity of the women's groups made them appear unprogressive. Ultimately, they detracted from professional women's status instead of enhancing it. Although professional women looked to the day when "science would regard only the work—not the worker," they found themselves little closer to acceptance within the men's groups at the end of the century than they had earlier.[2]

At the same time, women doctors of the period discovered that the public was less willing to patronize female physicians than they had anticipated. Restrictions on female medical practice undercut the clientele that the female culture of the late-nineteenth century had promised. The hospital-centered male medical elite monopolized advances in medical techniques—both touted and real. And as long as men denied women physicians hospital privileges and access to the latest medical advances, they were able to attract patients away by offering them a full range of services.

In addition to such institutional impediments, late-nineteenth-century physicians faced cultural barriers of a high order. Combining domestic responsibilities with demanding careers proved far more difficult than many had anticipated. Whether as wives and mothers, or as daughters and sisters, most women doctors owed allegiance to the family claim. While the vast majority maintained full-time practices, a few followed disjointed careers interrupted by the demands of children, husbands, or aged parents; a very few forsook publicly their own work to become unseen helpmates in the advancement of their husbands' career.

Embodying the cultural constructs of their time, later-nineteenth-century professional women—iconoclastic though they were in other respects—generally adhered to prevailing norms of ladylike behavior. The public criticism their outspoken predecessors had experienced—and the minimal gains seemingly they had achieved—forewarned their successors. With good reason, the post-pioneers avoided being branded "strong minded," an epithet that conjured up images of professional disparagement and rejection. Rather than challenge professional barriers and public prejudices head on, these doctors tried through alternative means to achieve the same ends, sometimes even capitalizing on their supposed distinctiveness as women professionals.

Not surprisingly, only a few women with social influence, charisma, or outstanding skills succeeded in transcending such cultural and professional obstacles; none attained the prominence of Washington's most elite male physicians. Ultimately, women doctors were unable to influence the misogynist form that the culture of professionalism was taking; the restructuring of American social roles lay beyond their ken. Along with their contemporary female colleagues, these women

watched the doors through which they had entered all but close behind them. Like the advance guard to which Dr. Francis White of
the Woman's Medical College of Pennsylvania had referred, late-
nineteenth-century Washington women physicians who served isolated outposts in alien territory waited in vain for replacements.

Women physicians were not unique in experiencing a reversal of
their opportunities at a moment in history usually regarded as socially
expansive. Washington's women journalists, scientists, and lawyers also
blazed trails few could follow. As the number of women correspondents admitted to the Capitol press galleries multiplied in the 1870s,
for instance, male opposition grew. Throughout the 1880s and 1890s,
Washington editors, largely in response to the objections of male re-
porters, relegated women to society news instead of allowing them to
cover the political scene as they had earlier. Those women who tried
to expand their opportunities by publishing independent, general interest journals, even with the aid of wealthy female patrons, failed because of competition and prohibitive costs.[3]

Women scientists employed by the federal government experienced
a comparable retrenchment. In the 1880s and 1890s, anthropologists
with the Bureau of Ethnology performed field studies and published
and lectured widely. Yet between the late 1880s and the 1920s, as the
field's base of operations shifted from a government bureau (under
the leadership of a supporter of women) to the universities, only one
American woman entered the field—and she had trained as a sociolo-
gist. The attitudes of those men who had orginally "sounded the bullroarer" at women's presence effectively barred women for thirty years.
In other federal scientific departments, women who hoped that Civil
Service reforms would allow them to advance on their merits, stood by
while covert practices and examination barriers perpetuated earlier
discrimination.[4]

Similarly, Washington's women lawyers who overcame obstacles in
the 1870s and 1880s—opening the Supreme Court and the Court of
Claims to women advocates, for example—faced other barriers in the
1890s. The decline of the apprenticeship system, which had enabled
some to enter the profession, and the exclusion of women from the
National University Law School when male students objected to their
presence, discouraged would-be lawyers. In 1896, a few prevailed
upon Washington's practicing female attorneys to open a modest law
school. Resistance from the male-dominated legal community forced
most of that school's graduates to use their legal training indirectly, as
administrators of social service agencies or as secretaries and jour-

nalists. The school, the Washington College of Law, ultimately became the law school of American University, its female origins lost until recent times.[5]

Black women doctors, lawyers, and teachers in Washington saw their opportunties reversed not only because they were women, but even more profoundly, because they were black. The material prosperity and enlarged opportunties that the city's black community enjoyed in the 1870s and 1880s declined sharply as racial hostilities increased. After the depression of 1893, black women found few opportunities in federal employment. At the same time, the segregated school system, earlier a mecca for black intellectuals, reached a limit on the number of educators it could hire. Women doctors and lawyers in the black community found it all but impossible to establish supporting private practices.

The decline in professional opportunities that Washington's career women faced found parallels throughout the United States. Women in various professions and cities experienced reversals in their opportunities at varying times and to varying degrees between 1900 and 1930. The vast increase in women college graduates in this period belied a decrease in their professional options. Female undergraduates gravitated to jobs where opportunities appeared to exist, such as the new fields of home economics and social work or the predominantly female occupations of teaching and nursing. The number of women engaged in graduate study did not match their increase. At the turn of the century, women's rapidly increasing numbers in the postgraduate schools fostered such concern about feminization at schools like the Universities of Chicago, Stanford, Wisconsin, and Tufts that their administrators adopted policies to either segregate women or limit their numbers. Women who did earn Masters and Ph.D. degrees between 1890 and 1930 faced limited options. Barred from the sciences and the emerging social scientific fields, they clustered in more hospitable occupations. Yet even in such an area as female higher education, they were denied top positions.[6]

Thus, as the culture of professionalism took shape, women professionals in medicine as well as in other fields found themselves restricted to positions at the periphery of the professional fraternity, denied the contacts and information that assured promotion and ultimate success. Diverse strategies proved unavailing. At the heart of the matter, women could not control the resources that provided entree to a field and sustained and nurtured a professional career. Limited in their ability to influence their access to education, postgraduate training, collegial networks of power and promotion, and real and symbolic positions of influence, late-nineteenth-century professional women struggled to retain the limited gains they had achieved. Black or white, these women discovered to their dismay that the "wheels of time" could indeed be set back. The consolidation of pervasive gender and race distinctions upon which the modern-day professions were built foreshortened their vision of a new age and left a legacy that remains to be fulfilled.

Notes

1. Most notably, Burton Bledstein focuses on the emergence of the professions themselves in *The Culture of Professionalism: The Middle Class and the Development of Higher Education in America* (New York: W. W. Norton, 1976); for
particular professions see, Maxwell Bloomfield, *American Lawyers in a Changing
Society, 1776–1876* (Cambridge: Harvard University Press, 1976); William R.
Johnson, "Education and Professional Life Styles: Law and Medicine in the
Nineteenth Century," *History of Education Quarterly* 14 (Summer 1974): 185–
207; Jerold Auerbach, *Unequal Justice* (New York: Oxford University Press,
1977), which analyzes how the emergence of a stratified bar discriminated
against "disfavored" groups but neglects women; Thomas Haskell, *The Emergence of Professional Social Science* (Urbana: University of Illinois Press, 1976);
and Paul Mattingly, *The Classless Profession: American Schoolmen in the Nineteenth
Century* (New York: New York University Press, 1975). Studies of the medical
profession likewise ignore women or relegate them to a footnote, see, for example, Thomas Bonner, *Medicine in Chicago, 1850–1950* (Madison: University of Wisconsin Press, 1957); Edward A. Atwater, "The Physicians of
Rochester, New York, 1860–1910: A Study of Professional History, II," *Bulletin of the History of Medicine* 51 (Winter 1977): 93–105; Joseph F. Kett, *The
Formation of the American Medical Profession, 1780–1860* (New Haven: Yale University Press, 1968); William G. Rothstein, *American Physicians in the Nineteenth
Century: From Sects to Science* (Baltimore: Johns Hopkins University Press,
1971). Two notable exceptions before 1975 are Richard Shryock's perceptive
essay, "Women in American Medicine," *Journal of the American Medical Women's
Association* 5 (Sept. 1950): 371–79, and Gerald Markowitz and David Karl
Rosmer, "Doctors in Crisis: A Study of the Use of Medical Education Reform
to Establish Modern Professional Elitism in Medicine," *American Quarterly* 25
(March 1973): 83–107. Standard works written about blacks in the professions similarly ignore women, for example, W. Montague Cobb, *Progress and
Portents for the Negro in Medicine* (New York: National Association for the Ad-
vancement of Colored People, 1948); Herbert M. Morais, *The History of the
Afro-American in Medicine*, vol. 1, International Library of Afro-American Life
and History (Cornwell Heights, Penn., Association for the Study of Afro-

American Life and History, 1976); Carter Godwin Woodson, *The Negro Profes-sional Man in the Community* (New York: Negro Universities Press, 1934).

For the focus on "subjective necessity," see Christopher Lasch, "Jane Ad-dams: The College Woman and the Family Claim," in *The New Radicalism in America, 1889–1963* (New York: Alfred A. Knopf, 1965).

For literature on nineteenth-century women in feminized fields, see Maris Vinovskis and Richard Bernard, "The Female School Teacher in Antebellum Massachusetts," *Journal of Social History* 10 (March 1977): 332–45; Redding Sugg, *Motherteacher: The Feminization of American Education* (Charlottesville: University Press of Virginia, 1978); Ann Douglas, *The Feminization of American Culture* (New York: Alfred A. Knopf, 1977), and "The 'Scribbling Women' and 'Fanny Fern': Why Women Wrote," *American Quarterly* 23 (Spring 1971): 3–14; Dee Garrison, *Apostles of Culture: The Public Librarian and American So-ciety, 1876–1920* (New York: Free Press, 1979); Roy Lubove, *The Professional Altruist: The Emergence of Social Work as a Career, 1880–1930* (Cambridge: Har-vard University Press, 1965); Alan Davis, *Spearheads for Reform* (New York: Ox-ford University Press, 1967).

2. For an excellent review of this literature, see Joan Jacobs Brumberg and Nancy Tomes, "Women in the Professions: A Research Agenda for Women Historians," *Reviews in American History* (June 1982): 275–96; see also demo-graphic surveys such as Richard Jensen's "Family, Career, and Reform: Women Leaders in the Progressive Era," in *The American Family in Social-Historical Per-spective*, ed. Michael Gordon (New York: St. Martin's Press, 1973) and Margaret Rossiter's "Women Scientists in America before 1920" in *American Scientist* 62 (May-June 1974): 312–23; Barbara Kuhn Campbell, *The "Liberated Woman" of 1914: Prominent Women in the Progressive Era* (Ann Arbor: University Micro-films International, Research Press, 1979), and Margaret Gibbons Wilson, *The American Woman in Transition: The Urban Influence, 1870–1920* (Westport, Conn.: Greenwood Press, 1979). Recent historical studies that focus on in-stitutional barriers to career success for turn-of-the century professional women include: Maurene H. Beasley, *The First Women Washington Correspon-dents*, George Washington Studies 4 (Washington: George Washington Uni-versity, 1976); Marion Marzolf, *Up from the Footnote: A History of Women Jour-nalists* (New York: Hastings House, 1977); Martha Blaxall and Barbara Reagan, eds., *Women and the Workplace: The Implications of Occupational Segrega-tion* (Chicago: The University of Chicago Press, 1976); William Chafe, *The American Woman: Her Changing Social, Economic, and Political Roles, 1920–1970* (New York: Oxford University Press, 1972); Estelle Freedman, "Separatism as a Strategy: Female Institution Building and American Feminism, 1870–1930," *Feminist Studies* 5 (Fall 1979): 512–29; Patricia M. Hammer, *The Decade of Elusive Promise: Professional Women in the United States, 1920–1930* (Ann Ar-bor: University Microfilms International, 1979); Sally Kohlstedt, "In from the Periphery: American Women in Science, 1830–1880," *Signs* 4 (Autumn 1978): 81–96; Stanley Leaman, *The Woman Citizen: Social Feminism in the 1920s* (Urbana: University of Illinois Press, 1973); Nancy Ostereich Lurie, "Women in Early American Anthropology," in *Pioneers of American Anthropology*, ed.

June Helm MacNeish (Seattle: University of Washington Press, 1966); D. Kelly Weisberg, "Barred from the Bar: Women and Legal Education in the United States, 1870–1890," *Journal of Legal Education* 28 (1977): 485–507. Regina Morantz-Sanchez provides a broad survey of women's experience as medical practitioner since the early period that looks both at the women's lives and the institutions they confronted in *Sympathy and Science: Women Physicians in American Medicine* (New York: Oxford University Press, 1985); valuable for their analyses of the misogynistic character of the emerging professions and their effect on women's career opportunites are Margaret Rossiter's "Sexual Segregation in the Sciences: Some Data and a Model," *Signs* 4 (Autumn 1978): 146–51 and *Women Scientists in America: Struggles and Strategies to 1940* (Baltimore: Johns Hopkins University Press, 1982), and Mary Roth Walsh, *"Doctors Wanted: No Women Need Apply:" Sexual Barriers in the Medical Profession, 1835–1975* (New Haven: Yale University Press, 1977). Useful sociological frameworks include Cynthia Fuchs Epstein, *Woman's Place: Options and Limits in Professional Careers* (Berkeley: University of California Press, 1970), and Harriet Zuckerman, "Stratification in American Science," *Sociological Inquiry* 40 (Spring 1979): 235–57. Classical sociology ignores women in fields in which they are underrepresented and defines feminized occupations as semi-professions. For the basic work in this regard, see Amatai Etzioni, ed., *The Semi-Professions and their Organization: Teaching, Nursing, Social Work* (Glencoe, Ill.: Free Press, 1967).

3. Karen Blair, *The Clubwoman as Feminist: True Womanhood Redefined, 1886–1914* (New York: Holmes and Meier, 1980); Barbara Epstein, *The Politics of Domesticity: Women, Evangelism and Temperance in Nineteenth Century America* (Middletown, Conn., Wesleyan University Press, 1981); Joyce Antler, "After College What? New Graduates and the Family Claim," *American Quarterly* 32 (Fall 1980): 409–33.

4. Ellen Hardin Walworth, "Washington: A Literary Center," *The Chautauquan* 13 (Sept. 1891): 768–69.

CHAPTER 1

1. Robert W. Weibe, *The Search for Order, 1870–1920* (New York: Hill and Wang, 1967), 111. The concepts signified by the phrases, "crucial moment" and "vertical vision" are central to Burton Bledstein's analysis, *The Culture of Professionlism: The Middle Class and the Development of Higher Education in America* (New York: W. W. Norton, 1976), 84.

2. Josephine St. Pierre Ruffin, in an address to the First National Conference of Colored Women published in the *Woman's Era* 2 (May 1895): 14; Lockwood in "My Efforts to Become a Lawyer," *Lippincott's* (June 1888): 215–29.

3. Thomas Woody, *A History of Women's Education in the United States*, vol. 2 (New York: Science Press, 1929; reprint, New York: Octagon Books, 1966), 229.

4. "Declaration of Sentiments and Resolution, Seneca Falls Convention," in *Up from the Pedestal*, ed. Aileen S. Kraditor (Chicago: Quadrangle Books,

1968), 185; Hale quoted in Esther Pohl Lovejoy, *Women Doctors of the World* (New York: Macmillan, 1957), 23; for female support networks, see Mary Roth Walsh, "Feminism: A Support System of Women Physicians," *Journal of the American Medical Women's Association* 31 (June 1976): 247–50.

5. The eclectics practiced botanic medicine and rigorously rejected the heavy drugging and bleeding practiced by the regulars. They claimed to utilize the best practices of all sects. All but one eclectic college accepted women. The homeopaths, a much larger group, believed in the efficacy of infintesimally reduced doses of medication. They drew their inspiration from the works of Samuel Hahnemann, a German physician who utilized drugs that induced the same symptoms in a healthy person that patients suffered. The homeopaths emphasized close doctor-patient relationships, the better to evaluate slight changes in the course of the illness, and they conducted experimental "provings" of drugs, based on scientific procedures then accepted. This approach—which succeeded as well as any methods then in use—appealed to the scientific perspective of the urban middle classes. For a discussion of these groups, see Paul Starr, *The Social Transformation of American Medicine* (New York: Basic Books, 1982); Martin Kaufman, *Homeopathy in America: The Rise and Fall of a Medical Heresy* (Baltimore: Johns Hopkins University Press, 1971); Harris Coulter, *Divided Legacy*, vol. 3 (Washington: McGrath Publishing, 1973); and George P. Peck, "Homoeopathy in the United States," *Hahnemannian Monthly* 35 (Sept. 1900): 559–66.

6. Coulter, *Divided Legacy*, 47.

7. William G. Rothstein, *American Physicians in the Nineteenth Century: From Sects to Science* (Baltimore: Johns Hopkins University Press, 1972), 287, 344. See also, Joseph F. Kett, *The Formation of the American Medical Profession: The Role of Institutions, 1780–1860* (New Haven: Yale University Press, 1968); Leo James O'Hara, "An Emerging Profession: Philadelphia Medicine, 1860–1900" (Ph.D. diss., University of Pennsylvania, 1976); Richard Harrison Shryock, *Medicine and Society in America: 1660–1860* (Ithaca: Cornell University Press, 1960); and Starr, *American Medicine*.

8. Mary Roth Walsh, *"Doctors Wanted: No Women Need Apply": Sexual Barriers in the Medical Profession, 1835–1975* (New Haven: Yale University Press, 1977), chap. 5, especially 176–80; Woody, *A History of Women's Education*, vols. 1 and 2, chap. 7, "Higher Professional Education," 321–81; *The Women's Medical Fund and the Opening of the Johns Hopkins School of Medicine* (Baltimore: Women's Medical Alumnae Association, [1978]).

9. See, for example, the column in the *Woman's Journal* entitled, "Medical Reporter," beginning 3 Jan. 1891; see also the *Woman's Tribune* and the *Alpha*, both nationally distributed journals edited by women; Meyers (New York: Ayer Co., 1891); Rayne (Albany: Eagle Publishing, 1893); Willard (New York: Mast Crowell & Kirkpatrick, 1897); Jewett (New York: Houghton, Mifflin, 1884); Twain and Charles D. Warner (Hartford: American Publishing, 1873). The Association for Collegiate Alumnae did much to publicize such efforts; see Roberta Frankfort, *Collegiate Women* (New York: New York University Press, 1977), 90. For a contemporary's reaction to this material, see Dr. Ross R.

Bunting, "The Doctor as Portrayed in Fiction," *North Carolina Medical Journal* 23 (Jan. 1889): 100–16.

10. Quoted in Ernest Samuels, *Henry Adams: The Middle Years* (Cambridge: Harvard University Press, 1958), 24. See also Henry L. Nelson, "Washington Society," *Harpers New Monthly Magazine* 86 (March 1893): 586–96.

11. Francis G. Carpenter, ed., *Carp's Washington* (authorized reproduction by microfilm, Ann Arbor, 1970), 9.

12. See James Kirkpartick Flack, *Desideratum in Washington: The Intellectual Community in the Capital City, 1870–1900* (Cambridge, Mass: Schenkman Publishing, 1975).

13. Gerri Major, *Black Society* (Chicago: Johnson Publishing, 1976), 175, 242; for economic opportunities for blacks in Washington, see Allan J. Johnston, "Surviving Freedom: The Black Community of Washington, D. C., 1860–1880" (Ph.D. diss., Duke University, 1980), and Constance Green, "Colored Washington, 1879–1901," in *Washington: Capital City, 1879–1950* (Princeton: Princeton University Press, 1962), 101–31; the Washington *Bee* listed jobs blacks held in the federal government, for example, 22 Jan. 1891; 14 Aug. 1897; and Laurence Hayes, *The Negro Federal Government Worker: A Study of His Classification Status in the District of Columbia, 1883–1928*, The Howard University Studies in Social Science 3 (Washington: Howard University Press, 1941). For black organizations in Washington, see Andrew F. Hilyer, *The Twentieth Century Union League Directory: A Compilation of the Efforts of Colored People of Washington for the Social Betterment* (Washington: The Union League, 1901).

14. Walworth, "Washington: A Literary Center," *The Chautauquan* 13 (Sept. 1891): 768; also see Caroline B. Winslow, ed., the *Alpha* 7 (Jan. 1882):8–9; for annual Washington activities of the National Woman Suffrage Association, see Elizabeth Cady Stanton, Susan B. Anthony, and Matilda J. Gage, *History of Woman Suffrage* vol. 2 (New York: Fowler and Wells, 1881; reprint, New York: Arno Press, 1969), especially chaps. 27–55; also see Susan B. Anthony's diaries for the appropriate months in the Susan B. Anthony Collection, Library of Congress, Washington, D.C.

15. Biographical sketches in Edward T. James and Janet Wilson James, eds., *Notable American Women, 1607–1950: A Biographical Dictionary* (Cambridge: Harvard University Press, 1972).

16. See Maurene H. Beasley, *The First Women Washington Correspondents*, George Washington University Studies 4 (Washington: George Washington University, 1976); Marion Marzolf, *Up from the Footnote: A History of Women Journalists* (New York: Hastings House, 1977). For a sample of their work, see: *Kate Field's Washington*, published 1891–95; Mary Clemmer Ames, *Ten Years in Washington, Life and Scenes in the National Capital as a Woman Sees Them* (Hartford: A. D. Worthington, 1874); Emily Edson Briggs, *The Olivia Letters, Being Some History of Washington City for Forty Years as Told by the Letters of a Newspaper Correspondent* (New York: Neale Publishing, 1906).

17. See James and James, *Notable American Women*, for biographies of Stevenson (vol. 3, 373–74), Fletcher (vol. 1, 630–33), Rathbun (vol. 3, 119–21),

de Graffenreid (vol.1, 452–54); see also Nancy Osterich Lurie, "Women in Early American Anthropology" in *Pioneers Of American Anthropology*, ed. June Helm MacNeish (Seattle: University of Washington Press, 1966), 29–81; Lola Carr Steelman, "Mary Clare de Graffenreid: The Saga of a Crusader for Social Reform," in *Studies in the History of the South, 1875–1922*, ed. Joseph Steelman (Greenville: East Carolina College, 1966), 53–84; Margaret Rossiter, *Women Scientists in America: Struggles and Strategies to 1940* (Baltimore: Johns Hopkins University Press, 1982), 51–73.

18. James and James, *Notable American Women*, vol 2, 413–16; Julia H. Winner, "Belva A. Lockwood," *New York History* 39 (Oct. 1958): 321–41; Grace Hathaway, *Fate Rides a Tortoise: A Biography of Ellen Spencer Mussey* (Philadelphia: John C. Winston, 1937); Charles Carusi, "Higher Education in the District of Columbia," in *Washington: Past and Present*, ed. John C. Proctor (New York: Lewes Historical Publishing, 1932), 458–94.

19. Mary Church Terrell, *A Colored Woman in a White World* (Washington: Ransdell Publishing, 1940), 148; Hilyer, *Directory; Sherman's Directory and Ready Reference of the Colored Population in the District of Columbia* (Washington: Sherman's Directory Co., 1913).

20. All statistics on the number of doctors in Washington drawn from *Boyd's Directory of the District of Columbia* (called *Polk's Directory* after 1907), and from *R. L. Polk's Medical Registry and Directory of North America* (Detroit: R. L. Polk) for appropriate years. Before 1873, the Washington city directory marked the names of homeopaths with an asterisk; other information derived from George Tully Vaughan, "Physicians and Surgeons in Washington," in *Washington*, ed. Proctor, 645–53; *Cleaves Biographical Cyclopaedea of Homeopathic Physicians and Surgeons* (Philadelphia: Galaxy Publishing, 1873); physicians listed in the annual reports of the local homeopathic dispensary and hospital.

21. The number of women doctors and medical students are derived from hand counts of physicians listed in the city directories and in Polk's medical directories as well as from lists of students registered at the city's five medical schools. For statistics on the number of women doctors in the United States, see Walsh, *Doctors Wanted*, 186, and Janet Hooks, "General Trends in the Numbers and Characteristics of Women Workers," in *Women's Occupations Through Seven Decades*, Women's Bureau Bulletin no. 218 (Washington: U. S. Government Printing Office, 1947), 124; for local students, see also H. L. Hodgkins, *Historical Catalogues of the Officers and Graduates of the Columbian University, Washington, D. C. 1821–1891* (Washington: Alumni Association, 1891); W. Maxwell, ed., *George Washington University General Alumni Catalogue* (Washington: George Washington University, 1919); Daniel S. Lamb, ed., *Howard University Medical Department: A Historical, Biographical, and Statistical Souvenir* (Washington: R. Beresford, 1900); and Lamb, ed., *History of the Medical Society of the District of Columbia, 1817–1909* (Washington: The Medical Society, 1909). A count of the doctors listed in the 1902 Polk medical directory shows that fewer than 1 percent of the doctors in Baltimore were women—even with John Hopkins in the city; in Charleston, one woman practiced with 71 men; in Cleveland, where several schools admitted women, approximately 30

of 1,020 physicians listed in 1905 were women—about 3 percent; Atwater in "The Physicians of Rochester" found less than 6 percent.

For historical discussions of women's entry into medicine, see John B. Blake, "Women and Medicine in Anti-Bellum America," *Bulletin of the History of Medicine* 39 (March-April 1965): 99–123; Regina Morantz-Sanchez, *Sympathy and Science* (New York: Oxford University Press, 1985); William H. Shryock, "Women in American Medicine," in *Journal of the American Medical Women's Association* 5 (Sept. 1950): 371–91; Walsh, *Doctors Wanted*, chaps. 1 and 2, 1–105. The names of several informally trained women practioners appeared in the city directories during the 1860s and through the mid-1870s. After 1876, the directory listed only homeopaths and regulars. The proportion and number of women doctors practicing in Washington is much lower than Walsh found for Boston.

For racial identification, see notes, chap. 2. According to Hilyer, *Directory,* there were twenty-two black physicians practicing in Washington in 1892 (twelve full time), and fifty-three in 1900 (thirty-six full time), 112; in 1923, a total of ninety-one black women had graduated from American medical colleges: thirty-nine from Meharry, twenty-five from Howard, twelve from integrated schools, in M. O. Bousefield, "An Account of Physicians of Color in the United States," *Bulletin of the History of Medicine* 17 (Jan. 1945): 61–84.

22. For historical accounts of Washington's white medical societies, see Lamb, *Medical Society*; John B. Nichols, *History of the Medical Society of the District of Columbia, 1833–1944*, part 2 (Washington: The Medical Society, 1947). The latter volume also contains the history of the District of Columbia Medical Association, a group that merged with the Society in 1911.

23. Elmer Louis Kayser, *A Medical Center: The Institutional Development of Medical Education in George Washington University* (Washington: George Washington University Press, 1973); Kayser, *Bricks without Straw: The Evolution of George Washington University* (New York: Appleton-Century-Crofts, 1970); Joseph T. Durkin, *Georgetown University: The Middle Years, 1840–1900* (Washington: Georgetown University Press, 1963), 84.

24. George M. Kober, *Charitable and Reformatory Institutions in the District of Columbia: A History of the Development of Public Charities and Reformatory Institutions and Agencies in the District of Columbia* (Washington: U. S. Government Printing Office, 1927); Louis G. Weitzman, "One Hundred Years of Catholic Charities in the District of Columbia" (Ph.D. diss., Catholic University, 1931); Charles W. Richardson, "Hospitals," in *Washington*, ed. Proctor; Samuel C. Busey, *Personal Reminscences and Recollections of Forty-Six Years' Membership in the Medical Society of the District of Columbia* (Philadelphia: Dornan Printers, 1895), 116–20; Lamb, *Medical Society*, 33–40.

25. For an account of the dramatic post-Civil War changes in Washington, see Constance McLaughlin Green, *Washington: Village and Capital, 1800–1878*, vol. 1 (Princeton: Princeton University Press,1967); and Green, *The Secret City: A History of Race Relations in the Nation's Capital* (Princeton: Princeton University Press, 1967). The number of doctors was derived from hand counts of the lists of physicians in the directories. Considerably more women

than men came to Washington in the post-Civil War period, see "Census of the District of Columbia," *Special Report of the Commissioner of Education* (Washington: U. S. Government Printing Office, 1871), 33.

26. For the role these hospitals played in doctors' careers, see discussions regarding "A Bill to Incorporate Garfield Hospital," H. R. 1278, *Congressional Record* (Jan. 1882): 431–34; In "An Emerging Profession," O'Hara discusses how the "medical aristocracy" uses such institutions to solidify their base of power, see especially, 231–37; for the role that dispensaries and hospitals played in physicians' careers, see Rothstein, *American Physicians*; Charles Rosenberg, "Social Class and Medical Care in Nineteenth-Century America: The Rise and Fall of the Dispensary," *Journal of the History of Medicine and the Allied Sciences* 29 (Jan. 1974): 32–54; Rosenberg, "Inward Vision and Outward Glance: The Shaping of the American Hospital, 1880–1914," *Bulletin of the History of Medicine* 53 (Fall 1979): 346–91; Morris Vogel "Boston's Hospitals, 1870–1930" (Ph.D. diss., University of Chicago, 1975).

27. Enrollments based on hand counts of students in successive medical school catalogs. There are several histories of Howard University, none recent. See Lamb, *Howard University*; Rayford W. Logan, *Howard University: The First One Hundred Years, 1867–1967* (New York: New York University Press, 1969). Little material remains for National University, see Thomas C. Smith, "History of the Medical Colleges," in *Washington*, ed. Proctor, 57–84; National University Medical Department, *Catalogue*, 1885, 1887, 1892, at the National Library of Medicine, Bethesda, Maryland.

28. For information about these institutions, see annual reports of the Homoeopathic Free Dispensary, 1882–93, and of the National Homoeopathic Hospital, 1885–1900, as well as annual Superintendent of Charity reports.

29. Walsh, *"Doctors Wanted,"* 185, 186, 193; see also, chap. 4, "Male Backlash," and 6, "Moving Backwards." The medical literature of the period is replete with articles about overcrowding in the professions. For a local reference, see the editorial in the *Maryland Medical Journal* 34 (1895–96): 18. There the author complains that the profession is "full to overflowing and we doubt very much if it is cruel and a great wrong on the part of anyone to advise young men to enter its ranks." Daniel W. Cathell, in his popular *The Physician Himself and What He Should Add to His Scientific Acquirements* (Baltimore: Cushings and Bailey, 1882), which went through seven printings in its first five years and was published through the 1920s, wrote more harshly in the 1890 edition about the problems of overcrowding and the declining value of diplomas than he had before. See also W. O. Hamaker, "Recent Advances in Medical Education," *The Chautauquan* 24 (Nov. 1896): 177–81.

30. Hand counts of the physicians in Washington city directories, 1900, 1320–36, and 1929, 2327–31.

Notes

1. Quotation in chapter title from Belva Lockwood, "My Efforts to Become a Lawyer," *Lippincott's* (June 1888): 215; Osler quoted in Lilian Welsh, *Reminiscences of Thirty Years in Baltimore* (Baltimore: Norman, Remington, 1925), 44.

2. All women doctors who practiced regular, homeopathic, or eclectic medicine in Washington or who studied medicine in Washington before 1884 comprise the pioneer group. Names were derived from city directories and Howard Medical Department class lists. The Howard Medical Department included programs in medicine, dentistry, and pharmacy. The overwhelming majority of women enrolled in the medical program, but women enrolled in all three programs were included in this survey as well. Between 1865 and 1884, another seven women for whom no information is available attended Howard. Thirty-two others, excluded here, advertised in the directory as physicians. Twenty-three of them were gone within a year; the remaining nine were apparently "irregulars." They listed themselves as "magnetic physician," "clairvoyant," "herbist," "electric physician," or "chiropodist." One of these practitioners, Charlotte Stegemeier, "herb doctress," practiced in the city for thirty years, 1868–98.

Information was obtained from city directories, medical school catalogs, alumni records, medical society membership lists, and national directories. For biographical directories that refer to the white women doctors, see *American Biographical Directories, District of Columbia: Concise Biographies of its Prominent Representative Contemporary Citizens, 1908–1909* (Washington: Potomac Press, 1908); William A. Boyd *The Elite List: A Compendium of Selected Names of Residents of Washington City, and Ladies Shopping Guide, Together with a List of the Members of the Most Prominent Clubs* (Washington: Elite Publishing, 1897); *Cleaves Biographical Cyclopaedia of Homoeopathic Physicians and Surgeons* (Philadelphia: Galaxy Publishing, 1873); William H. King, *The History of Homoeopathy and Its Institutions in America* (New York: Lewes Publishing, 1905); Daniel S. Lamb, ed., *History of the Medical Society of the District of Columbia, 1817–1909* (Washington: The Medical Society, 1909) and Lamb, ed., *Howard University Medical Department, A Historical, Biographical, and Statistical Souvenir* (Washington: R. Beresford, 1900); Mary Logan, *The Part Taken by Women in American History* (Wilmington, Del.: Perry Nalle Publishing, 1912); John B. Nichols, *The History of the Medical Society of the District of Columbia, part 2, 1822–1944* (Washington: The Medical Society, 1947); *Polk's Medical and Surgical Register of the United States* (Detroit: R. L. Polk, 1886–1920); *Who's Who in the Nation's Capital, 1921–22* (Washington: Consolidated Publishing, 1922); Frances E. Willard, ed., *American Women: Fifteen Hundred Biographies with over 1,400 Portraits*, vol. 2 (New York: Mast, Crowell, and Kirkpatrick, 1897). See also contemporary articles that define women by race, for example, the *Alpha* 10 (11 Jan. 1885): 7.

Information about black women and confirmation of their race was derived from census lists (the 1880 and 1900 note color); city directories (until 1869, city directories used a "c" to denote people of color), photographs in alumni bulletins, listings in black organizations, and journals, biographical directories, and historical accounts that refer to the women or to male members of their families; see for example, Steven Birmingham, *Certain People: America's Black Elite* (Boston: Little, Brown, 1977); Richard Bardolph, "The Distinguished Negro in America, 1770–1936," *American Historical Review* 61 (April 1955): 527–47; Joseph A. Boris, ed., *Who's Who in Colored America* (New York: Who's Who in Colored America Corporation, 1928); John M. Cromwell, "The First Negro Churches in the District of Columbia," *Journal of Negro History* 7 (Jan. 1922): 64–106; J. W. Gibson and W. H. Crogman, *The Colored American* (Atlanta: J. L. Nichols, 1902); Andrew Hilyer, *The Twentieth Century Union League Directory: A Compilation of the Efforts of the Colored People of Washington for Social Betterment* (Washington: The Union League, 1901); Allan J. Johnston, "Surviving Freedom: The Black Community of Washington, D. C., 1860–1880" (Ph.D. diss., Duke University, 1980); Rayford W. Logan and Michael Winston, eds., *Directory of American Negro Biography* (New York: W. W. Norton, 1982); Gerri Major, *Black Society* (Chicago: Johnson Publishing, 1976); M. Sammy Miller, "Slavery in an Urban Area: The District of Columbia," *Negro History Bulletin* 37 (Aug. 1974): 293–95; Frances J. Powell, "A Study of the Structure of the Freed Black Family in Washington, D. C., 1850–1880" (Ph. D. diss., Catholic University of America, 1980); Clement Richardson, ed., *The National Cyclopedia of the Colored Race* (Montgomery, Ala.: National Publishing, 1919); Wilhelmina Robinson, *Historical Negro Biographies*, International Library of Negro Life and History (New York: New York Publishers, 1967); *Sherman's Directory and Ready Reference of the Colored Population of the District of Columbia* (Washington: Sherman Directory Co., 1913); William J. Simmons, *Men of Mark* (Baltimore: G. M. Rewell, 1887; reprint, Chicago: Johnson Publishing, 1970); G. Smith Wormley, "Educators of the First Half Century of the Public Schools of the District of Columbia," *Journal of Negro History* 17 (April-July 1932): 124–40; Rosalyn Terborg-Penn, "Afro-Americans in the Struggle for Woman Suffrage" (Ph. D. diss., Howard University, 1977); Thomas Yenser, ed., *Who's Who in Colored America*, 1930, 1931, 1932 (Brooklyn: Thomas Yenser, 1932).

For sources devoted to black women themselves, see Hallie Quinn Brown, *Homespun Heroines* (Xenia, Ohio: Aldine Publishing House, 1935); Sara W. Brown, "Colored Women Physicians," *The Southern Workman* 52 (Dec. 1923): 580–94; Sylvia Dannett, *Profiles of Negro Womanhood*, vol. 1, *1619–1900* (Yonkers, N. Y.: Educational Heritage, 1964); Marianna W. Davis, ed., *Contributions of Black Women to America*, vol. 1–2 (Columbia, S. C.: Kenday Press, 1982); Gregoria Fraser-Goins, "Pioneer Negro Women in Medicine," unpublished paper, vertical file, Howard University Medical Library; Tulia Hamilton, "The National Association of Colored Women, 1896–1920" (Ph. D. diss., Emory University, 1978); Burt Loewenberg and Ruth Bogin, eds., *Black Women in Nineteenth-Century Life: Their Thoughts, Their Words, Their Feelings* (University Park: Pennsylvania State University Press, 1976); Monroe Majors, *Noted Negro Women* (Chicago: Donohue and Henneberry, 1893); Gertrude

Notes

Mossell, *Work of the Afro-American Woman* (Philadelphia: G. S. Ferguson, 1894; reprint, Freeport, N. Y. Books for Libraries Press, 1971); Jeanne Noble, *Beautiful Also Are the Souls of My Black Sisters: A History of the Black Woman in America* (Englewood Cliffs, N. J.: Prentice-Hall, 1978); Lawson A. Scruggs, *Women of Distinction* (Raleigh, N. C.: L. A. Scruggs Publishing, 1893); Susan McKinney Steward, "Women in Medicine," paper read before the National Association of Colored Women's Clubs, Wilberforce, Ohio, 6 Aug. 1914; see also Lenwood G. Davis, ed., *The Black Woman in American Society: A Selected Annotated Bibliography* (Boston: G. K. Hall, 1975).

This chapter also relies on information obtained from applications and records of employment for those medical women who held federal government clerkships. The Department of the Interior, which included the Patent Office, the Pension Bureau, the Census Office, the General Land Office, and the Bureau of Education among others, and the Treasury Department were the major employers of women during this period. Application files and work records for women who worked in these agencies before 1909 are accessed in the Applications and Appointments Files of the Department of the Interior, Record Group 48, or for the Treasury Department, in Record Group 56, National Archives Building, Washington, D. C. (RG48-NA, RG56-NA).

3. Constance McLaughlin Green, *Washington: A History of the Capital, 1800–1950*, vol. 1 (Princeton: Princeton University Press, 1962), 183. Howard University Medical School catalogs list place of birth as do Medical Society biographies. None of the women appeared in the city directories three years before entering school, which suggests that some came to Washington specifically to study or practice medicine.

4. Nannie Stafford was born in Brunswick, Georgia; Rebecca Cole, Georgiana Rumbley, and Caroline Still (Anderson) in Philadelphia; Sarah Loguen, Eunice Shadd, and Ella Simpson in northern New York or Canada; and Kate Beatty (Cook) in Illinois. See Janice Sumler Lewis, "The Fortens of Philadelphia: An Afro-American Family and Nineteenth-Century Reform" (Ph. D. diss., Georgetown University, 1978); Fred Landon, "Canadian Negroes and John Brown," *Journal of Negro History* 6 (April 1921): 174–82.

5. For Edson and Winslow, see *Cleaves Biographical Cyclopaedia*, 135, 264–66.

6. Walker in Siebert Goldowsky, "Mary Edwards Walker," *Rhode Island Medical Journal* 9 (March 1976): 118–42; Benisch, see city directories and 1880 census, Enumeration District (ED) 41:12.

7. Dent in successive city directories; 1880 census, ED 47:27; file folder 1457–1880, Agriculture Department, RG48-NA; brother Lewis Addison Dent cited in *American Biographical Directory*, 1908–9.

8. For Barrows, see Lamb, *Howard University*, 117; Hillyer, see 1880 census, ED 25:17, and successive city directories.

9. Letter quoted in "Miss Doc," unpublished manuscript, page 76, by Loguen-Fraser's daughter, Gregoria Fraser-Goins, in Fraser-Goins Manuscript Collection at the Moorland-Spingarn Research Center (M-SRC), Howard University; Shadd in Lamb, *Howard University*, 208; and Brown, *Homespun Heroines*, 92.

10. For Rice, see city directories, 1876–1882, and the 1880 census, ED 40:19, that shows a large and prosperous household: Elisha Rice, retired lawyer, lived with his wife, daughter Annie (aged twenty-six), son Nathan (physician), another son who was vice-consul general to Japan, the son's wife and three children, and three black servants; *Medical College Alumnae Association Proceedings*, 14 March 1884; for Sumner see 1880 census, ED 26:18, Nichols, *Medical Society*, 340.

11. Bland, 1880 census, ED 54:32; Mann, city directories; Sheldon in 1880 census, ED 48:28, and city directories, 1878–90; Spackman, see 1880 census, ED 17:3; city directories; Lamb, *Howard University*, 211; will filed 3 June 1904.

12. City directories, and Wooster's will filed 11 Nov. 1936; Interior files 3488–1882, 1888–1880, box 37, RG48-NA; 1880 census, ED 19:6.

13. Jermain Loguen, *The Reverend J. Loguen as a Slave and a Free Man* (Syracuse: J. G. K. Truair, 1866); Goins, "Miss Doc," 67, and chap. 3 for Underground Railroad activities; William Still, *The Underground Railroad: A Record of Facts, Authentic Narratives and Letters* (Philadelphia: Pennsylvania Anti-Slavery Society, 1871; reprint, Chicago, Johnson Publishing, 1970); for Abraham Shadd, see biography of Mary Shadd Cary in Edward T. James and Janet Wilson James, *Notable American Women, 1607–1950: A Biographical Dictionary*, vol. 3 (Cambridge: Harvard University Press, 1972), 300–1.

14. Brown, "Colored Women Physicians," 584; Goins "Pioneer Negro Women in Medicine," unpublished paper in Fraser-Goins Collection, M-SRC; Lamb, *Howard University*, 148.

15. Information about age obtained from Lamb, *Howard University*, 1880 and 1890 census records, obituaries, and Medical Society biographies; for Parsons, see Lamb, *Howard University*, 199, and Ibid., *Medical Society*, 330; Pile in Ibid., 344, and 1900 census, ED 48:7; Hartwell in Lamb, *Howard University*, 177.

16. Cole in 1900 census, ED 15:12; Cole and Still in Brown, "Colored Women Physicians," 585–86.

17. Brown, "Colored Women Physicians," 585–86; Goins, "Miss Doc," 2, and "Underground Railroad Princess," in Fraser-Goins Collection, M-SRC; letter from J. W. Loguen to William Still in *A Documentary History of the Negro People in the United States*, ed. Herbert Aptheker (New York: Citadel Press, 1951), 389–90, discusses family guests; Terborg-Penn, "Afro-Americans," 35.

18. Brown, "Colored Women Physicians," 584–85; Janice Sumler Lewis, "The Forten-Purvis Women of Philadelphia and the American Anti-Slavery Crusade," *Journal of Negro History* 66 (April 1981–82): 281–88; Cary in Brown, *Homespun Heroines*, 92; Terborg-Penn, "Afro-Americans," 58–62, 109; Mary Ann Shadd Cary papers, folder 43, M-SRC.

19. Gerda Lerner, "Establishing a Girls' Department in the Institute for Colored Youth," in *Black Women in White America*, ed. Lerner (New York: Pantheon Books, 1972), 85; Dannett, *Profiles*, 79; Rosalind Terborg-Penn in *The Afro-American Woman*, ed. Sharon Harley and Terborg-Penn (Port Washington, N. Y.: Kennikat Press, 1978) mentions Douglass's friendship with the

white women's rights activists; Logan and Winston, *Dictionary*, 186–87.

20. Lewis, "The Fortens of Philadelphia"; for Forten-Still-Purvis relationships, see Terborg-Penn, "Afro-Americans," 42–43, 60–64; for Purvis's commitment to women's rights, see Ibid., 35, 42, 61; letters from Frederick Douglass to Sarah Loguen, 14 Sept. 1882, 27 Oct. 1882, in Fraser-Goins collection; for the friendship between William Still and Mary Ann Shadd Cary, see letters 13 April 1871 and 30 July 1873 in Shadd-Cary Collection, M-SRC.

21. Madeline B. Stern, *We the Women: Career Firsts of Nineteenth-Century American Women* (New York: Schulte Publishing, 1963).

22. *Washington Evening Star* 3 June 1874 for Sargent's teaching position, and 15 June 1874 for notice of her graduation with Ida Heiberger, an 1880 Howard medical student.

23. *Cleaves Biographical Cyclopaedia*, 264–65; *Woman's Journal*, 10 Dec. 1892, 404. Rachel Gleason was in the first class of four students. Her physician husband reportedly persuaded the school to admit her, cited in Mary Putnam-Jacobi, "Women in Medicine," in *Woman's Work in America*, ed. Annie Nathan Meyers (New York: Ayer Publishing, 1891; reprint, New York: Arno Press, 1972), 159.

Water-cure resorts were popular among women's rights, temperance, dress, and health reform advocates in the two decades preceding the Civil War. Some attracted more than five hundred guests annually; two-thirds of whom were women. For their importance in female health reform and for the influence of Rachel Gleason on aspiring women doctors, see Regina M. Morantz, "Making Women Modern: Middle-Class Women in Health Reform in Nineteenth-Century America," *Journal of Social History* 10 (June 1977): 388–409. Also see Kathryn Kish Sklar, "All Hail Pure Cold Water!" in *Women and Health in America*, ed. Judith Walzer Leavitt (Madison: University of Wisconsin Press, 1984): 246–54.

24. City directories; letter from C. M. Melville to Mrs. Johnston, 14 June 1870, in Treasury Department files, RG56-NA; Lamb, Howard University, 153.

25. These women may have lived near each other because the senior physicians were serving as preceptors both before and during formal medical training. The 1880 census, however, shows no comparable residential pattern for male doctors. Historians of women physicians have remarked on the importance of female support networks. See Mary Roth Walsh, "Feminism: A Support System for Women Physicians," *Journal of the American Medical Women's Association* 31 (June 1976): 247–50. For a discussion of the Moral Education Society, see chapter 8. Data were obtained from city directories and census listings. See, for example, 1880 census, Edson and Burghardt, ED 47:14; Sheldon, 48:28; Winslow, 48:27.

26. Spencer in *Woman's Journal*, 21 Feb. 1892.

27. See city directories for information about Mabel Cornish Bond, George Cornish, and Mabel and Samuel Bond, 1865–1900; 1880 census, ED 73:32 (Cornish), 1900 census, 128:13 (Bond).

A study of female government clerks in Washington of the period shows that they resembled white medical women in the diversity of their geographic origins, see Cindy Aron, "'To Barter Their Souls for Gold'; Female Clerks in Federal Government Offices, 1862–1890," *Journal of American History* 67 (March 1981): 835–53. In 1890, 45.8 percent of the city's white residents were natives; 19.1 percent came from Maryland and Virginia, 18.4 percent from northern or western states, and 11.9 percent were foreign born, based on data from Green, *Washington: A History of the Capital*, vol. 2, 89.

28. City directories; 1900 census, ED 47 : 12. Foye's friends were Frederick Douglass and Eva Pitts. Pitts paid for Foye's tuition at Sidwell Friends' School in Washington, according to information obtained from Roderick Cox, historian of Sidwell Friends School; *Washington Post*, 18 Aug. 1894, 2.

29. Lamb, *Howard University*, 166.

30. See Margaret Magnon in city directories, 1886–87, and Ervine York, 1888–93; obituary from *Glendale News Press* in vertical file, Special Collections, George Washington University Library.

31. Strobel in 1900 census, ED 35 : 4; Ehrbach, 1900 census, ED 120 : 4; Bartsch-Dunne obituary, *Washington Post*, 1 July 1970.

32. For Datcher, see folders, 1, 19, 20–22, in box 20, Cook Family Papers, M-SRC; city directories; Letitia W. Brown, *Free Negroes in the District of Columbia, 1790–1846* (New York: Oxford University Press, 1972), appendix 2; *Union League Directory*, 162; Riggs, 1900 census, ED 17 : 21, and city directories. Johnston, "Surviving Freedom," 129. He found that 41.4 percent of blacks living in the District of Columbia in 1880 had been born there, 33–34.

33. Major, *Black Society*, 178; untitled manuscript on the Whipper family in Leigh Whipper Collection, M-SRC; Brown, "Colored Women Physicians," 589–90.

34. Lamb, *Howard University*, 136.

35. Dahlgren's book, originally published in 1873, went through numerous printings. For her opposition to female medical education, see letter from Mary Garrett to Phoebe Hearst, 10 June 1890, box 20, Phoebe Hearst Collection, Bancroft Library, University of California, Berkeley.

36. Rosalie Slaughter Morton, *A Woman Surgeon* (New York: Frederick A. Stokes, 1937), 15.

37. 1900 census, ED 73 : 43; Cowperthwaite letter from the Hon. J. P. Verre in Department of the Treasury application files, RG56-NA.

38. Major refers to this group in *Black Society*, 175, 242; Mary Church Terrell, *A Colored Woman in a White World* (Washington: Ransdell Publishing, 1940), 59, 62; for Terrell's father's background, see Elizabeth Chittenden, "As We Climb," *Negro History Bulletin* 38 (Feb.-Mar. 1975): 351; and Paula Giddings, *When and Where I Enter* (New York: William Morrow, 1984), 19–22, 109. See also Edward Ingle, *The Negro in the District of Columbia*, Johns Hopkins Studies in Historical and Related Sciences, 11th series, 3–4 (1893), 93, for negative attitudes toward female higher education in the elite black community.

39. Biography of Reyburn in Lamb, *Medical Society*, 280–81. See Ella

Marble, "National University Welcomes Women," *Woman's Journal,* 17 Dec. 1892 for reference to Reyburn's daughters in the medical school, and city directory physicians list, 1896 and 1900–1 for Eugenia Reyburn's office listing.

40. For Newcomb's ambitions and modest beginnings, see correspondence from Sara, 22 Oct. 1887, in box 11, "Family Correspondence," Simon Newcomb Collection, Library of Congress, Washington, D. C.; Newcomb letter to Donald McGee, 28 Aug. 1888, in family correspondence. Newcomb included women's rights activists Caroline Dall and Susan B. Anthony among his correspondents; see "Address Book," box 8, in the Anita Newcomb McGee Collection, Library of Congress.

41. Baker obituary, 22 Aug. 1955, in vertical file, Washingtoniana Collection, Martin Luther King Memorial Library, Washington, D. C., and Nichols, *Medical Society,* 321.

42. Kappelar, Interior Department, 2247:1889, RG48-NA; Hinds quoted in *Washington Post,* 6 June 1934.

43. The *Sentinel,* Washington's liberal German-American newspaper, 22 Dec. 1883, quoted in Green, *Washington,* vol. 1, 119, and Major, *Black Society,* 260–61.

44. Lamb, *Howard University,* 97–98, 123, 250; Major, *Black Society,* 395; Brown, "Colored Women Physicians," 588.

45. Lamb, *Howard University,* 152; see Simmons, *Men of Mark,* 805–8; Terborg-Penn, "Afro-Americans," 101–11; Logan and Winston, *Dictionary,* 68–69.

46. City directories for Holmes, Gunckel, Koogle, and Pettigrew; and 1900 census, ED 17:14, for Holmes.

47. City directories, especially 1860–70 and 1881 for Ehrbach, and 1891–97 for Lenman. See also 1900 census, ED 38:34, for Lenman and ED 120:4 for Ehrbach.

48. This lower-middle-class group made up approximately 7.6 percent of Washington's black population in 1880, see Johnston, "Surviving Freedom," 35, and description from Jane W. Gemmell, *Notes on Washington or Six Years at the National Capital* (Philadelphia: E. Claxton, 1884), quoted in Johnston, 37. For Tancil, see Lamb, *Howard University,* 153, city directories, and 1900 census, ED 34:9; for Moten, see city directories and 1880 census, ED 49:20, and Thomasene Corrothers, "Lucy Ellen Moten: 1851–1933," *Journal of Negro History* 19 (Jan. 1934): 102–6.

49. Male medical students were still considerably younger than women. Although the ages of women enrolling in medical schools were decreasing with each decade, so were the ages of men. Men's average age at entry dropped from 28.3 in the 1870s to 26.9 in the 1880s and 23.9 in the 1890s. Older men were enrolling in these schools, but young men still dominated. Age at medical school enrollment was obtained for 183 Howard University male students, 87 Columbian, and 215 Medical Society members; no difference emerged between Columbian and Howard men.

50. Lamb, *Howard University,* 182

51. Bertha Van Hoosen, *Petticoat Surgeon* (Chicago: Pellegrini and Cudahay, 1947), 54–55; Alice Hamilton, *Exploring the Dangerous Trades: The Autobiography of Alice Hamilton, M. D.* (Boston: Little, Brown, 1943), 38.

52. Welsh, *Reminiscences*, 46, 62.

53. The *Alpha* 8 (Dec. 1886): 13.

54. Anna Julia Cooper, in *A Voice from the South by a Black Woman of the South* (Xenia, Ohio: Aldine Printing House, 1892; reprint, Westport, Conn.: Negro Universities Press, 1969), 70; the *Bee*, 22 May 1897.

55. McGee, unpublished speech, dated 23 Dec. 1893, in box 4, Anita Newcomb McGee Collection; similar sentiments expressed in untitled papers in box 4 in folder labeled, "Women, General."

56. McGee, unpublished speech, "A Woman's Name," 21, in box 4, Ibid., probably written in 1898 for a DAR meeting.

57. Marital status was determined from census data, obituaries, wills, and interviews with family members. An 1881 survey of 189 graduates of the Woman's Medical College of Pennsylvania shows that 75 of the 189 (39 percent) had married before they enrolled in medical school, cited in Jacobi, "Woman in Medicine," 189. In 1894, William Osler of the Johns Hopkins Medical School reportedly complained that coeducation at Hopkins was a failure because one-third of the women students planned to marry at graduation. The editor of the *Woman's Medical Journal*, who quoted Osler, replied that "men objected that women doctors would not marry and now object because they do. . . . Our experience is that the majority of women in the profession are married and being married still maintain their profession," in *Woman's Medical Journal* 3 (Oct. 1894): 98–99.

58. Letters from Sara Merrick to Simon Newcomb, 6 June 1892 and 1 Dec. 1894 in box 10, "Family Correspondence," Simon Newcomb Collection.

59. Washington public schools were involved in a public controversy when they fired two teachers who married midyear. See the *Bee*, Nov. and Dec. 1889, especially 14 and 28 Dec.

60. City directories, medical biographies, census data, interviews. Daughters of physicians included Ella and Eugenia Reyburn, Isabel Barrows, Mary Walker, Lily Dent, Daisy Orleman, Clara Bliss Hinds, Rosalind Moore Baine, and Jeannette Sumner; sisters included Ellen Sargent, Susan Edson, Annie Rice, Rosalie Slaughter Morton, Rosalind Moore Baine, and Clara Bliss Hinds. Samuel Busey, a Washington doctor of the period, commented in *Personal Reminiscences*, 211, that it was a "common occurrence" for a son to succeed to his father's practice. He mentioned ten joint practices in Washington in 1895 alone. The majority were elite physicians.

61. Lamb, *Howard University*, 219–20, 225–26. Conversation with Dr. Margaret Parsons, Colebrook, New Hampshire, 5 Dec. 1978; Strobel, 1880 census, ED 35:4; Haslup, interview with niece Dolly Stackhouse, 30 March 1978; Whipper's mother's attendance at Howard mentioned in Davis, *Contributions of Black Women*, 68, but I was unable to find corroborating evidence in Howard medical school catalogs; for Loguen, see "Miss Doc," chap. 2, page 13; for

Haslup and Orleman, see Washington Training School for Nurses *Announce-ment,* 1890; for Portman, see will, filed 13 May 1922, Washington, D. C.; for Burritt, see city directories and 1880 census, ED 74 : 16, and 1900, 129 : 8; for Jones, see Brown, "Colored Women Physicians," 588.

CHAPTER 3

1. In 1868–69, eight men registered; in 1869–70, nineteen men registered with five women; Daniel Smith Lamb, ed., *Howard University Medical Department: A Historical, Biographical, and Statistical Souvenir* (Washington: R. Beresford, 1900), 143. For standard works on Howard University Medical Department, see Walter Dyson, *Founding the School of Medicine of Howard University, 1868–1873,* Howard University Studies in History 10 (Washington: Howard University Press, 1929), 11; Dyson, *Howard University: The Capstone of Negro Education; A History, 1867–1940* (Washington: The Graduate School, Howard University, 1941), 239–80; Rayford W. Logan, *Howard University: The First Hundred Years, 1867–1967* (New York: New York University Press, 1969); Dwight O. Holmes, "Fifty Years of Howard University," *Journal of Negro History* 3 (April 1918): 128–38. Samuel Pomeroy, an ardent suffragist, chaired the first woman suffrage convention in January 1869 in Washington, from Alma Lutz, *Created Equal: A Biography of Elizabeth Cady Stanton* (reprint ed., New York: Octagon Books, 1974), 168. The medical school's second catalog and subsequent catalogs carried the phrase, "without regard to race or sex," *Howard University Medical Department Catalogue (1868–69),* 36.

2. Lamb, *Howard University,* 21–22; Howard Medical School catalogs for 1873 and 1874, 6; see also *National Medical Journal* 1 (1870–71): 13; *Daily Morning Chronicle,* 10 Feb. 1870. Medical department classes met from 5 : 00 p.m. to 9 : 30 p.m., five days a week, as did other local schools. Federal government offices closed at 4:00 p.m. Because many students were inadequately prepared, the Howard faculty (as at other medical schools) insisted on only one entrance requirement: the ability to speak English well.

3. Howard's medical staff in 1869–70 included eight faculty members: five white men and three black. Purvis's activities on behalf of woman suffrage reported in Rosalyn Terborg-Penn, "Afro-Americans in the Struggle for Woman Suffrage," (Ph.D. diss., Howard University, 1977), 84, 35, 61; and Janice Sumler Lewis, "The Fortens of Philadelphia: An Afro-American Family and Nineteenth-Century Reform" (Ph. D. diss., Georgetown University, 1978), 233–40.

4. Loomis presented the paper at the February 9, 1870, meeting of the Medical Society and published it in the *National Medical Journal* 1 (April 1870–71): 13; see *Daily Morning Chronicle,* 10 Feb. 1870. For an examination of such attitudes, see Carroll Smith-Rosenberg, "The Female Animal: Medical and Biological Views of Woman and Her Role in Nineteenth-Century America," *Journal of American History* 60 (Sept. 1973): 332–56.

5. Lamb, *Howard University,* 28.

6. Quoted in Madeline B. Stern, *We the Women: Career Firsts of Nineteenth-Century American Women* (New York: Schulte Publishing, 1962), 184.

7. Cora Hawkins, *Buggies, Blizzards, and Babies* (Ames: The Iowa State University Press, 1971), 155; boycott cited in Thomas Bonner, *Medicine in Chicago, 1850–1950: A Chapter in the Social and Scientific Development of the City* (Madison: American History Research Center, 1957), 61–62; only one woman finished her degree. Male students of the John Hopkins School were just as rude to women students; see Bertram Bernheim, *The Story of the Johns Hopkins: Four Great Doctors and the Medical School They Created* (New York: Whittlesly House, 1948), 33.

8. Dyson, *Howard University*, 28; Lamb *Howard University*, 33, 67, 29. For Augusta's tenure, see Rayford Logan and Michael Winston, *Dictionary of American Negro Biography* (New York: W. W. Norton, 1982), 19–20.

9. Lamb, *Howard University*, 28.

10. See "First Woman Stenographic Reporter for Congressional Committee: Isabel Barrows," in *We the Women*, ed. Stern; Busey in *National Medical Journal* 2 (Sept. 1871): 275.

11. *Howard University Alumni Catalogue, 1867–96* (Washington, 1896), list of instructors; *Howard University Medical Department Catalogue (1897–98)*, 14; Lamb, *Howard University*, 99–107, for a list of all faculty members; see also 46, 56, 57, 72, 77.

12. In 1875, six women studied with nineteen men; in 1876, seven women with twenty-four men. These numbers derived from Lamb, *Howard University*, 143. Hand counts of students in available catalogs between 1870–1900 are slightly higher than Lamb's figures. Lamb explains that the catalog lists students still under consideration in October, but his counts refer to those who formally matriculated, see Lamb, *Howard University*, 142.

13. Race for women students is derived from several sources: Lamb's biographical sketches occasionally refer to the respondent's race or include a photograph; several women had well-known male relatives whose names and family backgrounds appear in biographical dictionaries; records of federal employment sometimes mention race; records of the D. C. public school system list the schools where women taught, indicating a segregated black school; D.C. directories before 1870 and 1880 and 1900 census sheets note households of color. Sherman's 1913 directory of black residents of the District of Columbia and newspaper accounts were useful as was the Washington *Bee*, for example, 15 May 1897; and the *Alpha* 10 (1 Jan. 1885): 1. Biographical dictionaries and medical society records list white male and female doctors.

14. Lamb, *Howard University*, 142, chart of students' race.

15. Logan, *Howard University*, 40, 27, 25; Dyson, "Founding the School," 17, 19, 25; Dyson, *Howard University*, 247, 264.

Much of this money was derived from a special head tax paid by black laborers working in Washington during the war; see also Thomas Holt, Cassandra Smith-Parker, Rosalyn Terborg-Penn, *A Special Mission: The Story of Freedmen's Hospital, 1862–1962* (Washington: Howard University Press, 1975),

12; Dyson, *Howard University*, 247, 264; Ibid., "Founding the School," 25; Logan, *Howard University*, 63.

For medical education programs of the period, see William G. Rothstein, *American Physicians in the Nineteenth Century: From Sects to Science* (Baltimore: Johns Hopkins University Press, 1972), chap. 15, pp. 278–98; and Paul Starr, *The Social Transformation of American Medicine* (New York: Basic Books, 1982), chap. 3, "Medical Education and the Restoration of Occupational Control," 112–16.

16. Johnson's letter published in Dyson, "Founding the School," 15; Lamb, *Howard University*, 169; Holt, et al., *Freedmen's Hospital*, 14; Dyson, *Howard University*, 263. Dyson concluded that very few students actually paid fees because of the many exemptions.

17. Palmer quoted in Dyson, *Howard University*, 246; Logan, *Howard University*, 43.

18. Samuel Busey, *Personal Reminiscences and Recollections of Forty-Six Years' Membership in the Medical Society of the District of Columbia* (Philadelphia: Dornan Printers, 1895), 274, 287; Lamb, *Howard University*, 22; *National Medical Journal* 2 (Oct. 1871): 315.

19. For white Medical Society members, see Busey, *Personal Reminiscences*, 275–78, 318–25; for black doctors and their supporters, see Lamb, *Howard University*, 22, and William Montague Cobb, *Progress and Portents for the Negro in Medicine* (New York: National Association for the Advancement of Colored People, 1948), 16.

20. See letter, 22 Oct. 1875, in Georgetown University letter file, "Medical School, 1874–79," regarding the refusal of Georgetown and Columbian's faculties to allow Howard students reciprocal courtesies. See Lamb, *Howard University*, 52, quoting black physician Charles Purvis, who stated in 1890 that "caste prejudice" prohibited Howard's black students from observing at clinics in area hospitals.

21. Logan, *Howard University*, 42, 140, 91; Dyson, *Howard University*, 247.

22. Lamb, *Howard University*, 142–43. In 1892, the federal government granted sizeable appropriations to all departments except the medical school, which charged tuition, see "Report of the President of Howard University to the Secretary of the Interior," 1892, 1895, 1896. In 1892, medical education at Howard cost $240 plus $30 for graduation fees; at Columbian, $265 plus graduation fees.

Between 1890 and 1900, the number of black male doctors in the United States doubled, from 909 to 1734; the majority of these graduated from Howard, see Gilbert F. Edwards, *The Negro Professional Class* (Glencoe, Ill.: Free Press, 1959), 26.

23. Ella Marble, "The Real Facts," *Woman's Medical Journal* 1 (July 1893): 149.

24. A hand count of students in Howard catalogs from 1900 to 1912 shows that the number and proportion of women attending the medical school declined:

Year	Men	Women	Percent Women
1900	138	12	8.0
1902	131	10	7.1
1903	127	14	9.9
1904	135	13	8.8
1905	147	12	7.5
1908	171	4	2.3
1909	205	3	1.4
1912	174	2	1.1

See also Mary Roth Walsh, *"Doctors Wanted: No Women Need Apply": Sexual Barriers in the Medical Profession, 1835–1975* (New Haven: Yale University Press, 1977), 242–45.

CHAPTER 4

1. Joseph T. Durkin, *Georgetown University: The Middle Years, 1840–1900* (Washington: Georgetown University Press, 1963), especially chap. 6, "Building a University," 78–102, and chap. 8, "Georgetown's Various Treasures," 119–29.

2. Durkin, *Georgetown University*, 78.

3. Ibid., 85–88.

4. William G. Rothstein, *American Physicians in the Nineteenth Century: From Sects to Science* (Baltimore: Johns Hopkins University Press, 1972), especially, "Medical Education After the Civil War," 288. Harvard was one school that reverted to the shorter term; University of Pennsylvania enrollments dropped 22 percent when trustees forced the faculty to adopt the longer term. See Paul Starr, *The Social Transformation of American Medicine* (New York: Basic Books, 1982), 113–15.

5. Enrollment figures from the archivist of the Georgetown University Library, 23 Oct. 1978; quote from Durkin, *Georgetown University*, 39.

6. Rice obituary in *Proceedings of the Woman's Medical College of Pennsylvania Alumnae* (March 1884); for Sumner, see Daniel S. Lamb, *History of the Medical Society of the District of Columbia, 1817–1909* (Washington: The Medical Society, 1909), 340, and 1880 census, Enumeration District (ED) 26:18.

7. Johnson, a graduate of Georgetown, was elected president of the Medical Society in 1887. He operated the largest private obstetrical and gynecological hospital in the city; see Lamb, *Medical Society*, 153.

8. Samuel C. Busey, *Personal Reminiscences and Recollections of Forty-Six Years' Membership in the Medical Society of the District of Columbia* (Washington: Dornan Printers, 1895), 343.

9. Busey, *Personal Reminiscences*, 322.

10. Letter from Mary McCay, 3 Aug. 1885, Special Collections, Georgetown University Library; Durkin, *Georgetown University*, 203. For the school's admis-

sion of women in 1947, see Lois Irene Platt, "Women Doctors in Washington," *Journal of the American Medical Women's Association* 6 (Nov. 1951): 446–49. Histories of Georgetown overlook the presence of Rice and Sumner in 1880, although their names appear in the school catalog. Durkin assumed that the medical faculty's "first timid venture" into coeducation occurred in 1898 when it allowed Louise Tayler to attend a special class in anatomy, *Georgetown University*, 203.

11. Thomas C. Smith, "History of Medical Colleges," in *Washington: Past and Present*, ed. John C. Proctor (New York: Lewes Historical Publishing, 1932), 78–80. Few printed documents survive regarding National's existence; see *National University Medical Department Announcement* for 1885, 1887, and 1892 at the National Library of Medicine, Bethesda, Maryland; annual announcements in Washington city directories, 1885–1902; and an advertisement in *Polk's Medical and Surgical Register of the United States* (Detroit: R. L. Polk, 1902), 413. For references to the school, see *National Medical Journal* 2 (May 1871): 50, and *Evening Star*, 16 May 1894, 19 May 1895, and *National Medical Review* 1 (Nov. 1892): 133–34; Ella Marble, "National University Welcomes Women," *Woman's Journal*, 17 Dec. 1892; Marble, "The Real Facts," *Woman's Medical Journal* 1 (July 1893): 149–50, for later developments.

12. Smith, "History," 78; see also *National Medical Review* 1 (1892–93).

13. Marble, "The Real Facts," 149; medical school notices in the city directories list Gallagher as demonstrator between 1893 and 1903. For insight into the low regard such positions carried, see letter from Dr. Llewellyn Eliot, 18 Feb. 1884, resigning from his job as demonstrator, folder "1880–1884," Georgetown University Medical School Collection, Georgetown University Library.

14. Smith, "History," *National Medical Review*, 133.

15. Ella Marble, "Women's Contribution to Medical Literature," *Woman's Journal* 5 (March 1896): 60–62; Marble, "National University Welcomes Women."

16. Marble, "The Real Facts," 150; Smith, "History," 79; *Transactions and Proceedings of the Washington Medical Society* (1894), 9; Elmer Louis Kayser, *A Medical Center: The Institutional Development of Medical Education in George Washington University* (Washington: George Washington University Press, 1973), 133.

17. *Evening Star*, 2 March 1896; C. Willard Camalier, *One Hundred Years of Dental Progress in the Nation's Capital* (Washington: District of Columbia Dental Society, 1966), 17. See Rothstein, *American Physicians*, 293, for the difficulties that undercapitalized schools faced in this period.

18. Elmer Louis Kayser, *Bricks without Straw: The Evolution of George Washington University* (New York: Appleton-Century-Crofts, 1970), especially, chap. 11, "The Age of Welling, 1871–1894," 141–72.

19. Kayser, *Bricks*, 159.

20. Ibid.; "Minutes of the Board of Trustees," vol. 3 (18 June 1881), Special Collections, George Washington University Library.

21. Kayser, *Bricks*, 150.

22. Ibid., 166.

23. Ibid., 152–53; *Annual Report to the President* (1897), 13.

24. Elliot Coues, "A Woman in the Case," address delivered to the commencement, 16 March 1887, Columbian University National Medical College (Washington, 1887; reprinted by George Washington University Library, 1972), 11.

25. Kayser, *Bricks*, 166. See Margaret Rossiter, *Women Scientists in America: Struggles and Strategies to 1940* (Baltimore: Johns Hopkins University Press, 1982), 31.

26. "First Woman M.D. Here Fought a Pioneer Battle," *Washington Post*, 6 June 1934; White appears only in the 1885 directory.

27. See city directories for Cathcart and Scull, and catalogs for the Mt. Vernon School for Girls.

28. Hinds, et al., "Letter to the Faculty of the Medical Department," 10 Dec. 1884, quoted from faculty minutes, 17 Dec. 1884, in a correspondence from Dr. Kayser, 15 Nov. 1978; Cynthia Epstein in *Woman's Place: Options and Limits in Professional Careers* (Berkeley: University of California Press, 1970), 85, discusses the often used excuse of inadequate bathroom facilities to disqualify women. As Dr. Mary Putnam Jacobi noted in 1891, "it is amazing how many invincible objections on the score of feasibility, modesty, propriety, and prejudice will melt away before the charmed tool of a few thousand dollars," quoted in Mary Roth Walsh, *"Doctors Wanted: No Women Need Apply": Sexual Barriers in the Medical Profession, 1835–1975* (New Haven: Yale University Press, 1977), 169.

29. Kayser, *Bricks*, 166–67.

30. "Report of the Dean of the Medical School, 1883–1884," in Special Collections, George Washington University Library. For biography of Lee, see Lamb, *Medical Society*, 274.

31. Coues, "A Woman in the Case," 19; see also *Evening Star*, 27 April 1887.

32. From Daniel W. Prentiss eulogy on Fristoe in *Address Delivered at the Opening of the Medical Depatment of the Columbian University, with a Sketch of the Life and Work of Edward T. Fristoe* (Washington: The National Medical Review, 1892), 11. Fristoe also contributed generously to the Woman's Clinic run by women doctors, see Woman's Clinic, *Souvenir* (Washington: Gill and Son, 1892–93), 5.

33. In *A Woman's Quest: The Life of Maria E. Zakrzewska, M.D.*, ed. Agnes Vietor (New York: D. Appleton, 1924; reprint, New York: Arno Press, 1972), 441; Albert Freeman Africanus King, "The Physiological Argument in Obstetrical Studies," *Journal of Obstetrics and Diseases of Women and Children* 29 (April 1888): 17. For a rebuttal of King's views, see W. H. Studley, "Is Menstruation a Disease?" A Review of Professor King's Article Entitled, 'A New Basis of Uterine Pathology'," *American Journal of Obstetrics* 8 (Nov. 1875); King quoted in Kayser, *A Medical Center*, 114.

34. Figures derived from successive class lists, 1885–92, published in annual medical department catalogs.

35. Edna Clarke statement in file entitled "Clubs, Societies, Organizations—

Columbian Women," Special Collections, George Washington University Library; Vietor, *A Woman's Quest,* 441; Hinds, "First Woman M.D."

36. Marble, "National University Welcomes Women." That same year the National University Law School closed enrollment to women after four had graduated. Administrators claimed it had a "deterring" effect on enrollment; Grace Hathaway, *Fate Rides a Tortoise: The Biography of Ellen Spencer Mussey* (Philadelphia: John C. Winston, 1937), 81.

37. Marble, "National University Welcomes Women"; Vietor, *A Woman's Quest,* 441.

38. For Orleman, see letter of application, 26 Jan. 1888, file folder, 279: 1888, U.S. Department of Interior, Application and Appointment Files, Record Group 48, National Archives Building, Washington, D. C.; "Woman Surgeon of the U.S. Medical Corps," *Woman's Medical Journal* 29 (Aug. 1922): 185; for McGee, Mary Dearing, "Anita Newcomb McGee," in *Notable American Women, 1607–1950: A Biographical Dictionary,* vol. 2, ed. Edward T. James and Janet Wilson James (Cambridge: Harvard University Press, 1972), 464–66; for York, city directories, and obituary from Glendale *News Press,* 26 Feb. 1946, in obituary file, Special Collections, George Washington University Library.

39. "To the Faculty of the Medical Department of the Columbian University," box 1, folder "M" in Anita Newcomb McGee Collection, Library of Congress.

40. McGee, "To the Faculty," draft 2; letter to *Washington Post,* box 7, McGee Collection.

41. McGee, "To the Faculty."

42. Ibid.

43. Ibid.; Muncaster interview reported by Ella Marble in letter printed in *Washington Post,* 29 Jan. 1893.

44. McGee, "To the Faculty."

45. Jacobi, "Woman in Medicine," 148.

46. Marble, "Women's Contribution to Medical Literature," 60; *New York Times,* 3 Jan. 1892; William B. Daniels, "Albert Freeman Africanus King," *Medical Annals of the District of Columbia* 29 (Sept. 1950): 499–506. For the concern of local doctors about overcrowding in the profession, see *Maryland Medical Journal* 34 (1895–96): 18.

47. Kayser, *A Medical Center,* 109, 111; McGee, 28 May 1892, "To the President, Trustees, and Overseers of Columbian University," in box 1, folder "M," McGee Collection.

48. McGee, "To the President."

49. Ibid.

50. Ibid.

51. Quoted by Kayser, April 1978, from the minutes of the faculty, 22 March 1892.

52. An article in the *Washington Post* refers to the petition, 19 June 1893. For biographical information on Blount, see Walter M. Whitehill, *Dumbarton Oaks* (Cambridge: Harvard University Press, 1967) and *American Biographical Dic-*

tionary, District of Columbia, (Washington: Potomac Press, 1908). For ProRe-Nata, see Jane Cunnigham Croly, *The History of the Women's Club Movement in America* (New York: H. G. Allen, 1898), 346.

53. Croly, *History of the Women's Club Movement.* Blount directed ProReNata until 1895, when she resigned to assume the presidency of the 5,000-member District of Columbia Federation of Women's Clubs.

54. Marble, "The Real Facts," 149.

55. Diaries for 1892 and 1893 in Susan B. Anthony Collection, Library of Congress; *The Woman's Journal,* 7 May 1892.

56. McGee "To the President."

57. Ella Marble, "Caroline Winslow's Birthday Party," *Woman's Journal,* 10 Dec. 1892, 404; McGee, April 1892, in "Women, General," box 4, McGee Collection. This attitude was common among professional women, see interview in *Washington Post,* 23 Dec. 1889, when a woman lawyer replied to a reporter's question, "Do you believe in woman's rights?" with "I have all the rights I want except the right to practice law."

58. Coues's letter in Wright Collection of Individual Manuscripts, Special Collections. George Washington University Library. There is no clue to what Coues meant by the "electric shock."

59. "Why Women Are Excluded," *Washington Post,* 20 Jan. 1893.

60. Unpublished letter to the editor in box 7, McGee Collection. There are three different drafts of this letter with numerous strikeovers. See also Ella Marble, "Women and Columbian University: A Reply to the Faculty from the ProReNata Club of this City," *Washington Post,* 29 Jan. 1893. This letter is signed by Marble, but contains many of the phrases from McGee's own letter in her handwriting.

61. Marble, "Women and Columbian University." For King's conduct, see Daniels, "A. F. A. King." Despite King's notoriety for his imitations of pregnant women, according to Daniels, his colleagues knew that he had little first-hand obstetrical experience.

62. Dr. Charles Stowall, "A New College Needed," *National Medical Review* 1 (Oct. 1892); see also the medical faculty's letter to the *Washington Post,* 20 Jan. 1893.

63. McGee's unpublished letter.

64. Ibid., and Marble's "Women and Columbian University." For women's heightened expectations, see *Woman's Journal,* 24 Sept. 1892, 310.

65. For women in chemistry, see *Report of the Dean of the Corcoran Scientific School,* vol. 73, 109; and Kayser, *Bricks,* 153–54. Statistics on graduate school attendance from correspondence with archivist of Special Collections, George Washington University Library.

66. See Thomas Woody, *A History of Women's Education in the United States* (New York: Science Press, 1929; reprint, New York: Octagon Books, 1966), 546–48, for the increase in female graduate school enrollment and for the multiplication of high schools in the period. Woody shows that the number of high school students increased nationally from approximately 296,000 in 1890, to 630,000 in 1900, and to 1,032,000 in 1910.

67. Starr, *American Medicine*, 22. For the best account of the male backlash, see Walsh, *"Doctors Wanted,"* chap. 4, "Moving Backward," 135–36; see also Bertram Bernheim, *The Story of the Johns Hopkins: Four Great Doctors and the Medical School They Created* (New York: Whittlesy House, 1948), chaps. 4 and 8; *The Women's Medical Fund and the Opening of the Johns Hopkins School of Medicine* (Baltimore: Women's Medical Alumnae Association, 1978).

68. *The Report of the President, 1888–1889*, 5, in Special Collections, George Washington University Library; *Report of the President, 1892–93*, 15; Kayser, *Bricks*, 98, and *A Medical Center*, 112. See *National Medical Review* 2 (June 1893): 52, and 2 (Oct. 1893): 118, for enhancement of the medical program; *Washington Star*, 30 Oct. 1894.

69. Kayser, *Bricks*, 177, and *A Medical Center*, 120.

70. George Washington University *Bulletin* 6 (1907): 34; also see Winnifred Black, *The Life of Phoebe Hearst* (San Francisco: J. H. Nash, 1928) and the Hearst Collection, Bancroft Library, University of California, Berkeley. Hearst was known for interceding in women's behalf. See, for example, letter in box 3, Phoebe A. Hearst Collection, 2 Jan. 1900, from the president of the San Francisco Association for Collegiate Alumnae thanking her for using her influence to secure the appointment of a woman to the San Francisco school board. Northwestern's medical school, closed to women after 1902, restored coeducation in 1920 when potential contributor Mrs. Montgomery Ward merely expressed surprise that women were denied admission, in Walsh, *Doctors Wanted*, 205.

71. The women matriculated "by special permission" of the board of trustees, George Washington University *Bulletin*, 34. One of the women admitted under this change of policy already had a Ph.D., see *George Washington University Annual Report to the President*, 11 Jan. 1911 (1910–11), and Kayser, *Bricks*, 194–204. In 1910, women made up 4.5 percent of the class (5 of 109), in 1915, 2 percent (3 of 147), and in 1925, 3.6 percent (9 of 250). Figures based on hand counts of the medical students in George Washington University Medical School bulletins.

CHAPTER 5

1. District of Columbia Board of Health, *Annual Report* (Washington: U. S. Government Printing Office, 1877), 9; Drs. Philip Male, Joseph T. Johnson, and Charles Hagner to the Georgetown faculty (1879) in folder labeled "Undated" in the medical school file, Special Collections, Georgetown Library (SC-GUL) ; see also *Evening Star*, 4 Oct. 1884. For another contemporary view, see Charles C. Savage, "Dispensaries, Historically Considered," in *Hospitals, Dispensaries, and Nursing*, ed. John S. Billings and Henry M. Hurd (Baltimore: Johns Hopkins University Press, 1894), 649. For a description of a local clinic "service," see the *Evening Star*, 13 Aug. 1887. In 1904, the Council on Medical Education of the American Medical Association estimated that 50 percent of medical school graduates received hospital training; by 1911, that proportion had increased to 75 percent, in Mary Roth Walsh, *"Doctors Wanted: No Women*

Need Apply": Sexual Barriers in the Medical Profession, 1835–1975 (New Haven: Yale University Press, 1977).

For secondary accounts, see Paul Starr, *The Social Transformation of American Medicine* (New York: Basic Books, 1982), chap 5; George Rosen, *The Structure of American Medical Practice, 1875–1941* (Philadelphia: University of Pennsylvania Press, 1983), 70–80; Charles Rosenberg, "Social Class and Medical Care in Nineteenth-Century America: The Rise and Fall of the Dispensary," *Journal of the History of Medicine and the Allied Sciences* 29 (Jan. 1974): 32–54; Rosenberg, "Inward Vision and Outward Glance: The Shaping of the American Hospital, 1884–1914," *Bulletin of the History of Medicine* 53 (Fall 1979): 346–91; Morris Vogel, "Patrons, Practitioners and Patients: The Voluntary Hospital in Mid-Victorian Boston," in *Victorian America*, ed. Daniel Howe (Philadelphia: University of Pennsylvania Press, 1976); Michael Davis and Andrew Warner, "The Beginnings of Dispensaries," *Boston Medical and Surgical Journal* 178 (May 23, 1918): 712–15.

This chapter does not include the medical services women doctors performed for orphanages, old-age homes, and homes for unwed mothers; for example, the Woman's Christian Association, a residence for homeless women, listed at least six women doctors on its staff between 1885 and 1900.

2. Blackwell quoted in Dorothy Clarke Wilson, *Lone Woman: The Story of Elizabeth Blackwell* (Boston: Little, Brown, 1970), 402; Jacobi in "Woman in Medicine," in *Woman's Work in America*, ed. Annie Nathan Meyers (New York: Henry Holt, 1891; reprint, New York: Arno Press, 1972).

3. *Woman's Journal*, 14 Feb. 1891. As late as 1916, only two of one hundred Chicago hospitals admitted women as interns, *Woman's Medical Journal* 26 (May 1916): 132.

4. "The National Homeopathic Hospital," *Report of the U. S. Congress Joint Select Committee to Investigate the Charities and Reformatory Institutions in the District of Columbia* (Washington: Government Printing Office, 1897), 69; "The Proposed Garfield Memorial Hospital," *Evening Star*, 4 Oct. 1881. Some legislators opposed the hospital on the grounds that it was to be used for the advancement of a select group of doctors, in *Congressional Record*, H.R. 1278, 20 Dec. 1880, 433. For further details regarding the dispute, see Samuel C. Busey, *Personal Reminiscences and Recollections of Forty-Six Years' Membership in the Medical Society of the District of Columbia* (Philadelphia: Dornan Printers, 1895), chap. 15.

5. Homoeopathic Free Dispensary Association *Annual Report*, 1882, 16–19; see *Report*, 1882–93, mixed numbers at the National Library of Medicine, Bethesda, Maryland; see also city directories and annual reports. Lenman was related to Louease Lenman, who graduated from the Washington Homoeopathic Medical College in 1895. Of twelve women officers in 1885, four were widows, two were married to lawyers, one to a druggist, and the others to owners of small shops.

6. In 1889, of 2,194 patients, 1,234 were black, of whom 954 were women; 960 were white, 726 of whom were women; 40 percent suffered respiratory

and digestive disorders, 11 percent reported gynecological problems; *Fourth Annual Report*, (1885) 7, 9. The hospital plan is mentioned in the *Alpha*, 8 (May 1883): 9; *Sixth Annual Report*, (1888) 5–6.

7. National Homoeopathic Hospital, *Annual Report* (31 Dec. 1891), 5; *Report*, 1890–1900; *Annual Report* of the Commissioner of the District of Columbia, 30 June 1895, 413.

8. *Announcement and Catalogue* of the National Medical College, Medical Department of the Columbian University (1890), 11; Hinds quoted in "First Woman M.D. Here Fought a Pioneer Battle," *Washington Post*, 6 June 1934. Women students at Howard had requested residency appointments in 1876; their request was tabled, in *Howard University Medical Department: A Historical, Biographical, and Statistical Souvenir*, ed. Daniel S. Lamb (Washington: R. Beresford, 1900), 33.

9. *Congressional Record*, 419, House of Representatives, 16 Jan. 1882; "A bill providing for the admission of women to clinics and as resident students in Columbia Hospital for women," 47 Cong. 1st sess., H.R. 2879.

10. For Barrows, see Madeline Stern, *We the Women: Career Firsts of Nineteenth-Century American Women* (New York: Schulte Publishing, 1963), 178–204. Information on Heiberger obtained from "History of the Heiberger Family," unpublished manuscript in the possession of Kenneth Kelly, Bethesda, Maryland.

11. Jeanette Sumner, "A Puzzling Case of Uterine Disease," *Report of the Proceedings of the Eleventh Annual Meeting of the Alumnae Association of the Woman's Medical College of Pennsylvania* (12 March 1882): 52–53.

12. Jane C. Hitz, Annie Rice, Jeanette Sumner to Dr. James W. H. Lovejoy, dean of the faculty, 19 June 1883, in folder, "Medical School, 1880–1884," SC-GUL.

13. For a list of incorporators, see *Washington Post*, 19 June 1883, and *Women's Hospital and Dispensary*, 1890–91 (Washington: Gibson Brothers, 1892); occupations listed in city directory.

14. *Polk's Medical and Surgical Directory of the United States* (Detroit: R. L. Polk, 1886), 207; District of Columbia, *Report of the Health Officer* (Washington: Government Printing Office, 1878), 107, for mortality by area; for patients treated, see District of Columbia, *Report of the Superintendent of Charitable and Reformatory Institutions*, for example, 30 June 1891, 36, and 1897, 96–97.

15. Rice, "Obituary," in *Proceedings of the Alumnae*, 14 March 1884; successive city directories for Sumner's addresses; D.C. *Directory* (1887), 942.

16. For pressure on medical school professors to provide clinic opportunities for their students, see folder labeled "1890–1900," in medical school file, SC-GUL; letter, Dr. P. Murphy to Joseph T. Johnson, 13 Sept. 1884; see also Johnson to Lovejoy, 13 Sept. 1884. Several years later the situation was as critical. Then, James Kerr punished fellow faculty members in a personal dispute by refusing to allow Georgetown students to visit his private clinic, 23 Sept. 1895, SC-GUL. In 1894, the Georgetown faculty discharged one of its members to hire Morris Murray, head of a clinic at the Central Dispensary, so that

they could use those facilities for their students. See also a student petition complaining of the need for clinical training in obstetrics in "Undated" folder, SC-GUL.

17. City directories; information about Heiberger's early affiliation with the dispensary from Kelly, "History of the Heiberger Family."

18. City directories; for biographies of Kerr and Wilner, see Daniel S. Lamb, ed., *History of the Medical Society of the District of Columbia, 1817–1909* (Washington: The Medical Society, 1909), 332; also see John C. Proctor, ed., *Washington: Past and Present* (New York: Lewes Historical Publishing, 1932): 518–80, for Kerr biography.

19. See city directories, 1890–99 and Superintendent of Charity, *Report* for lists of affiliated doctors; for their biographies and subsequent success, see Lamb, *Medical Society*, 336, 342, 348, 352, 358. Five of the men had graduated from Georgetown between 1889 and 1891.

20. City directories, 1891–96; Anita Newcomb McGee's doctor's visiting card listing her as attending physician in folder labeled, "Cards and Invitations," box 8, Anita Newcomb McGee Collection, Library of Congress.

21. "Women's Hospital and Dispensary" in District of Columbia, *Report of the Commissioner*, 1890–1891, 5–9; Mrs. M. J. Stroud gave the largest donation, $127.50 (she also owned the building that housed the dispensary); for comparable contributions, see "Contributors to the Central Dispensary," District of Columbia, *Report of the Commissioner*, 24 March 1896, 180.

22. See *Report* for 1898, 31, and 1899, 672. Doctors nationwide were alarmed at the increase in gynecological surgery. William Keen, professor of medicine at the University of Pennsylvania, was one critic who feared that the abdomen and pelvic areas were becoming a "playground in which surgeons deport to their hearts' content and invent new operations as children invent new games," in *Addresses and Other Papers* (Philadelphia: W. B. Saunders, 1905), 117; see also Busey, *Personal Reminiscences*, 338–39, and *Evening Star*, 23 April 1897, for criticism of such excesses.

23. See Elmer Louis Kayser, *A Medical Center: The Institutional Development of Medical Education in George Washington University* (Washington: George Washington University Press, 1973); and Richardson, "Hospitals," in *Washington*, ed. Proctor, 674–75. For the importance of these hospitals in the development of a "medical aristocracy," see Leo James O'Hara, "An Emerging Profession: Philadelphia Medicine, 1860–1900" (Ph.D. diss., University of Pennsylvania, 1976).

24. District of Columbia, Superintendent of Charities, *Report* (1897) 22; also see *Report on Hospital and Dispensary Abuse in the City of Washington* (1896), 15–16; George W. Kober, *Charitable and Reformatory Institutions in the District of Columbia: A History of the Development of Public Charities and Reformatory Institutions and Agencies in the District of Columbia* (Washington: U. S. Government Printing Office, 1927); also Rosenberg, "Social Class and Medical Care," 49–52.

25. Superintendent *Report* (1898), 22.

26. Hinds in *Washington Post*, 6 June 1934; see also "Woman's Clinic has

Blazed Path for Medical Care," *Washington Times*, 19 Aug. 1914; see also Starr, *American Medicine*, 182–84.

27. Woman's Clinic *Souvenir* (1892–93) for early members; see successive years of Woman's Clinic listing in the city directories under "Medical Societies" rather than under "Clinics and Dispensaries." The staff at the clinic also trained nurses, *Fourteenth Annual Announcement*, Washington Training School for Nurses (1891), 19.

28. Letter to Emily, 26 March 1892, in folder "1892-A," box 10, Simon Newcomb Collection, Library of Congress.

29. In Gregoria Fraser Goins, "Miss Doc," 180, unpublished biography of Loguen, in Gregoria Fraser Goins Collection, Moorland-Spingarn Research Center, Howard University.

30. "Articles of Incorporation, 1891," included in *Souvenir* (1905).

31. *Souvenir* (1892–93), 7; "Healing the Sick at the Woman's Clinic," *Evening Star*, 17 Dec. 1911. The National Homeopathic Hospital opened an evening clinic for working women, but closed it for lack of patients. Administrators attributed its failure to the hospital's dangerous neighborhood; see *Report of the Medical Staff of the Board of Trustees of the National Homoeopathic Hospital* (1890), 13.

32. *Souvenir* (1893, 1905); District of Columbia Superintendent of Charities *Report*, vol. 2 (1896), 38.

33. *Souvenir*, (1893), 10, 15, 17, 18; *Report of the Commissioners of the District of Columbia*, successive years, 1899–1910.

34. *Souvenir*, (1893), 9–11. For the importance of hospital privileges in a private practice, see Starr, *American Medicine*, 167, where he reports that in 1900, 15.6 percent of physicians enjoyed such privileges, but by 1910, 42.3 percent did. Unaffiliated doctors suffered "enormous pecuniary losses," according to a contemporary cited in Starr.

35. Ibid., 11; Anita to Emily, 26 March 1892, Simon Newcomb Collection; McGee received honorable mention for the casework done under Dr. Johnson's supervision, box 4, McGee Collection; "Report of the Central Dispensary and Emergency Hospital," in *Report of the Commissioners of the District of Columbia*, successive years, 1895–1910; "Minutes of the Board of Directors of the Central Dispensary and Hospital," especially 11 Oct. 1895, 10 Oct. 1896, in Archives of the Washington Hospital Center; for Gunckel's appointment, see *Washington Post*, 25 May 1896.

36. City directories; see Mrs. Spofford to daughter Ellen, 23 Feb. 1887, in "Correspondence, 1880–1889," box 1, Ainsworth Rand Spofford Collection, Library of Congress. The female board included other members of Washington's professional middle class: Mrs. Arnold Haye, for example, was married to a geologist, and Mrs. F. E. Chadwick to a U.S. Navy bureau chief.

37. *The Woman's Clinic* (Washington: The Woman's Clinic, 1916), 20–21.

38. From an interview with Dr. Margaret Nicholson, 1925 Georgetown University Medical School graduate, Washington, 29 July 1977.

39. In Elizabeth McCracken, *The Women of America* (New York: Macmillan, 1904), 354.

40. White in "American Medical Woman," *The Woman's Medical Journal* 4 (April 1895): 244.

CHAPTER 6

1. John C. Proctor, "Medico-Body More Than Century Old,"*Sunday Star,* 29 April 1934, 6 : 1; for standard histories of the two organizations, see Daniel S. Lamb, ed., *History of the Medical Society of the District of Columbia, 1817–1909* (Washington: The Medical Society, 1909), and John B. Nichols, "History of the Medical Association of the District of Columbia, 1833–1911," in *History of the Medical Society of the District of Columbia,* part 2, *1833–1944,* ed. John B. Nichols (Washington: The Medical Society, 1947); Theodore Wiprud, "History of the Medical Society of the District of Columbia," *Medical Annals* 39 (July-Sept. 1970): 379–89, 459–67, 515–26, 603, 695; also see Samuel C. Busey, *Personal Reminiscences and Recollections of Forty-Six Years' Membership in the Medical Society of the District of Columbia* (Washington: Dornan Printers, 1895). These works mention women's membership only briefly: Lamb devotes two pages to the events surrounding women's admission, 119–21; Nichols, two paragraphs, 25; and Busey, in passing, when it relates to other issues such as the admission of black doctors or the status of "sundown doctors" (those who worked at other jobs and practiced only evenings and weekends) or military physicians. For the exact wording of the licensing law, see Lamb, *Medical Society,* 6.

2. Busey, *Personal Reminiscences,* 323. In the early years, the same men presided over both societies, Nichols, "History of the Medical Association," 45.

3. The best summary of early licensing requirements is in William Rothstein, *American Physicians in the Nineteenth Century: From Sects to Science* (Baltimore: Johns Hopkins University Press, 1972); see also Richard H. Shryock, *Medical Licensing in America, 1650–1965* (Baltimore: Johns Hopkins University Press, 1967), and Paul Starr, *The Social Transformation of American Medicine* (New York: Basic Books, 1982), 40–58.

A comparison of doctors listed in the city directory in 1883 with those 185 who applied for licenses shows that the licentiates were more likely to establish successful, longlasting practices; 141 (76.2 percent) also joined the Medical Association; see "A List of the Licentiates of the Medical Society of the D of C," in folder, "Medical Lists—D.C.," box 171, and "Medical Association of the District of Columbia," in scrapbook folder, box 171, both in Joseph Toner Collection, Library of Congress. Sixty percent of 1883 Medical Association members were still in practice in 1888 compared to 40 percent of nonaffiliated doctors.

4. Nichols, "History of the Medical Association," 29.

5. For details concerning Washington's nineteenth-century black medical community, see W. Montague Cobb, "The Door that Stayed Closed," *The First Negro Medical Society: A History of the Medico-Chirurgical Society of the District of Columbia, 1884–1939* (Washington: Associated Publishers, 1939), especially

Notes

9–10; Herbert M. Morais, *The History of the Afro-American in Medicine*, vol. 1 (Cornwall Heights, Penn.: Association for the Study of Afro-American Life and History, 1976); Dietrich Reitzes, ed., *Negroes and Medicine* (Cambridge: Harvard University Press, 1958). For evidence regarding the licensing of black physicians in Washington, see reference to "Washington, Geo. [col'd]" in "List of Licenses issued to Physicians in the District of Columbia, from May 1 '66 to date," [date unknown, est. 1867]; the "List of Licentiats [sic]," 1883, included Augusta, Purvis, and George W. Cook, Toner Collection.

6. W. Montague Cobb, *First Negro Medical Society*, 19; for further details of that struggle, see Cobb, 11–21; Busey, "The Disturbances of 1869–1872," in *Personal Reminiscences*, 243–84; Lamb, *Medical Society*, 100–5. For contemporary accounts, see *Daily Morning Chronicle*, 9 Feb. 1870, 10 Feb. 1870; Medical Society of the District of Columbia, *An Appeal to Congress* (Washington: District of Columbia Medical Society, 12 Jan. 1870); *National Medical Journal* 1 (Jan. 1870–71): 68. One prominent member of the society had been Jefferson Davis's personal physician, see Nichols, "Medical Society," 43.

7. Cobb, *First Negro Medical Society*, 14.

8. Quoted from *The New Era* (Washington), 27 Jan. 1870, in Herbert Aptheker, *A Documentary History of The Negro People in the United States* (New York: Citadel Press, 1951), 618–69; Cobb, *First Negro Medical Society*, 15–16.

9. "Memorial of the National Medical Society of the District of Columbia," printed in *The New Era*, 27 Jan. 1870, reprinted in Aptheker, *Negro People*, 618; Cobb, *First Negro Medical Society*, 20. Further efforts to repeal the charter in 1871 and 1872 and as late as 1890 and 1892 also failed to be reported out of committee, Ibid., 20–21, and Lamb, *Medical Society*, 100–5.

10. Verdi discusses the hardships faced by local homeopaths in "Report of the Committee on Legislation," American Institute of Homoeopathy, *Proceedings of the 24th Session* (June 1871): 104–6. For the homeopathic struggle, see Martin Kaufman, *Homeopathy in America: The Rise and Fall of a Medical Heresy* (Baltimore: Johns Hopkins University Press, 1971), and Harris Coulter, *Divided Legacy*, vol. 3 (Washington: McGrath Publishing, 1973), 291–96.

11. Coulter, *Divided Legacy*, 296, quoted from *Hahnemannian Monthly* 7 (April 1871): 84. At first few women joined the homeopathic society, but after 1890, they regularly attended sessions; see *Report of the National Homoeopathic Hospital* (1891), 5; Edwin M. Williams, "Homeopathy in the District of Columbia," in *Washington: Past and Present*, ed. John C. Proctor (New York: Lewes Historical Publishing, 1932): 651–53. The *Evening Star*, 6 Oct. 1892, mentions a meeting of the local committee to prepare for the National Congress of American Institute of Homoeopathy scheduled for Washington that included several women. The American Institute of Homoeopathy admitted women in 1869, see Coulter, *Divided Legacy*, 296. There is evidence that women experienced discrimination despite Verdi's welcome. In 1885, a Washington homeopath, Mary E. Hart, a Howard graduate and a postgraduate of the Chicago Homoeopathic Medical College, objected to a statement made by one of her former professors that women "subjected themselves to dangers [when they]

stepped out of social restrictions." He had also insulted her by referring to her as "Miss Hart." "Would he so address any male graduate?" Hart fumed in the *Alpha* 10 (March 1885): 9.

12. Cobb, *First Negro Medical Society*, 22–38.

13. Ibid., 30–34, quoting from *Transactions of the American Medical Association* 21 (1870): 23.

14. Busey, *Personal Reminiscences*, 275–76; *Transactions of the American Medical Association* 23 (1872): 53.

15. Busey, *Personal Reminiscences*, 287, and Cobb, *First Negro Medical Society*, 18–19. For the esteem in which Bliss was held in the black community, see John Mercer Langston, *From Virginia Plantation to the Nation's Capital* (Hartford, Conn.: American Publishing, 1894), 327.

16. Coulter, *Divided Legacy*, 90; Busey, *Personal Reminiscences*, 289–90; *National Medical Journal* 2 (Oct. 1871): 379.

17. Busey, *Personal Reminiscences*, 249, 267.

18. Ibid., 319; for Barrows, see Daniel S. Lamb, ed., *History of Howard University Medical Department* (Washington: R. Beresford, 1900): 117.

19. Busey, *Personal Reminiscences*, 282. See "Barred on Account of His Color," the *Bee*, 4 April 1891. In 1894, John R. Francis, a prominent black physician who ran one of the largest private hospitals in the city, where he treated both black and white patients, received just five votes short of the eighty-one he needed for membership (76 of 124). The following year, the opposition came well prepared and rejected his application, 145 to 30, in Cobb, *First Negro Medical Society*, 9–10.

20. In 1873, when Spackman entered practice, six other women listed themselves as physicians in the city directory: Two were homeopaths, one an herbist, one the widow of a homeopath, and two listed no affiliation. Midwives also listed themselves in the physicians column; see, for example, Anna Benisch in 1876 directory. Renner ads in the *Bee*, 12 June 1897, and *Washington Times*, 12 Nov. 1895. For a discussion of abortionists and their threat to marginally practicing physicians, see James Mohr, *Abortion in America: Origins and Evolution of National Policy* (New York: Oxford University Press, 1978).

21. Lee quoted in Lamb, *Medical Society*, 119; Edith Seville Coale, "Women Physicians in the District of Columbia," in *Washington*, 656–57; "List of Licenses," Toner Collection.

22. Busey, *Personal Reminiscences*, 322. For a discussion of similar debates in other societies, see Martin Kaufman, "The Admission of Women to Nineteenth-Century American Medical Societies," *Bulletin of the History of Medicine* 50 (1976): 251–60; and Mary Roth Walsh, *"Doctors Wanted: No Women Need Apply": Sexual Barriers in the Medical Profession, 1835–1975* (New Haven: Yale University Press, 1977), 147–54.

23. Busey, *Personal Reminiscences*, 324; *Washington Star*, 18 Jan. 1875; 23 Jan. 1875; *Congressional Record*, 23 Jan. 1875, 43rd Cong., 2nd sess., vol. 3:24, 14, 19, 23. For Thompson's support of women's application, see Parsons's eulogy, District of Columbia Medical Society, *Medical Annals* 6 (1907–8): 107.

24. By 1882, seventeen state societies admitted women, from Mary Putnam

Jacobi, "Woman in Medicine," in *Woman's Work in America*, ed. Annie Nathan Meyers (New York: Henry Holt, 1891; reprint, New York: Arno Press, 1972), 188.

25. Busey, *Personal Reminiscences*, 318.

26. Ibid., 322.

27. Ibid., 165.

28. Ibid., 282.

29. Statistics based on physicians listed in city directories and Medical Society membership lists. Women joined an average of 13 years following graduation, men, 7.7 years. If extreme cases are removed, the average for women is eight years, for men, six.

30. See, for example, "Lady Physicians Are Also Invited," *Washington Post*, 1 May 1895; Rosalie Slaughter Morton, *A Woman Surgeon* (New York: Frederick A. Stokes, 1937), 73.

31. See published minutes of the Medical Society in *National Medical Review*, especially 3 (June 1894); 3 (Feb. 1895); 4 (March 1895); 4 (June 1895); 7 (July 1897); 8 (May 1899); 9 (July 1899); and the *Maryland Medical Journal* 32 (Feb. 23, 1895), 32 (April 6, 1895); *Transactions of the Medical Society of the District of Columbia*, 27 March 1897; 12 May 1897; 19 May 1897; *Food: A Journal of Hygiene and Nutrition* 5 (May 1894): 441–46. Anecdote about Parsons reported by Dr. Margaret Nicholson, 1925 George Washington University Medical School alumnae, Washington, 29 July 1977.

32. *Transactions of the Medical Society of the District of Columbia*, 23 Feb. 1895 and 9 June 1895. For the current debate about a distinctively female therapeutic viewpoint, see Regina Morantz-Sanchez and Sue Zschoche, "Professionalism, Feminism, and Gender Roles: A Comparative Study of Nineteenth-Century Therapeutics," *Journal of American History* 67 (Dec. 1980): 568–88.

33. Nichols, *History of the Medical Society*, 46; *Transactions of the Medical Society of the District of Columbia*, 6 (18 Dec. 1901): 332; Coale, "Women Physicians," 656–57. Over the next twenty years, three other women served as vice-president—Phoebe Norris in 1907 (information from alumni biography, Juniata College, Huntington, Penn.), Ada Thomas in 1919, and Amelia Foye, 1920 (information from District of Columbia Medical Society, *Medical Annals* 19 [1920]). None of these women were included in the list of officers in Nichols, *History of the Medical Society*. Nichols listed no other women in that office until 1945. None had held office in the Medical Association before 1911, when it merged with the society.

34. See Margaret W. Rossiter, "Sexual Segregation in the Sciences: Some Data and a Model," *Signs* 4 (Autumn 1978): 146–51. Nationally, in 1932, only one woman was in the American Gynecological Society, and two served on the American Board of Obstetrics and Gynecology, see Kate C. Hurd-Mead, *Medical Women of America* (New York: Froben Press, 1933), 32. For membership rosters of Washington medical organizations, see *Maryland Medical Journal and R. L. Polk, Polk's Medical and Surgical Register of the United States and Canada* (Detroit: R. L. Polk, 1902); successive years of D.C. directories, 1890–1910, under "Medical Societies."

35. Quoted in Cora Bagley Marritt, "Nineteenth-Century Associations of Medical Women: The Beginnings of a Movement," *Journal of the American Medical Women's Association* 32 (Dec. 1977): 470.

36. *Woman's Medical Journal* 18 (March 1908): 45; Coale, "Women Physicians"; Elizabeth Kittredge, "Woman's Medical Society of the District of Columbia," *Journal of the American Medical Women's Association* 6 (Nov. 1951): 443–45.

37. Cobb mentions these clubs in *First Negro Medical Society*, 66, 123; only one has a female member. Williams quoted by Helen Buckler in manuscript of biography, "Doctor Dan," in folder labeled, "Chapter 6," Daniel Hale Williams Collection, Moorland-Spingarn Research Centrer, Howard University Library.

38. Daniel S. Lamb, ed., *Howard University Medical Department: A Historical, Biographical, and Statistical Souvenir* (Washington: R. Beresford, 1900), 182.

CHAPTER 7

1. Comparisons are based on hand counts of men and women who entered Columbian University Medical Department between 1885 and 1892, the years women attended. Other surveys of women doctors of the period also show a high proportion of graduates, see, for example, "What Becomes of Women Medical Students," *Woman's Medical Journal* 3 (July 1894): 98; at least five of Columbian's women graduates received honors: Anita McGee '92, Fannie Brewer '95, Mary Stanton '94, Carolyn Kiefe '94, and Margaret York '93. Ella Marble and Anna Dickerson received honors from National, see *Washington Post*, 3 May 1895, and "Biographical Series," *Woman's Medical Journal* 5 (March 1896): 69. An 1890 survey of 430 women medical who graduated from seven schools between 1870 and 1889 showed the average time of completion to be 4.5 years, *Woman's Medical Journal* 3 (July 1894): 17.

2. Figures for Columbian women and men based on reported employment in city directories; *National Medical Review* 1 (Nov. 1892): 133.

3. Lucille F. McMillan, *Women in the Federal Service* (Washington: U. S. Government Printing Office, 1938), 4, 10; see also Paul Van Riper, *History of the U.S. Civil Service* (Evanston, Ill.: Row, Peterson, 1958), 58, 158–59. Journalist Mary Clemmer Ames called civil service reform a "mockery" for women in *Ten Years in Washington: Life and Scenes in the Nation's Capital as a Woman Sees Them* (Hartford: A. D. Worthington, 1874), 67; for the frequent occurrence of reductions-in-force, see Cindy Aron, " 'To Barter Their Souls for Gold': Female Clerks in Federal Government Offices, 1862–1890," *Journal of American History* 67 (March 1981): 833–53.

4. For Harvey, see file folder 440:1890, Department of the Interior, Records of the Appointments Division, Record Group 48, National Archives Building, Washington, D. C., hereafter referred to as Interior, RG 48-NA; for teachers' salaries, see District of Columbia Board of Education, Personnel Records, Division of Research and Evaluation, and Henrietta R. Hatter,

"History of the Miner Teachers' College," (M.A. thesis, Howard University, 1939), 32.

5. Brewer, Interior, file folder 1846:1890, RG 48-NA; Adelaide Johnson diary, 7 Aug. 1895, file "1895–99," box 1, Adelaide M. Johnson Collection, Library of Congress; Frank Carpenter ("Carp") in the *Cleveland Leader,* 1882, in box 2, Frank Carpenter Collection, Library of Congress.

6. Jacobi in "Woman in Medicine," in *Woman's Work in America,* ed. Annie Nathan Meyers (New York: Henry Holt, 1891; reprint, New York: Arno Press, 1972), 199; for Lenman employment, see city directories, 1892–94.

7. Hart, 1880 Census, Enumeration District (ED) 39:37 and file folder 1878:1883, Department of the Treasury, Records of the Division of Appointments, Record Group 56, National Archives Building, hereafter referred to as Treasury, RG 56-NA; for Rochefort, see Josiah McLeod to Alonzo Bell, assistant secretary of the Interior, letters dated 26 Aug. 1881 and 29 Sept. 1881.

8. Edith Seville Coale, "Women Physicians of the District of Columbia," in *Washington: Past and Present,* ed. John C. Proctor (New York: Lewes Historical Publishing, 1932), 654–62.

9. Osler quoted in William G. Rothstein, *American Physicians in the Nineteenth Century: From Sects to Science* (Baltimore: Johns Hopkins University Press, 1971), 286. In 1904, the AMA estimated that 50 percent of physicians went on to hospital training, in Paul Starr, *The Social Transformation of American Medicine* (New York: Basic Books, 1982), 124.

10. Alice Hamilton, *Exploring the Dangerous Trades: The Autobiography of Alice Hamilton, M. D.* (Boston: Little, Brown, 1943), 47.

11. Daniel S. Lamb, ed., *Howard University Medical Department: A Historical, Biographical, and Statistical Souvenir* (Washington: R. Beresford, 1900), 29; for Barrows, see Madeline Stern, *We the Women: Career Firsts of Nineteenth-Century American Women* (New York: Schulte Publishing, 1963), 178–204; Lamb, ed., *History of the Medical Society of the District of Columbia* (Washington: The Medical Society, 1909), 340, 351, 358, 370. Nordhoff-Jung obituary, *Washington Times-Herald,* 9 June 1943; Bartsch-Dunne obituary, *Washington Post,* 1 July 1970.

12. Biographical sketches in Lamb, *Medical Society,* 356, 360; Lamb, *Howard University,* 136, 77.

13. Jacobi, "Woman in Medicine," 169; for Low and McCormick, see Lamb, *Howard University,* 152, 192, 194, 218; for Burritt, see Harold J. Abrahams, *Extinct Medical Schools of Baltimore, Maryland* (Baltimore: Maryland Historical Society, 1965), 301, 311. Between 1891 and 1895, the New England Hospital for Women accepted only twenty-six of sixty-one applicants, in Virginia Drachman, *Hospital with a Heart: Women Doctors and the Paradox of Separatism at the New England Hospital, 1862–1969* (Ithaca: Cornell University Press, 1984), 227–28.

14. Sara Loguen to "Sister Meal," 14 Feb. 1877, in file labeled, "Letters and Documents," Fraser-Goins Collection, Moorland-Spingarn Research Center (M-SRC), Howard University.

15. Drachman, *Hospital,* 158–59.

16. These figures based on information obtained from alumni records, city directories, obituaries, biographical dictionaries, medical society biographical sketches, and personnel records. For Brewer, see file folder 1846:1890, Interior, RG 48-NA; for Pettigrew, see "Augusta Pettigrew Shute," in vertical file, Special Collections, George Washington University Library (SC-GUL); Margaret Schneider, in an eighty-year "Survey of Women Graduates from Cincinnati Medical Colleges, 1873–1953," *Journal of the American Medical Women's Association* 9 (Dec. 1954): 400–10, finds that only 6 of 133 women, 4.5 percent, never used their education. An 1892 study by Dr. Emily Pope of 390 American women medical graduates shows that only 12 of 390 in her group never practiced (3 percent), quoted in Mary A. Spink, "Women in Medicine," *Woman's Medical Journal* 3 (July 1894): 17.

17. City directories; Samuel C. Busey, *Personal Reminiscences and Recollections of Forty-Six Years' Membership in the Medical Society of the District of Columbia* (Philadelphia: Dornan Printers, 1895), 322–23.

18. *Washington Post,* 29 Dec. 1889; survey of school catalogs, city directories, alumni bulletins; Lamb, *Medical Society,* Ibid., *Howard University.*

19. *Kate Field's Washington,* 21 Sept. 1892, 192; Washington *Bee,* 3 June 1893, 3. Salaries based on a review of government records of Howard and Columbian graduates hired as pension examiners, see, for example, John Raymond, file folder 2268-1889, and Richard Parrott, file folders 3996-1890 and 738-1891, Interior, RG 48-NA. According to the *Evening Star,* 13 Jan. 1890, pension surgeons earned $3,000 a year, examiners, $2,500 a year.

20. Daniel W. Cathell, *The Physician Himself and What He Should Add to His Scientific Acquirements* (Baltimore: Cushings and Bailey, 1882), chap. 11, "The Business of Medicine"; study conducted by Emily F. Pope cited in Spinks, "Woman in Medicine," 17–19. Pope also found that 111 of 390 women doctors (28 percent) were able to support themselves by the end of the first year, but 138 (35 percent) had insufficient income even after the third year. An earlier study of 1870–79 graduates of the Woman's Medical College of Pennsylvania by Dr. Rachel Bodley showed the average income of 76 women doctors to be $2,907. Removing the handful of women who earned more than $10,000 annually left an average for the majority of $1,300, quoted in Jacobi, "Woman in Medicine," 200, and "Women as Physicians," *The Medical and Surgical Reporter* 44 (March 1881): 354–56. M. L. Rayne in *What Can a Woman Do: Or Her Position in the Business and Literary World* (Petersburgh, N. Y.: Eagle Publishing, 1893), 79, estimated that women doctors earned $1,000 a year. An informal survey of Washington male doctors reported in the *National Medical Review* 4 (Feb. 1895): 23, indicated that the average Washington male practitioner earned $2,000 a year, the next hundred earned $3,500, and the ten wealthiest, $9,500; Lilian Welsh quoted in *Reminiscences of Thirty Years in Baltimore* (Baltimore: Norman Remington, 1925), 37.

21. For McGee, see "Physicians Visiting List, 1894," box 4, Anita Newcomb McGee Collection, Library of Congress; Julia Green's diary for 1904 lent to the author by Dr. Maesimund Panos, Tipp City, Ohio.

22. Letter quoted from Dr. Hunter Robb in folder "R," Correspondence File, McGee Collection. Information about Parsons provided by Dr. Margaret Nicholson, a graduate of George Washington University Medical Department, 1925, Washington, D.C., 29 July 1977. McGee listed first names only of her 50 cent clients: These were probably neighborhood servants, because children's first and last names were included, for example, "Lizzie Hardie [mumps]"; all others are "Miss" or "Mrs".

23. Appropriate medical school catalogs; Superintendent of Charities *Report on Charitable Institutions in the District of Columbia* (Washington: U. S. Government Printing Office, 1895); *Hearings before the Subcommittee of the House Committee on Appropriations in Charge of the District of Columbia Appropriations Bill for 1894* (Washington: U. S. Government Printing Office, 1892), 25; District of Columbia Board of Health, *Report of the Health Officer,* 30 June 1900, 12–13.

24. Pope survey, reported in Jacobi, "Woman in Medicine"; information on Heiberger and Erbach based on interviews with Kenneth Kelly, Elizabeth Newby, and Amalia Perry, family members; Strobel, see 1900 census, ED 35:4; Hartman in 1880 census, ED 423:22. Edson also supported her mother and her unmarried sister who lived with her; for Spackman, Hinds, and Kappelar, see chap. 2.

25. Winslow, city directories, 1868–72; Hinds, "The Woman's Gymnasium," in *Washington Post,* 11 Dec. 1889, and "First Woman M.D. Here Fought Pioneer Battle," *Washington Post,* 6 June 1934. Hinds charged adults $10 a year and children $5. Ella Marble managed a gym before she entered medical school, see "Biographical Series" *Woman's Medical Journal* 5 (1896), 69; 1894 and 1895 city directories for Harvey and Hartman.

26. Mount Vernon Seminary for Girls, *Catalogue,* 1892/93-1918/19; Welsh, *Reminiscences,* 53; Reville, 1900 census, ED 76:13; Alice Burritt, 1900 census ED 76:12; Bland kept eight boarders, 1880 census, ED 54:32; Jacobi referred to the common practice of taking in boarders in "Woman in Medicine," 199; for a male physician's household, see, Dr. Aurelius Shands, 1900 census, ED 80:13. Busey objected to these informal registries that competed with the one run by the Medical Society, see *Personal Reminiscences,* 344.

27. More than one-half of these women married, see chap. 2. Schneider's study of 133 women medical graduates, 1879–1953, shows that 71.4 percent married, almost 40 percent to physicians; they averaged 2.3 children per mother, in "Survey of Women Graduates," 405. Pope's 1892 study showed that 6 percent of the women were widowed and 19 percent had married, but many in that sample were still of marriageable age, in "Woman in Medicine," 17. For McGee's arrangements, see McGee to Tilly, 18 Nov. 1891, file 8, box 1, in Matilda Coxe Stevenson Collection, National Anthropological Archives, National Museum of Natural History, Washington, D.C.; 3 May 1893 and March to June, 1893, diary of Caroline Hassler Newcomb, box 3, Simon Newcomb Collection, Library of Congress.

28. For Burritt, see Abrahams, *Extinct Medical Schools,* 301, 311; 1900 census, ED 129:8; Baker obituary in Washingtoniana Collection vertical file, Martin Luther King Library, Washington, D. C.

29. Birthrate based on information from census, alumni lists, and biographical records; Xarifa Sallume and Frank Notestein, "Trends in the Size of Families Completed Prior to 1910 in Various Social Classes," *American Journal of Sociology* 38 (Nov. 1932): 406–7. The birthrates for women doctors were similar to those of better educated middle-class women; see Louise Newman, *Men's Ideas/Women's Realities: Popular Science, 1870–1915* (New York: Pergamon Press, 1985), 105–6. Based on an examination of census and survey data, Norman E. Himes concluded that physicians practiced birth control before other segments of the professional population, in *Medical History of Contraception* (Baltimore: Williams and Wilkins, 1936; reprint, New York: Gamut Press, 1963), 370–71.

30. "Anita to Don, from Paris," 14 May 1897, box 1, McGee Collection; for information about access to the Mensinga diaphragm, see Himes, *Contraception*, 248–49, 252, 305.

31. McGee list written on stationery from Hotel Buckingham, New York, in box 7, McGee Collection.

32. For a sardonic account of changing attitudes of supportive husbands, see Mabel S. Ulrich, "Men Are Queer that Way: Extracts from the Diary of an Apostate Woman Physician," *Scribner's* 93 (June 1933): 365–66; Lamb, *Howard University*, 150.

33. Stern, *We the Women*, 178–204.

34. Prentiss, "Address to the Graduating Class, 1892," in Special Collections, George Washington University Library.

35. "Physicians Visiting List, 1894" and diary, Feb. 1895; McGee Collection.

36. Obituary, vertical file, Washingtoniana Collection.

37. Daniel S. Lamb, "Address to the Graduates of the Medical Department of Howard University," Washington, 9 March 1885, 17.

38. *Medical Woman's Journal* 29 (Aug. 1922): 185.

39. Central Dispensary and Emergency Hospital, Board of Directors, "Minutes," 1880–1898, 11 Oct. 1895; 10 Oct. 1896; 9 Nov. 1896, Archives of Washington Hospital Center, Washington, D. C.; for Hearst philanthropies, see miscellaneous items in the Phoebe Hearst Collection, Bancroft Library, University of California, Berkeley.

40. Central Dispensary, "Minutes."

41. Green diary; interviews with Dr. Margaret Parsons, niece of Mary Parsons, and Amalia Perry, niece of Amelia Erbach; Kenneth Kelly, nephew of Ida Heiberger.

42. Based on survey of locations of offices of Medical Society members in 1900; William A. Boyd, ed., *Boyd's Elite List: A Compilation of Selected Names of Residents of Washington City, District of Columbia, and Ladies' Shopping Guide, Together with a List of the Members of the Most Prominent Clubs* (Washington: Elite Publishing, 1897); *Who's Who in the Nation's Capital*, 1921, mentions Bond, McGee, Thomas; register of wills: Brosius, filed 23 Jan. 1948; Erbach, 3 June 1941; Thomas, 7 May 1925; Bartsch-Dunne bequest reported in *Journal of the National Medical Association* 60 (March 1968): 161.

43. Howard University Medical Department catalogs and city directories.
44. Sara Brown, "Colored Women Physicians," *The Southern Workman* 52 (Dec. 1923): 591–92.
45. *Medical Woman's Journal* 46 (Oct. 1939): 299; Brown, "Colored Women Physicians," 584–86.
46. Gregoria Fraser-Goins, "Miss Doc," 110, 111, Fraser-Goins Collection, M-SRC.
47. Fraser-Goins, "Miss Doc," 210. In 1911, interns at the New England Hospital for Women refused to work with a newly appointed black physician. Hospital directors overruled the resident physicians who had asked her to leave, cited in Drachman, *Hospital with a Heart*, 175–76.
48. B. M. Rhetta, "Negro Physicians of Baltimore," *Opportunity* 1 (May 1923): 21–22; see also Kelly Miller, "The Historic Background of the Negro Physician," *Journal of Negro History* 1 (April 1916): 107, for blacks' unwillingness to patronize physicians of their own race; the *Colored American*, 14 May 1898, 132.
49. Hughes quoted in Lamb, *Howard University*, 182.
50. Brown, "Colored Women Physicians," 591–92.
51. For Gilbert, Jones, Hall, and Whipper, see Lamb, *Howard University*, 168, 181–82, 173, and chap. 2 above.
52. Thomas, M. L. Brown, and S. W. Brown are listed in city directories; District of Columbia Department of Education personnel records; Thomas is listed as a midwife in *Sherman's Directory and Ready Reference of the Colored Population in the District of Columbia* (Washington: Sherman Directory, 1913); see also Lamb, *Howard University*, 152, 221.
53. District of Columbia, Board of Education Personnel Records for Thomas and Brown, Office of Director of Research and Evaluation, Washington, D.C.; G. F. A. Key, librarian, Washingtoniana Collection, Martin Luther King Memorial Library, Washington, D.C. In 1890, the District of Columbia Department of Education employed 265 black teachers, 225 were women; cited in Lawson A. Scruggs, *Women of Distinction* (Raleigh, N. C.: L. A. Scruggs, 1893), 313; Department of Education records; Mary Church Terrell, "History of the High School for Negroes in Washington," *Journal of Negro History* 2 (July 1917): 252–67; Bernard Nelson, "Miner Teachers' College: The First Century, 1851–1951," (M.A. thesis, District of Columbia Teachers College, 1973), 51, 57–9; see also the *Bee*, Aug. 1897; Hatter, "Miner Teachers' College," 24–26, 33; Sharon Harley, "Black Women in the District of Columbia, 1890–1920: Their Economic, Social, and Institutional Activities" (Ph.D. diss., Howard University, 1981), 183, 282–3.
54. Board of Education Personnel Records for Riggs, Moten, Gibbs; see also Thomasene Corruthers, "Lucy Ellen Moten, 1851–1933," *Journal of Negro History* 19 (Jan. 1934): 102–7.

CHAPTER 8

1. Washington women established more than fifty organizations that received public notice in this period. Excluded from examination in this chapter are: church societies such as the popular Twentieth Century Club, affiliated with the All Souls Unitarian Church, and the Women's Alliance; groups that attracted few women doctors such as the Professional Women's League, the Women's Christian Temperance Union Hartwell Chapter, the Legion of Loyal Women, and the Women's National Press Club; and charitable groups that served women doctors' professional needs directly, such as those connected to women's clinics and institutions like the Woman's Christian Home, the Florence Crittenton Home, and St. Rose's Industrial School for Girls.

Two-thirds of the forty-five pre-1900 white women who practiced in the city for more than five years participated in the groups considered here. Evidence regarding their activities was derived from newspaper reports, accounts in women's periodicals like the *Woman's Journal*, the *Woman's Council*, and the *Woman's Tribune*, published club reports, manuscript collections, wills, obituaries, and articles in books and national magazines.

2. For feminists and homeopathy, see Gena Corea, *The Hidden Malpractice* (New York: William Morrow, 1977), chap. 1; see also Susan B. Anthony diary, 20 June 1892, regarding her visit to Chicago homeopath Julia Holmes Smith, box 3, Anthony Collection, Library of Congress.

3. Winslow quoted by Ella S. Marble in "Caroline Winslow's Birthday Party," *The Woman's Journal*, 10 Dec. 1892, 404; details about Winslow's struggle reported in *Cleaves Biographical Cyclopaedia of Homoeopathic Physicians and Surgeons* (Philadelphia: Galaxy Publishing, 1873), 254–65.

4. An 1867 meeting of the UFA included Washington activists Belva Lockwood, Josephine Griffing, doctors Caroline Winslow and Susan Edson, and Senator Samuel Pomeroy, a founder of Howard University; for a discussion of the UFA, see Ellen DuBois, *Feminism and Suffrage* (Ithaca: Cornell University Press, 1978), 64; for the founding of the NWSA, see DuBois, *Feminism*, and Mari Jo Buhle and Paul Buhle, *The Concise History of Woman Suffrage* (Urbana: University of Illinois Press, 1979). In 1875, Winslow founded the Washington Woman's Club, a shortlived association for which there is no information, see announcement in *Washington Star*, 22 July 1875.

5. See, for example, "Tobacco, Temperance, Religion, and Purity," the *Alpha* 7 (Sept. 1881): 10; "A Woman's Medical College," the *Alpha* 8 (Feb. 1883): 8–9; "Feticide," the *Alpha* 8 (May 1883): 1; "Women—The Strike at Yonkers" and "Medical Women," the *Alpha* 10 (Dec. 1885): 8; "Concubinage," the *Alpha* 11 (Nov. 1886): 11. For a historical overview of the MES, see the *Alpha* 7 (1882): 3–5. For a reference to the *Alpha* and the MES, see Frances Willard and Mary Livermore, *American Women: A Complete Encyclopedia of the Lives and Achievements of American Women of the Nineteenth Century*, vol. 2 (New York: Mast, Crowell, and Kirkpatrick, 1897). David Pivar, *Purity Crusade: Sexual Morality and Social Control, 1868–1900* (Westport, Conn.: Greenwood Press, 1973) mentions the journal. Membership in these groups was derived from

lists of elected officers and meeting attendees in annual February editions of the *Alpha;* see, for example, the *Alpha* 8 (1883): 9. Names were checked in city directories and in the 1880 census for occupation.

6. Katherine Hosmer, "What Women Have Done in Washington's City Affairs," *Municipal Affairs* 2 (Sept. 1898): 514–23; selected issues of the *Woman's Journal,* see, for example, 7 Oct. 1899, 27 April 1901, and 11 May 1901; see also Susan B. Anthony diary, 9 Jan. 1890, box 1, Anthony Collection. For membership, see 1884 National Woman Suffrage Association brochure in Mary Church Terrell Collection, reel 15, Manuscript Division, Library of Congress. Names were checked in appropriate city directories for occupations of women, spouses, and relatives. DuBois noticed a similar shift in emphasis and membership with the Working Woman's Association, *Feminism and Suffrage,* 48. Winslow and Edson also belonged to the Hartwell chapter of the WCTU, which met twice monthly in Winslow's home. Reports concerned legislation on women, temperance, arbitration, peace, and "social purity," see the *Alpha* 13 (Feb. 1888): 8.

7. Lockwood's visit and the attempt to have a woman doctor placed in Columbia Hospital in "Minutes, 29 Jan. 1896," 2, District of Columbia Federation of Women's Clubs Scrapbook, District of Columbia Federation of Women's Club Collection, Washington, D. C. See also *Proceedings of the Twenty-fifth Annual Convention of the NWSA* (1893) on reel 15, Terrell Collection, which reported that women succeeded in winning a $35,000 appropriation from Congress for the girls' reform school, which was then put in charge of a male governing board. For other DWSA projects, see Mrs. William B. Sennot and Mrs. Arthur G. Davis, eds., *History of the District of Columbia Federation of Women's Clubs, 1894–1962* (Washington: District of Columbia Federation of Women's Clubs, 1962); "District of Columbia" column in the *Woman's Journal,* 30 Jan. 1892; the *Alpha* 13 (Feb. 1888): 8; *Evening Star,* 9 April 1895.

At meetings, lawyer Ellen Spencer Mussey spoke on the "Legal Status of Women in the District of Columbia"; others reported on the progress of te girls' reform school, the status of women in local medical and law schools, the protection of women prisoners, improvements in the condition of the poor, and the admission of black organizations. After repeated tabling of the latter issue, members voted against admitting black groups but for the admission of integrated clubs, in "Minutes," 19 April 1902.

8. For "strong minded" as an epithet of derision, see the article on the founding of the Washington Woman's Club, in *Evening Star,* 22 July 1875.

9. Lilian Whiting, "Women's Organizations in Boston," the *Chautauquan* 27 (May 1898): 197–99; for membership, see the *Alpha* 13 (June 1888): 9.

10. The *Alpha* 13 (June 1888): 9.

11. Jane Cunningham Croly, *The History of the Women's Club Movement in America* (New York: Henry G. Allen, 1898): 340–50; the *Woman's Column,* 7 June 1890, 17 Jan. 1891, and 8 Aug. 1891; "The Wimodaughsis Elections," *Evening Star,* 17 May 1894. A check of 1892 members against D. C. directory listings reveals that 60 percent of Wimodaughsis members were government clerks.

12. Croly, *Women's Club Movement*, 348.

13. "Washington Letter," *Woman's Journal*, 7 May 1892, 17 Jan. 1891, 14 Nov. 1891, 8 Aug. 1891, 7 May 1891, and 21 Feb. 1892; the *Woman's Tribune*, 21 Feb. 1891; the *Woman's Column*, 7 June 1890; Croly, *Women's Club Movement*, 348.

14. Edward Ingle, *The Negro in the District of Columbia*, Johns Hopkins Studies in Historical and Related Sciences. 11th series, 3–4 (Baltimore: Johns Hopkins University Press, 1893), 59–60, contains a copy of Desha's letter of resignation; also see *Woman's Tribune*, 21 Feb. 1891, 92.

15. Ingle, *The Negro in the District of Columbia*, 60.

16. *Proceedings of the Twenty-sixth Annual Convention of the National American Woman Suffrage Association*, 15–20 Feb. 1894 (Washington: National American Woman Suffrage Association, 1894), 186.

17. Marble, "Caroline Winslow's Birthday Party."

18. Spencer in *Woman's Journal*, 21 Feb. 1892, 58; Ella Marble, "The First Pan American Medical Congress: Some Women Who Took Part," the *Woman's Medical Journal* 1 (Sept. 1893): 200.

19. Croly, *Women's Club Movement*, 344–45; *Boyd's Elite List: A Compilation of Selected Names of Residents of Washington City, District of Columbia, and Ladies' Shopping Guide, Together with a List of the Members of the Most Prominent Clubs* (Washington: Elite Publishing, 1897), 249.

20. "A Mart for Women's Work," *Washington Post*, 17 March 1894, 4.

21. Marion Talbott and Lois Kimball Matthews Rosenberry, *The History of the American Association of University Women, 1881–1931* (Boston: Houghton Mifflin, 1931), 190; the group had thirty-four members; see also "Learned Women of Washington," *Evening Star*, 3 Aug. 1889, 11.

22. *Washington Post*, 13 July 1890; "Inception and Organization of the National Society of the Daughters of the American Revolution," *Report of the National Society of the DAR*, vol. 1 (Washington: National Society of the Daughters of the American Revolution, 1890–93), 3; Mrs. Robert Duncan, ed., *In Washington: The National Society of the Daughters of the American Revolution* (Washington: National Society of the Daughters of the American Revolution, 1965), 15; Ellen Hardin Walworth, "Mary Ellen Cabell," *The American Monthly Magazine* 1 (Jan. 1892): 119.

23. *Second Report of the National Secretary of the DAR*, 11 Oct. 1897–11 Oct. 1898 (Washington: National Society of the Daughters of the American Revolution, 1900), 15, 18; *Fourth Report*, 11 Oct. 1900–11 Oct. 1901; *Evening Star*, 29 Nov. 1893, 8.

24. McGee justified DAR involvement in the nurses corps project on the basis of women's assistance in the Revolution, see *Second Report*, 46; see also Dita H. Kinney, "Dr. Anita McGee and What She Has Done for the Nursing Profession," the *Trained Nurse and Hospital Review* 26 (March 1901): 129–34. For a perspective that places McGee's activities in the context of the professionalization of nursing, see Susan Armeny, "Organized Nurses, Women Philanthropists and the Intellectual Bases for Cooperation Among Women,

Notes

1898–1920," in *Nursing History: New Perspectives, New Possibilities*, ed. Ellen Condliffe Lagemann (New York: Teachers College Press, 1983), 13–46, especially 19–25.

25. *Second Report* (1897–98): 46, 47, 50, 51; "A National University," *Report* 2 (1893): 630. Several committee members, including Jane Stanford and Mary Parke Foster, had contributd to the Johns Hopkins Women's Medical Fund.

26. *Report* 8 (1896): 511; the *American Monthly Magazine* 8 (1896); 11 (1900): 756; 20 (1902): 1326; 22 (1904): 453.

27. For information about these groups and the network which they comprised, see James Kirkpatrick Flack, *Desideratum in Washington: The Intellectual Community in the Capital City, 1870–1900* (Cambridge, Mass.: Schenkman Publishing, 1975). Robinson Lappin, in *Lappin's Club Book of Washington* (Washington: R. L. Lappin, 1894) remarked on the expansion of clubs and societies in the period.

28. Tylor in Nancy Ostereich Lurie, "Women in Early Anthropology," in *Pioneers of American Anthropology*, ed. June Helm MacNeish (Seattle: University of Washington Press, 1966), 34; for biographical sketch, see "Matilda Coxe Evans Stevenson," in *Notable American Women, 1607–1950*, vol. 3, ed. Edward T. James and Janet Wilson James (Cambridge: Harvard University Press, 1971), 373–74. Stevenson had other reasons to hope for acceptance: Her colleagues Erminnie Smith and Alice Cunningham Fletcher were elected fellows in the American Assocation for the Advancement of Science in 1880 and 1883, respectively; see Margaret W. Rossiter, *Women Scientists in America: Struggles and Strategies to 1940* (Baltimore: Johns Hopkins University Press, 1982), 76–77.

The society could hardly have objected to Stevenson's lack of credentials, because few members were themselves professional anthropologists. In 1889, for instance, only 5 percent of the members of the Anthropological Society of Washington could have been considered anthopologists; physicians, clergy, lawyers, government scientists, high-level administrators, artists, bankers, and clergy comprised the rest; see Daniel S. Lamb, "The Story of the Anthropological Society of Washington," *American Anthropologist* 8 (July-Sept. 1906): 564–79.

29. "The Minervas of Washington," *Sunday Star*, 6 July 1889. For more information about the organization, see Croly, *Women's Club Movement*, 341, and Flack, *Desideratum*, 128–30. Anita Newcomb McGee, *General Report of the Recording Secretary* (Washington: Women's Anthropological Society, 1889), 1; *Organizational and Historical Sketch*, (Washington: Women's Anthropological Society, 1889), 19; and *Statistical Sketch of the Women's Anthropological Society* (Washington: Women's Anthropological Society, 1893). The statement regarding the lack of aid from the men's societies exists in McGee's handwritten draft only, not in the published document; "Draft of the Woman's Anthropological Society General Report, 25 Feb. 1899," in folder, "Speeches, Articles, and Book File," box 4, Anita McGee Collection. Local members included the wives

of Washington's prominent citizens; four were married to senators, one to the minister of Hawaii, one to a judge, and several to high-ranking government scientists.

Tylor wrote Stevenson in 1887 congratulating her on the continued success of the Women's Anthropological Society, "Tylor to Stevenson," box 1, file 18, 25 Sept. 1897, in Matilda Coxe Stevenson Collection, National Anthropological Archives, National Museum of Natural History, Washington, D.C. Just six years before Stevenson organized the society, Maria Mitchell tried to found a comparable section in the AAAS. "We have been so long accustomed to listen in silence and not speak that we felt inadequate before groups of scientific men," said Mitchell. Her plan failed because there were too few women scientists for such a venture. See Sally Gregory Kohlstedt, "Maria Mitchell: The Advancement of Women in Science," *New England Quarterly* 51 (March 1978): 39.

30. "Minervas," *Sunday Star*.

31. Clara B. Hinds, *Child Growth*, (Washington: Women's Anthropological Society, 1886), 1; *Constitution and Bylaws* and *List of Members* (Washington: Women's Anthropological Society, 1886).

32. Otis T. Mason, *What Is Anthropology? A Lecture Given at the National Museum, 18 March 1882* (Washington: Women's Anthropological Society, n.d., probably 1885), 10.

33. McGee, *General Report of the Recording Secretary* (Washington: Women's Anthropological Society, 1889), 1, 2; and "Draft of the General Report."

34. Mason, *What Is Anthropology?* 9, 11.

35. "First Woman M. D. Here Fought Pioneer Battle," *Washington Post*, 6 June 1934. For the popularity of this subject, see James Allen Young, "Height, Weight, and Health: Anthropometric Study of Human Growth in Nineteenth-Century American Medicine," *Bulletin of the History of Medicine* 53 (Summer 1979): 214–43.

36. Hinds, *Child Growth*, 4, 5–6; also see notice, "Child Growth" in the *Alpha* 1 (Nov. 1886): 9.

37. McGee, *General Report*, 1–2; also see page 2 of the handwritten draft of that report in McGee Collection; draft titled "A Woman's Name," 3, box 9, McGee Collection.

38. *Catalog of Books* (Washington: Women's Anthropological Society, 1889); Lamb, "Anthropological Society of Washington," 564–79.

39. Sample questions included, "Do women seem to prefer particular phases or kinds of this work? If so, what phases? Do they show aptitudes unlike those displayed by men in the same service? If so, what are the special aptitudes manifested by women?", *Scheme of Work of the Committee on the Investigative and Directive Forces in Society* (Washington: Women's Anthropological Society, 1893).

40. Anita McGee to Stevenson on the results of the close election, 18 Nov. 1891, box 1, file 8, Stevenson Collection. Stevenson was elected to the AAAS the next year.

41. Lamb, "Anthropological Society of Washington," 577–78; Joint Com-

mission of the Scientific Societies of Washington, *Notice of Meetings* (April 1895-May 1896): 5–7; Regna Diebold Darnell, "Development of American Anthropology, 1879–1920: From the Bureau of American Ethnology to Franz Boas," (Ph.D. diss., University of Pennsylvania, 1969).

42. Flack, *Desideratum*, chap. 4, "By a Social Tie," 77–106, see especially, 77, 82, 84; for Cosmos membership, see William A. DeCaindry, Marcus Benjamin, and Cyrus Adler, eds., *The Twenty-fifth Anniversary of the Founding of the Cosmos* (Washington: The Cosmos, 1904); Thomas M. Spaulding, *The Cosmos Club on Lafayette Square* (Washington: George Bank, Publishing, 1949), 2, 45; and Wilcomb E. Washburn, *The Cosmos Club of Washington, A Centennial History 1878–1978* (Washington: The Cosmos Club, 1978); Billings quoted in Flack, *Desideratum*, 94. For the club's rules, see Denys P. Myers, *Cosmos Club Bulletin* 2 (Oct. 1958): 2; see also Washburn, *The Cosmos*, 112–14.

43. *Washington Mirror*, 7 April 1900.

44. See Fletcher diary, 1 and 8 April 1888, and 23 Jan. 1893, Fletcher Collection, box 6, MS number 4558, Anthropology Archives, Smithsonian Institution, Washington, D.C.

45. For male colleagues' attitudes toward Stevenson, see Neil P. Judd, *The Bureau of American Ethnology: A Partial History* (Norman: University of Oklahoma Press, 1967), 57; and Lurie, "Women in Anthropology," 5, 55, 59, 234; McGee, *General Report*, 1–2; Nordhoff-Jung letter in Stevenson Collection, box 1, file 18.

46. Nannie Burroughs in the *Bee*, 4 Jan. 1902, quoted in Sharon Harley, "Black Women in the District of Columbia: Their Economic, Social, and Institutional Activities, 1890–1920" (Ph.D. diss., Howard University, 1980), 289.

47. "Statement of Purpose," Colored Women's Professional Franchise Association, in Mary Ann Shadd Cary Papers, 13–1, Manuscript Division, Moorland-Spingarn Research Center, Howard University (M-SRC).

48. Ibid.; "Minutes of the first meeting," folder 5.

49. Ibid.

50. Carter Godwin Woodson, *The Negro Professional Man and the Community* (New York: Negro Universities Press, 1934), 105–6.

51. Andrew Hilyer, *The 20th Century Union League Directory: A Compilation of the Efforts of the Colored People of Washington for the Social Betterment* (Washington: The Union League, 1901), 117.

52. For Colored Women's League activities, see Mary Church Terrell, *A Colored Woman in a White World* (Washington: Ransdell Publishing, 1940), 148; *Evening Star*, 10 April 1895, 12. Like Wilson, Terrell helped to create and sustain an extraordinary network of women's groups. In addition to the Washington Colored Women's League and the College Alumnae Club, she helped to found, and served as leader of, the National Association of Colored Women, the Colored YWCA, the Colored Social Settlement, the Colored Women's Republican League, and the NWSA. See her autobiography, *A Colored Woman in a White World* (Washington: Ransdell Publishing, 1940), and Beverly Washington Jones, "Quest for Equality: The Life of Mary Church Terrell, 1863–

1954" (Ph.D. diss., University of North Carolina, 1980); Paula Giddings, *When and Where I Enter* (New York: William Morrow, 1984), 93, 97–100, 179–80, 218–19. See Harley, "Black Women," chap. 8, especially 296–97, for Hearst's contribution to the kindergarten project.

53. *Journal of the College Alumnae Club of Washington, Twenty-fifth Anniversary* (Washington: College Alumnae Club, 1935), 3, in box 102–12, Mary Church Terrell Collection, M-SRC; Terrell, "The Story of the National Unfolds," *Journal of the National Association of College Women* 18 (1941): 6–23. Women doctors also participated with men in the Bethel Literary and Historical Society, the foremost group in the black upper-middle-class community. While women did hold positions of leadership (Laura Joiner, for example, a teacher and Howard medical student, was recording secretary in 1897) and gave papers, they were significantly underrepresented. Male physicians and ministers held the key posts and delivered the vast majority of papers. See Papers of the Bethel Literary and Historical Society, M-SRC.

54. Mary Church Terrell, "How and When the College Alumnae Club Was Founded," *Journal of the College Alumnae Club* 8 (Oct. 1935): 4–5. In subsequent years, the CAC supported suffrage, established scholarship funds, and furnished a room at the YWCA.

55. Nannie Burroughs, the *Bee*, 4 Jan. 1902 and 30 Oct. 1897, and see 2 May 1896, 9 July 1898, and 25 June 1899; Cary, in a letter to the editor of the *Colored American*, undated clipping in Mary Ann Shadd Cary papers, M-SRC; see Harley, "Black Women," 32, and Allan J. Johnston, "Surviving Freedom: The Black Community of Washington, D. C., 1860–1880" (Ph.D. diss., Duke University, 1980), 94.

CONCLUSION

1. Sara Spencer, owner of the popular Spencerian Business Academy to Lucretia Garfield, 19 June 1870, in President James A. Garfield Papers, Library of Congress; at the end of the period, see the remarks of Mrs. W. A. Kellerman, "Presidential Address," *Journal of the National Science Club* 1 (May 1898): 9.

2. Anita N. McGee in *General Report of the Recording Secretary* (Washington: Women's Anthropological Society, 1889), 1–2.

3. See Maureen Beasley, *The First Women Washington Correspondents*, George Washington University Studies 4 (Washington: George Washington University, 1976), 28, 21–3; Mrs. Elden E. Billings, "Early Women Journalists of Washington," in *Records of the Columbia Historical Society of Washington, D.C., 1966–68*, ed. Francis C. Rosenberger (Washington: The Historical Society, 1969), 84–97; for Kate Field's difficulties in publishing *Kate Field's Washington*, see correspondence with Phoebe Hearst, especially 12 July 1893, in folder titled, "Kate Field," box 18, Phoebe Hearst Collection, Bancroft Library, University of California, Berkeley.

4. Nancy Ostereich Lurie, "Women in Early American Anthropology," in

Notes

Pioneers of American Anthropology, ed. June Helm MacNeish (Seattle: University of Washington Press, 1966), 34; Regna Diebold Darnell, "The Development of American Anthropology, 1879–1920: From the Bureau of American Ethnology to Franz Boas," (Ph.D. diss., University of Pennsylvania, 1969); Margaret W. Rossiter, *Women Scientists in America: Struggles and Strategies to 1940* (Baltimore: Johns Hopkins University Press, 1983), esp. chaps. 2 and 8, "'Women's Work' in Science" and "Government Employment: Paper Reforms but Expanded Segregation"; Lucille Foster McMillan, *Women in the Federal Service* (Washington: U. S. Government Printing Office, 1938); Laura Puffer Morgan, "Report on the Status of Women in Classified Civil Service of the United States Government in the District of Columbia," *Journal of the Association of Collegiate Alumnae* 1 (April 1913).

5. Madeline Stern, "The First Woman Admitted to Practice Before the U. S. Supreme Court: Belva Ann Lockwood," in *We the Women: Career Firsts of Nineteenth Century American Women,* ed. Stern (New York: Schulte Publishing, 1963): 205–34. Lockwood and other women completed the law course at National, but administrators refused to grant them diplomas because "some Gentlemen . . . did not choose to graduate with women," quoted in Stern, 211; also see Belva A. Lockwood, "My Efforts to Become a Lawyer," *Lippincott's* (June 1888): 215–29. For information about the women's law school, see Catherine M. Rottier, "Ellen Spencer Mussey and the Washington College of Law," *Maryland Historical Magazine* 69 (Winter 1974): 361–82; Charles Carusi, "Higher Education in the District of Columbia," in *Washington: Past and Present,* ed. John C. Proctor (New York: Lewes Historical Publishing, 1932): 458–94; see also *Woman's Tribune,* 18 May 1899 and 3 June 1899; *The Crescent of the League of Loyal Women* (Washington: 1901): 1, 49; advertisements in the D.C. Federation of Women's Clubs annual *Yearbooks,* especialy its first year of operation, 1896, 22; Elizabeth Kemper Adams, *Women Professional Workers* (Washington: U. S. Government Printing Office, 1921), 71–7. For optimism regarding the profession for women, see Winona B. Sawyer, "The Legal Profession for Women," in *The Congress of Women,* ed. Mary K. Oldham Eagle (Chicago: W. B. Conkey, 1894; reprint, New York: Arno Press, 1974): 273–76; Ada M. Bittenbinder, "Women in the Law," in *Woman's Work in America,* ed. Annie Nathan Meyers (New York: Henry Holt, 1891, reprint, New York: Arno Press, 1972).

6. Thomas Woody, *A History of Women's Education in the United States,* vol. 2 (New York: The Science Press, 1929; reprint, New York: Octagon Press, 1966), 280, 381, chap. 5, "Coeducation"; Sophonisba Breckenridge, *Women in the Twentieth Century: A Study of their Political, Social, and Economic Activities* (Recent Social Trends Monographs, 1933; reprint, New York: Arno Press, 1972), chap. 12, "Professional and Near-Professional Women"; Margaret Rossiter, "Women Scientists in America Before 1920," *American Scientist* 62 (May-June 1974): 312–23; Barbara Miller Solomon, *In the Company of Educated Women: A History of Women and Higher Education in America* (New Haven: Yale University Press, 1985), 58–61, chap. 8, 115–40.

Selected Bibliography

PRIMARY SOURCES

Manuscripts and Collections
(All located in Washington, D. C., unless otherwise noted.)

Susan B. Anthony Collection. Manuscript Division, Library of Congress.

Anthropological Society of Washington. National Anthropological Archives, National Museum of Natural History.

Clara Barton Collection. Manuscript Division, Library of Congress.

Bureau of Ethnology, 1879–94. National Anthropological Archives, National Museum of Natural History.

Frank Carpenter Collection. Manuscript Division, Library of Congress.

Mary Ann Shadd Cary Collection. Manuscript Division, Moorland-Spingarn Research Center, Howard University Library.

Central Dispensary and Emergency Hospital, Board of Directors' Minutes, 1880–98, contained in the Archives of the Washington Hospital Center.

Cook Family Papers. Manuscript Division, Moorland-Spingarn Research Center, Howard University Library.

William W. Corcoran Collection. Manuscript Division, Library of Congress.

Madeline Vinton Dahlgren Collection. New York Public Library, New York, New York.

District of Columbia. Board of Education Personnel Records, Office of Director of Research and Evaluation.

District of Columbia Federation of Women's Clubs. Minutes and yearbooks, 1898–1905, District of Columbia Federation of Women's Clubs Archives.

Alice Cunningham Fletcher Collection. National Anthropological Archives, National Museum of Natural History.

Gregoria Fraser-Goins Collection. Manuscript Division, Moorland-Spingarn Research Center, Howard University Library.

President James A. Garfield Papers. Manuscript Division, Library of Congress.

Lucretia Garfield Collection. Manuscript Division, Library of Congress.

Georgetown University. Medical School Collection. Georgetown University Library.

————. Special Collections, Georgetown University Library.
George Washington University. Alumni Association Records, Special Collections, George Washington University Library.
————. Wright Collection of Individual Manuscripts. Special Collections, George Washington University Library.
Diary of Julia Green. In possession of Dr. Maesimond Panos, Tipp City, Ohio.
Phoebe Apperson Hearst Collection. Bancroft Library, University of California, Berkeley.
Sara L. Adelaide Johnson Collection, Manuscript Division, Library of Congress.
Federick West Lander and Jean Margaret Lander Collection. Manuscript Division, Library of Congress.
Mary Logan Collection. Manuscript Division, Library of Congress.
Anita Newcomb McGee Collection. Manuscript Division, Library of Congress.
Simon Newcomb Collection. Manuscript Division, Library of Congress.
New England Hospital for Women Collection. Sophia Smith Collection, Smith College, Northampton, Massachusetts.
Ainsworth Rand Spofford Collection. Manuscript Division, Library of Congress.
Matilda Coxe Stevenson Collection. National Anthropological Archives, National Museum of Natural History.
Mary Church Terrell Collection. Manuscript Division, Library of Congress.
Joseph M. Toner Collection. Manuscript Division, Library of Congress.
United States Census. 1880, 1900.
United States Department of the Interior. Application and Appointments File, Record Group 48, National Archives Building.
United States Department of the Treasury. Records of the Division of Appointments, Record Group 56, National Archives Building.
Washington. Board of Education Pesonnel Records, Department of Research Services.
Washington Hospital Center Archives. Washington Hospital Center.
Washingtoniana Collection. Martin Luther King Memorial Library.
Leigh Whipper Collection. Moorland-Spingarn Research Center, Howard University Library.

Announcements, Proceedings, Pamphlets, and Professional Journals

Alpha. Published by the Moral Education Society of Washington, vols. 7–13 (1881–88), Library of Congress, Washington, D. C.
American Institute of Homeopathy. *Directory,* 1925.
————. *Journal,* 1909–26.
————. *Transactions,* 1870–1909.
American Medical Association. *Transactions,* vols. 21–53 (1870–72).
Association of Collegiate Alumnae. *Bulletin,* 1889–99.
Biological Society of Washington. *Proceedings,* vol. 4–5 (1886–90).

Bibliography

Charity Organization Society of the District of Columbia. *Annual Report and Addresses,* 1883–86.

Chemical Society of Washington. *Bulletin,* 1884–95.

Colored Young Women's Christian Association. *Pamphlet,* 1907–9.

Columbian University. *Catalogue of the Officers and Students,* 1872–95.

———. *Catalogue,* 1895–1905.

———. National College of Medicine. *Annual Catalogue,* 1877–1903.

———. *Report of the Dean of the Corcoran Scientific School,* vol. 73, 1895.

———. *Report of the President,* 1897.

Council of Social Agencies of the District of Columbia and Vicinity. *Health and Hospital Survey,* 1929.

District of Columbia. Board of Charities. *Report,* 1900–10.

———. Board of Health. *Report of the Health Officer,* 1878–1900.

———. Charities Board. *Report on Charitable and Reformatory Institutions,* vol. 2., 1896.

———. Commissioner. *Report,* 1895–1910.

———. Department of Public Health. *Report,* 1873–1888.

———. Health Department. *Report,* 1870–71.

———. *Special Report of the Committee of Education on the Condition and Improvement of the Public Schools,* 1871.

———. Superintendent of Charities. *Report on Charities and Reformatory Institutions,,* 1891–1900.

———. Superintendent of Charities. *Report on Hospital and Dispensary Abuse in the City of Washington,* 1896.

District Of Columbia Federation of Women's Clubs. *Directory,* 1898–1905.

District of Columbia Medical Society. *Medical Annals,* 1907–70.

———. *National Medical Journal,* April 1870–Feb. 1872.

———. *National Medical Review,* March 1892–June 1901.

———. *Transactions,* 1874–1901.

———. *Transactions and Proceedings of the 75th Anniversary,* ed. Thomas C. Smith, 1894.

Georgetown University, College of Medicine. *Catalogue.* 1875–1900.

George Washington University. *Annual Report of the President,* 1907–14.

———. *Bulletin,* 1907–14.

———. *General Alumni Catalogue,* ed., W. J. Maxwell, 1919.

Hahnemannian Monthly, 1871.

Homoeopathic Free Dispensary Association. *Annual Report,* 1882–93, 1881–1925.

Howard University Medical Department. *Catalogue,* 1868/69–1924/25 (mixed nos.).

———. *Report of the President to the Secretary of the Interior,* 1892, 1895, 1896.

Maryland Medical Journal, 1895–96.

Mount Vernon Seminary for Girls. *Catalogue,* 1885–95.

National American Woman Suffrage Association. *Proceedings of the Twenty-fifth Annual Convention,* 1893.

National Homoeopathic Hospital. *Annual Report,* 1889–1910.
———. *Report of the Medical Staff to the Board of Trustees,* 1890.
National Society of the Daughters of the American Revolution. *American Monthly Magazine,* 1895–1905.
———. *Annual Report,* 1890–1927.
———. *Proceedings of the Continental Congress,* 1910–31.
National University Medical Department. *Announcement,* 1885, 1887, 1892.
United States Congress. House. *A Bill to Incorporate Garfield Hospital.* H. R. 1278. 47th Cong., 1st sess., 1882.
———. House. *A Bill Providing for the Admission of Women to Clinics and as Resident Students in Columbia Hospital for Women.* H. R. 2879, 47th Cong., 1st sess., 1882.
———. House of Representatives Appropriations Committee. *Hearings before the Senate of the House Committee on Appropriations in Charge of the District of Columbia Appropriations Bill for 1894.* Washington: U. S. Government Printing Office, 1892.
———. *Joint Select Committee to Investigate the Charities and Reformatory Institutions in the District of Columbia,* 1887.
Washington College of Law. *Announcement,* 1899–1900, 1904–16, 1940–41.
Washington Training School for Nurses. *Announcement,* 1882–92.
Woman's Clinic. *Pamphlet,* 1902, 1916.
———. *Souvenir.* 1892–93, 1905.
Woman's Medical College of Pennsylvania Alumnae Association. *Proceedings,* 1884.
Women's Anthropological Association. *Proceedings of the 100th Meeting,* 1893.
Women's Christian Association. *Annual Report,* 1871–1916.
Women's Hospital and Dispensary. *Pamphlet,* 1890–91.

Periodicals and Newspapers

The Colored American, 1898–1904.
Daily Morning Chronicle, 1870.
Glendale News Press, 1946.
Kate Field's Washington, 1891–1895.
New York Times, 1875–1900.
Washington Bee, 1885–1900.
Washington Evening Star, 1874–1905.
Washington Mirror, 1899–1901.
Washington Post, 1885–1905.
Washington Sunday Star, 1874–1905.
Washington Times, 1895–1915.
Woman's Column, 1890–94.
Woman's Journal, 1885–99.
Woman's Medical Journal, 1893–1919.
Woman's Tribune, 1892–1900.

Bibliography

Directories

American Biographical Directory, District of Columbia: Concise Biographies of its Prominent and Representative Contemporary Citizens, 1908–1909. Washington: Potomac Press, 1908.

American Medical Directory, 2nd ed.: *A Register of Legally Qualified Physicians of the United States and Canada.* New York: American Medical Association, 1909.

Biographical Cyclopedia of Representative Men of Maryland and the District of Columbia. Baltimore: National Biographical Publishing, 1879.

Boris, Joseph J., ed. *Who's Who in Colored America.* New York: Who's Who in Colored America, 1928.

Boyd, William A. *Boyd's Directory of the District of Columbia Together with a Compendium of its Government, Institutions, and its Trades.* Washington: William H. Boyd Publishing, 1860–1907.

———. *Boyd's Elite List: A Compilation of Selected Names of Residents of Washington City, District of Columbia and Ladies' Shopping Guide, Together with a List of the Members of the Most Prominent Clubs.* Washington: Elite Publishing, 1897.

Cattell, J. McKeen, and Jacques Cattell. *American Men of Science: A Biographical Dictionary.* New York: Science Press, 1927.

Cleaves Biographical Cyclopaedia of Homeopathic Physicians and Surgeons. Philadelphia: Galaxy Publishing, 1873.

Directory of Scientific Societies of Washington: Comprising the Anthropological, Biological, Chemical, Entomological, National Geographic, and Philosophical Societies. Washington: Joint Commission of the Scientific Societies of Washington, 1890, 1891, 1892.

Gibson, J. W., and W. H. Crogman. *The Colored American.* Atlanta: J. L. Nichols, 1902.

Hilyer, Andrew F. *The Twentieth Century Union League Directory: A Compilation of the Efforts of the Colored People of Washington for Social Betterment.* Washington: Union League, 1901.

Hodgkins, H. L. *Historical Catalogue of the Officers and Graduates of the Columbian University, Washington, D. C. 1821–1891.* Washington: Alumni Association, 1891.

James, Edward T., and Janet Wilson James, eds. *Notable American Women, 1607–1950: A Biographical Dictionary,* vols. 1–3. Cambridge: Harvard University Press, 1972.

Lappin, Robinson. *Lappin's Club Book of Washington, 1894. Containing the Names and Addresses of the Members of Thirty-one Prominent Clubs and Societies.* Washington: R. L. Lappin, 1894.

Logan, Rayford, and Michael Winston, eds. *Dictionary of American Negro Biography.* New York: W. W. Norton, 1982.

Mather, Frank L. *Who's Who of Colored Race,* vol. 1. Chicago: Gail Research, 1915.

Maxwell, W. J., ed. *George Washington University General Alumni Catalogue.* Washington: George Washington University, 1919.

Medical Directory of Physicians, Dentists, and Druggists in the District of Columbia and Maryland: Also a List of Trained Nurses. Baltimore: Guggenheim, Weil, 1901.
Polk's Directory of the District of Columbia. Detroit: R. L. Polk, 1907–30.
Polk's Medical and Surgical Directory of the United States. Detroit: R. L. Polk, 1886–90.
Polk's Medical and Surgical Register of the United States and Canada. Detroit: R. L. Polk, 1890–1920.
Richardson, Clement, ed. *The National Cyclopedia of the Colored Race.* Montgomery, Ala.: National Publishing, 1919.
Robinson, Wilhelmina S. *Historical Negro Biographies: International Library of Negro Life and History.* New York: New York Publishing, 1967.
Sherman's Directory and Ready Reference of the Colored Population in the District of Columbia. Washington: Sherman Directory, 1913.
Simmons, Rev. William J. *Men of Mark.* Baltimore: G. M. Rewell, 1887; reprint, Chicago: Johnson Publishing, 1970.
Who Was Who in America. Chicago: Marquis, 1960.
Who's Who in the Nation's Capital, 1921–1922. Washington: Consolidated Publishing, 1922.
Willard, Frances E., ed. *American Women: Fifteen Hundred Biographies with over 1,400 Portraits.* New York: Mast, Crowell, and Kirkpatrick, 1897.
———, and Mary Livermore. *American Women: A Comprehensive Encyclopedia of the Lives and Achievements of American Women of the Nineenth Century,* vol. 2. New York: Mast, Crowell, and Kirkpatrick, 1897.
Yenser, Thomas. *Who's Who in Colored America.* Brooklyn: Thomas Yenser, 1932.

Interviews and Correspondence

Gershon Bradford, patient of Dr. Julia Green. Washington, 10 April 1978.
Roderick Cox, Sidwell Friends School. Washington, 15 April 1978.
Dr. Dorothy Ferebee. Washington, 15 Jan. 1978.
Pauline Fisher, Haslup family. Washington, 15 May 1978.
Ruth H. Green, niece of Dr. Julia Green. Boston, 15 Oct. 1977.
Elmer Louis Kayser. George Washington University, Washington, 22 Sept. 1977, 15 Nov. 1978.
Kenneth Kelly, nephew of Dr. Ida Heiberger. Bethesda, Md., 15 March 1978.
G. F. A. Key, librarian, Washingtoniana Collection, Martin Luther King Memorial Library. Washington, 1978–80.
Elizabeth Newby, niece of Dr. Ida Heiberger. Washington, 18 Sept. 1978.
Dr. Margaret Nicholson. Washington, 29 July 1977.
Dr. Maesimond Panos, partner of Dr. Julia Green. Bethesda, Md. 21 Oct. 1977.
Dr. Margaret Parsons, great-niece of Dr. Mary Parsons. Colebrook, N. H., 18 Nov. 1978, 15 Dec. 1978.
Amalia Perry, niece of Dr. Amelia Erbach. Bethesda, Md., 2 May 1978.
Dolly Stackhouse, niece of Dr. Isabel Haslup Lamb. Washington, 15 May 1978.

Bibliography

OTHER SOURCES

Abrahams, Harold J. *Extinct Medical Schools of Baltimore, Maryland.* Baltimore: Maryland Historical Society, 1969.

Adams, Elizabeth Kemper. *Women Professional Workers.* Washington: U. S. Government Printing Office, 1921.

Adams, Herbert Baxter, ed. *Studies in History and Political Science,* series 8, no. 1. Baltimore: Johns Hopkins University Press, 189–91.

"A Mart for Women's Work," *Washington Post,* 17 March 1894.

Ames, Mary Clemmer. *Outline of Men, Women, and Things.* New York: Hurd and Houghton, 1873.

———. *Ten Years in Washington: Life and Scenes in the Nation's Capital as a Woman Sees Them.* Hartford: A. D. Worthington, 1874.

Antler, Joyce. "After College, What? New Graduates and the Family Claim," *American Quarterly* 32 (Fall 1980): 408–33.

Aptheker, Herbert, ed. *A Documentary History of the Negro People in the United States.* New York: Citadel Press, 1951.

Armeny, Susan. "Organized Nurses, Women Philanthropists, and the Intellectual Bases for Cooperation Among Women, 1898–1920," in *Nursing History: New Perspectives, New Possibilities,* ed. Ellen C. Lagemann. New York: Teachers College Press, 1983.

Aron, Cindy. "'To Barter Their Souls for Gold': Female Clerks in Federal Government Offices, 1862–1890." *Journal of American History* 67 (March 1981): 833–53.

Atwater, Edward A. "The Physicians of Rochester, New York, 1860–1910: A Study of Professional History, II." *Bulletin of the History of Medicine* 51 (Winter 1977): 93–106.

Auerbach, Jerold. *Unequal Justice: Lawyers and Social Change in Modern America.* New York: Oxford University Press, 1976.

Bardolph, Richard. "The Distinguished Negro in America, 1770–1936." *American Historical Review* 60 (April 1955): 527–47.

Barus, Annie Howes. *Health Statistics of Women College Graduates: Report of a Special Committee of the Association of Collegiate Alumnae.* Boston: Massachusetts Bureau of Statistics of Labor, 1885.

Beasley, Maurene H. *The First Women Washington Correspondents.* George Washington University Studies 4, Washington: George Washington University, 1976.

Bernheim, Bertram. *The Story of the Johns Hopkins: Four Great Doctors and the Medical School They Created.* New York: Whittlesly House, 1948.

Billings, Mrs. Elden E. "Early Women Journalists of Washington." In *Records of the Columbia Historical Society of Washington, D. C., 1966–68,* ed. Francis C. Rosenberger. Washington: The Society, 1969, 84–89.

Billings, John S., and Henry M. Hurd, eds. *Hospitals, Dispensaries and Nursing.* Baltimore: Johns Hopkins University Press, 1894.

Billingsly, Andrew. *Black Families in White America.* Englewood Cliffs, N. J.: Prentice-Hall, 1968.

Birmingham, Stephen. *Certain People: America's Black Elite.* Boston: Little, Brown, 1977.

Bittenbinder, Ada M. "Women in the Law." In *Woman's Work in America,* ed. Annie Nathan Meyers. New York: Henry Holt, 1891; reprint, New York: Arno Press, 1972, 218–44.

Black, Winfred. *The Life and Personality of Phoebe Hearst.* San Francisco: J. H. Nash, 1928.

Blair, Karen. *The Clubwoman as Feminist: True Womanhood Redefined, 1886–1914.* New York: Holmes and Meier, 1980.

Blake, John. "Women and Medicine in Ante-Bellum America." *Bulletin of the History of Medicine* 39 (March–April 1965): 99–123.

Blaxall, Martha, and Barbara Reagan, eds. *Women and the Workplace: The Implications of Occupational Segregation.* Chicago: University of Chicago Press, 1976.

Bledstein, Burton J. *The Culture of Professionlism: The Middle Class and the Developmemnt of Higher Education in America.* New York: W. W. Norton, 1976.

Bloomfield, Maxwell. *American Lawyers in a Changing Society, 1776–1876.* Cambridge: Harvard University Press, 1976.

Bolton, Henrietta Irving. "Women in Science." *Popular Science* 53 (May–Oct. 1898): 506–11.

Bonner, Thomas. *Medicine in Chicago, 1850–1950: A Chapter in the Social and Scientific Development of the City.* Madison: American History Research Center, University of Wisconsin Press, 1957.

Bousefield, M. O. "An Account of Physicians of Color in the United States." *Bulletin of the History of Medicine* 17 (Jan. 1945): 61–84.

Breckinridge, Sophonisba. *Women in the Twentieth Century: A Study of Their Political, Social, and Economic Activities.* Chicago: Recent Social Trends Monographs, 1933; reprint, New York: Arno Press, 1972.

Briggs, Emily Edson. *The Olivia Letters, Being Some History of Washington City for Forty Years as Told by the Letters of a Newspaper Correspondent.* New York: Neale Publishing, 1906.

Brown, Hallie Quinn. *Homespun Heroines.* Xenia, Ohio: Aldine Publishing House, 1935.

Brown, Letitia Woods. *Free Negroes in the District of Columbia, 1790–1846.* New York: Oxford University Press, 1972.

———. "Residence Patterns of Negroes in the District of Columbia, 1800–1860." In *Records of the Columbia Historical Society of Washington, D.C.,* ed. Francis C. Rosenberger. Washington: Columbia Historical Society, 1971, 66–79.

Brown, Sara W. "Colored Women Physicians." *The Southern Workman* 52 (Dec. 1923): 580–93.

Brownlee, S. "Where Is the Professional Woman?" *Woman Lawyers Journal* 53 (Winter 1967): 14–15.

Brumberg, Joan Jacobs, and Nancy Tomes. "Women in the Professions: A Research Agenda for American Historians." *Reviews in American History* 10 (June 1982): 275–96.

Bibliography

Buckler, Helen. *Dr. Dan: Pioneer in American Surgery.* Boston: Little, Brown, 1954.

Bunting, Ross R. "The Doctor as Portrayed in Fiction," *North Carolina Medical Journal* 23 (Jan. 1889): 100–16.

Busey, Samuel C. "Howard University." *National Medical Journal* 2 (Sept. 1871): 275.

———. *Personal Reminiscences and Recollections of Forty-Six Years' Membership in the Medical Society of the District of Columbia.* Philadelphia: Dornan Printers, 1895.

Camalier, C. Willard. *One Hundred Years of Dental Progress in the Nation's Capital.* Washington: District of Columbia Dental Society, 1966.

Campbell, Barbara Kuhn. *The "Liberated Woman" of 1914: Prominent Women in the Progressive Era.* Ann Arbor: University Microfilms International Research Press, 1979.

Carpenter, Francis G., ed. *Carp's Washington.* Ann Arbor: Authorized Reproductions by Microfilm, 1970.

Cartwright, Lillian Kaufman. "Continuity and Discontinuity in the Careers of a Sample of Young Women Physicians." *Journal of the American Medical Women's Association* 32 (Sept. 1977): 318–21.

Carusi, Charles. "Higher Education in the District of Columbia." In *Washington: Past and Present*, ed. John C. Proctor. New York: Lewes Historical Publishing, 1932, 458–94.

Cathell, Daniel W. *The Physician Himself and What He Should Add to His Scientific Acquirements.* Baltimore: Cushings and Bailey, 1882.

Chafe, William. *The American Woman: Her Changing Historical, Social and Economic Role, 1920–1970.* New York: Oxford University Press, 1972.

Chaff, Sandra, et al., eds. *Women in Medicine: A Bibliography of the Literature on Women Physicians.* Metuchen, N.J.: Scarecrow Press, 1977.

Chesney, Alan M. *The John Hopkins Hospital and the Johns Hopkins School of Medicine:—the Early Years*, vol. 1, *1867–1893.* Baltimore: Johns Hopkins University Press, 1943.

Chittenden, Elizabeth. "As We Climb." *Negro History Bulletin* 38 (Feb.–March 1975): 351.

Coale, Edith Seville. "Women Physicians of the District of Columbia." In *Washington: Past and Present*, ed. John C. Proctor. New York: Lewes Historical Publishing, 1932, 654–62.

Cobb, William Montague. *The First Negro Medical Society: A History of the Medico-Chirurgical Society of the District of Columbia, 1884–1939.* Washington: Associated Publishers, 1939.

———. *Progress and Portents for the Negro in Medicine.* New York: National Association for the Advancement of Colored People, 1948.

Cooper, Anna Julia. *A Voice From the South by a Black Woman of the South.* Xenia, Ohio: Aldine Printing House, 1892; reprint, New York: Negro Universities Press, 1969.

Corea, Gena. *The Hidden Malpractice.* New York: William Morrow, 1977.

Corrothers, Thomasene. "Lucy Ellen Moten, 1851–1933." *Journal of Negro History* 19 (Jan. 1934): 102–7.

Coues, Elliot. *"A Woman in the Case": Address Delivered at the Annual Commencement of Columbian University Medical Department. 16 March 1887.* Washington: George Washington University Library, 1976.

Coulter, Harris. *Divided Legacy,* vol. 3. Washington: McGrath Publishing, 1973.

Croly, Jane Cunningham. *The History of the Woman's Club Movement in America.* New York: H. G. Allen, 1898.

Cromwell, John W. "The First Negro Churches in the District of Columbia." *Journal of Negro History* 7 (Jan. 1922): 64–106.

Crossette, George. *Founders of the Cosmos Club of Washington: A Collection of Biographical Sketches and the Likenesses of the Sixty Founders.* Washington: Cosmos Club, 1966.

Dabney, Lillian G. *The History of Schools for Negroes in the District of Columbia, 1807–1947.* Washington: Catholic University of America Press, 1949.

Dahlgreen, Madeleine Vinton. *Etiquette of Social Life in Washington.* Washington: J. A. Winburger, 1873.

"Daisy Orleman." *Medical Woman's Journal* 29 (Aug. 1922): 185.

Daniel, Sadie Iola. *Women Builders.* Washington: Associated Publishers, 1931.

Daniels, William B. "Albert Freeman Africanus King." *Medical Annals of the District of Columbia* 29 (Sept. 1950): 499.

Dannett, Sylvia G. *Profiles of Negro Womanhood,* vol. 1, *1619–1900.* Yonkers, N.Y.: Educational Heritage, 1964.

Darnell, Regna D. "The Development of American Anthropology, 1879–1920: From the Bureau of American Ethnology to Franz Boas," Ph.D. diss. University of Pennsylvania, 1969.

Davis, Alan. *Spearheads for Reform.* New York: Oxford University Press, 1967.

Davis, Elizabeth Lindsay. *Lifting as They Climb: The History of the National Association of Colored Women.* Washington: National Association of Colored Women, 1933.

Davis, Lenwood G., ed. *The Black Woman in American Society: A Selected Annotated Bibliography.* Boston: G. K. Hall, 1975.

Davis, Marianna W. ed. *Contributions of Black Women to America,* vols. 1–2. Columbia, S. C.: Kenday Press, 1982.

Davis, Michael, and Andrew Warner. "The Beginnings of Dispensaries." *Boston Medical and Surgical Journal* 178 (May 1918): 712–15.

DeCaindry, William A., Marcus Benjamin, and Cyrus Adler, eds. *The Twenty-fifth Anniversary of the Founding of the Cosmos.* Washington: The Cosmos, 1904.

de Graffenreid, Mary Clare. *The Needs of Self-Supporting Women.* Studies in History and Political Science, series 8, no.1, ed. Herbert Baxter Adams. Baltimore: Johns Hopkins University Press, 1890–91.

Desha, Mary. *The True Story of the Origins of the National Society of the Daughters of the American Revolution.* Washington: Daughters of the American Revolution [?], 1892 [?].

Douglas, Ann. *The Feminization of American Culture*. New York: Alfred A. Knopf, 1977.

Drachman, Virginia. *Hospital with a Heart: Women Doctors and the Paradox of Separatism at the New England Hospital, 1862–1969*. Ithaca: Cornell University Press, 1984.

DuBois, Ellen. *Feminism and Suffrage*. Ithaca: Cornell University Press, 1978.

Duffy, John. *The Healers: The Rise of the Medical Establishment*. New York: McGraw Hill, 1976.

Duncan, Mrs. Robert, ed. *In Washington: The National Society of the Daughters of the American Revolution*. Washington: The National Society of the Daughters of the American Revolution, 1965.

Dunnahoo, Terry. *Before the Supreme Court: The Story of Belva A. Lockwood*. Boston: Houghton Mifflin, 1974.

Dupree, A. Hunter. *Science in the Federal Government: A History of Policies and Activities to 1940*. Cambridge: Harvard University Press, 1957.

Durkin, Joseph T. *Georgetown University: The Middle Years 1840–1900*. Washington: Georgetown University Press, 1963.

Dyson, Walter. *Founding the School of Medicine of Howard University, 1868–1873*. Howard University Studies in History 10. Washington: Howard University Press, 1929.

———. *Howard University: The Capstone of Negro Education: A History, 1867–1940*. Washington: The Graduate School, Howard University, 1941.

Eagle, Mary K. Oldham, ed. *The Congress of Women*. Chicago: W. B. Conkey, 1893; reprint, New York: Arno Press, 1974.

Edwards, Gilbert Franklin. *The Negro Professional Class*. Glencoe, Ill.: Free Press, 1959.

Epstein, Barbara. *The Politics of Domesticity: Women, Evangelism and Temperance in Nineteenth Century America*. Middletown, Conn.: Wesleyan University Press, 1981.

Epstein, Cynthia Fuchs. "Motivation versus Social Structure." In *Women in the Professions*, ed. Laurily Kerr Epstein. Lexington, Mass.: D. C. Heath, 1975.

———. *Woman's Place: Options and Limits in Professional Careers*. Berkeley: University of California Press, 1970.

Epstein, Laurily Kerr, ed. *Women in the Professions*. Lexington, Mass.: D. C. Heath, 1975.

Etzioni, Amatai, ed. *The Semi-Professions and their Organization: Teaching, Nursing, Social Work*. Glencoe, Ill.: Free Press, 1967.

"First Woman M. D. Here Fought a Pioneer Battle." *Washington Post*, 6 June 1934.

Fishbein, Morris. *A History of the American Medical Association, 1847–1947*. Philadelphia: Saunders, 1947.

Flack, James Kirkpatrick. *Desideratum in Washington: The Intellectual Community in the Capital City, 1870–1900*. Cambridge, Mass.: Schenkman Publishing, 1975.

Fox, Mary Virginia. *Lady for the Defense: A Biography of Belva Lockwood*. New York: Harcourt Brace Jovanovich, 1975.

Frankfort, Roberta. *Collegiate Women: Domesticity and Careers in Turn-of-the-Century America.* New York: New York University Press, 1976.

Freedman, Estelle. "Separatism as a Strategy: Female Institution Building and American Feminism, 1870–1930." *Feminist Studies* 5 (Fall 1979): 512–29.

Garrison, Dee. *Apostles of Culture: The Public Librarian and American Society, 1876–1920.* New York: Free Press, 1979.

———. "The Feminization of Librarianship." In *Clio's Consciousness Raised,* ed. Mary Hartman and Lois Banner. New York: Octagon Press, 1972.

Giddings, Paula. *When and Where I Enter.* New York: William Morrow, 1984.

Goins, Gregoria Fraser, "Pioneer Negro Women in Medicine," unpublished paper in vertical file, "Physicians, Women," at Howard University Medical Library.

Goldowsky, Siebert. "Mary Edwards Walker." *Rhode Island Medical Journal* 9 (March 1976): 118–42.

Gordon, Linda. *Women's Body, Women's Right: A Social History of Birth Control in America.* New York: Viking, 1976.

Gordon, Michael, ed. *The American Family in Social and Historical Perspective.* New York: St. Martin's Press, 1973.

Green, Constance McLaughlin. *The Secret City: A History of Race Relations in the Nation's Capital.* Princeton: Princeton University Press, 1967.

———. *Washington, A History of the Capital, 1800–1950,* vol. 1, 2. Princeton: Princeton University Press, 1963.

Hamaker, W. O. "Recent Advances in Medical Education in the United States." *Chautauquan* 24 (Nov. 1896): 177–81.

Hamilton, Alice. *Exploring the Dangerous Trades: The Autobiography of Alice Hamilton, M.D.* Boston: Little, Brown, 1943.

Hamilton, Tulia. "The National Association of Colored Women, 1896–1920," Ph.D. diss., Emory University, 1978.

Harley, Sharon. "Black Women in the District of Columbia, 1890–1920: Their Economic, Social, and Institutional Activities, Ph.D. diss., Howard University, 1981.

———. and Rosalyn Terborg-Penn, eds. *The Afro-American Woman.* Port Washington, N. Y.: Kennikat Press, 1978.

Hartman, Mary, and Lois Banner, eds. *Clio's Consciousness Raised.* New York: Octagon Press, 1972.

Haskell, Thomas. *The Emergence of Professional Social Science.* Urbana: University of Illinois Press, 1976.

Hathaway, Grace. *Fate Rides a Tortoise: A Biography of Ellen Spencer Mussey.* Philadelphia: John C. Winston, 1937.

Hatter, Henrietta R. "History of the Miner Teachers' College," M.A. thesis, Howard University, 1939.

Hawkins, Cora. *Buggies, Blizzards, and Babies.* Ames: Iowa State University Press, 1971.

Haycock, Robert L., "Sixty Years of the Public Schools of the District of Columbia, 1885–1945." In *Records of the Columbia Historical Society,* ed. Francis C. Rosenberger. Washington: The Society, 1949, 29–92.

Bibliography

Hayes, Laurence. *The Negro Federal Government Worker: A Study of His Classification in the District of Columbia, 1883–1938*, Howard University Studies in the Social Sciences 3. Washington: Howard University Press, 1941.

Hill, Joseph A. *Women in Gainful Occupations, 1870–1920: A Study of the Trend of Recent Changes in Numbers, Occupations, Distribution, and Family Relationships of Women Registered in the Census.* Census Monographs. Washington: U. S. Government Printing Office, 1929.

Himes, Norman. *Medical History of Contraception.* Baltimore: Williams and Wilkins, 1936; reprint, New York: Gamut Press, 1963.

Hinds, Clara Bliss. *Child Growth.* Washington: Women's Anthropological Society, 1886.

Holmes, Dwight O. " Fifty Years of Howard University." *Journal of Negro History* 3 (April, 1918): 128–38.

Holt, Thomas, Cassandra Smith-Parker, and Rosalyn Terborg-Penn, *A Special Mission: The Story of Freedman's Hospital, 1862–1962.* Washington: Howard University Press, 1975.

Hooks, Janet M. "General Trends in the Numbers and Characteristics of Women Workers." In *Women's Occupations Through Seven Decades.* Women's Bureau Bulletin no. 218. Washington: U. S. Government Printing Office, 1947.

Hosmer, Katherine. "What Women Have Done in Washington's City Affairs." *Municipal Affairs* 2 (Sept. 1898): 514–23.

Howe, Daniel W., ed. *Victorian America.* Philadelphia: University of Pennsylvania Press, 1976.

Hummer, Patricia M. *The Decade of Elusive Promise: Professional Women in the United States, 1920–1930,* Studies in American History and Culture, 5. Ann Arbor: UMI-Research Press, 1979.

Hurd-Meade, Kate C. *Medical Women of America.* New York: Froben Press, 1933.

Hutchins, Stilson, and Joseph West Moore, eds. *The National Capital, Past and Present.* Washington: Post Publishing, 1885.

"Inception and Organization of the National Society of the Daughters of the American Revolution," *Report of the National Society of the Daughters of the American Revolution,* vol. 1. Washington: Daughters of the American Revolution, 1893.

Ingle, Edward. *The Negro in the District of Columbia.* Johns Hopkins Studies in Historical and Related Sciences, 11th series. Baltimore: Johns Hopkins University Press, 1893, 3–4.

Jacobi, Mary Putnam. "Woman in Medicine." In *Woman's Work in America,* ed. Annie Nathan Meyers. New York: Henry Holt, 1891; reprint, New York: Arno Press, 1972, 139–205.

Jensen, Richard. "Family, Career, and Reform: Women Leaders of the Progressive Era." In *The American Family in Social and Historical Perspective,* ed. Michael Gordon. New York: St. Martin's Press, 1973.

Johnson, Leonard W. "History of the Education of the Negro Physician." *Journal of Medical Education* 42 (May 1967): 439–46.

Johnson, William R. "Education and Professional Life Styles: Law and Medicine in the Nineteenth Century." *History of Education Quarterly* 14 (Summer 1974): 185–207.

Johnston, Allan J. "Surviving Freedom: The Black Community of Washington, D. C., 1860–1880," Ph.D. diss., Duke University, 1980.

Jones, Beverly Washington. "Quest for Equality: The Life of Mary Church Terrell, 1863–1954," Ph.D. diss., University of North Carolina, 1980.

Judd, Neil P. *The Bureau of American Ethnology: A Partial History.* Norman: University of Oklahoma Press, 1967.

Kaufman, Martin. "The Admission of Women to Nineteenth-Century American Medical Societies." *Bulletin of the History of Medicine* 50 (Summer 1976): 251–60.

———. *Homeopathy in America: The Rise and Fall of a Medical Heresy.* Baltimore: Johns Hopkins University Press, 1971.

Kayser, Elmer Louis. *Bricks without Straw: The Evolution of George Washington University.* New York: Appleton-Century-Crofts, 1970.

———. *A Medical Center: The Institutional Development of Medical Education in George Washington University.* Washington: George Washington University, 1973.

Keen, William W. *Addresses and Other Papers.* Philadelphia: W. B. Saunders, 1905.

Kellerman, Mrs. W. A. "Presidential Address." *Journal of the National Science Club* 1 (May 1898): 9.

Kenny, John A. *The Negro in Medicine.* Tuskegee, Ala.: Tuskegee Institute Press, 1912

Kett, Joseph F. *The Formation of the American Medical Profession: The Role of Institutions, 1780–1860.* New Haven: Yale University Press, 1968.

King, Albert Freeman Africanus. "The Physiological Argument in Obstetrical Studies." *American Journal of Obstetrics and Diseases of Women and Children* 21 (April 1888): 3–17.

King, William H. *The History of Homoeopathy and Its Institutions in America.* New York: Lewes Publishing, 1905.

Kinney, Dita H. "Dr. Anita McGee and What She Has Done for the Nursing Profession." *Trained Nurse and Hospital Review* 26 (March 1901): 129–34.

Kittredge, Elizabeth. "Woman's Medical Society of the District of Columbia." *Journal of the American Medical Women's Association* 6 (Nov. 1951): 443–45.

Kober, George M. *Charitable and Reformatory Institutions in the District of Columbia: A History of the Development of Public Charities and Reformatory Institutions and Agencies in the District of Columbia.* Washington: U. S. Government Printing Office, 1927.

Kohlstedt, Sally Gregory. "In From the Periphery: American Women in Science, 1830–1880." *Signs* 4 (Autumn 1978): 81–96.

———. "Maria Mitchell: The Advancement of Women in Science." *New England Quarterly* 51 (March 1978): 39–59.

Kraditor, Eileen S., ed. *Up from the Pedestal.* Chicago: Quadrangle Books, 1968.

Bibliography

Lagemann, Ellen C., ed. *Nursing History: New Perspectives, New Possibilities.* New York: Teachers College Press, 1983.

Lamb, Daniel S., ed. *History of the Medical Society of the District of Columbia, 1817–1909.* Washington: The Medical Society, 1909.

———, ed. *Howard University Medical Department: A Historical, Biographical, and Statistical Souvenir.* Washington: R. Beresford, 1900.

———. "The Story of the Anthropological Society of *Washington.*" *American Anthropologist* 8 (July–Sept. 1906): 564–79.

Landon, Fred. "Canadian Negroes and John Brown." *Journal of Negro History* 6 (April 1921): 174–82.

Langson, John M. *From Virginia Plantation to the Nation's Capital.* Hartford, Conn.: American Publishing, 1894.

Lankton, F. M. "The Medical Profession for Women." In *The Congress of Women,* ed. Mary K. Oldham Eagle. Chicago: W. B. Conkey, 1893; reprint, New York: Arno Press, 1974.

Lasch, Christopher. *The New Radicalism in America, 1889–1963:* New York: Alfred A. Knopf, 1965.

Leaman, J. Stanley. *The Woman Citizen: Social Feminism in the 1920s.* Urbana: University of Illinois Press, 1973.

"Learned Women of Washington." *Washington Evening Star,* 3 Aug. 1888, 11.

Leavitt, Judith Walzer, ed. *Women and Health in America.* Madison: University of Wisconsin Press, 1984.

Lerner, Gerda, ed. *Black Women in White America: A Documentary History.* New York: Pantheon Books, 1972.

Lewis, Janice Sumler. "The Forten-Purvis Women of Philadelphia and the American Anti-Slavery Crusade." *Negro History Bulletin* 66 (Winter 1981–82): 281–88.

———. "The Fortens of Philadelphia: An Afro-American Family and Nineteenth-Century Reform," Ph.D. diss., Georgetown University, 1978.

Lindsay, Inabel. "Participation of Negroes in the Establishment of Welfare Services, 1865–1900," Ph.D. diss., University of Pittsburgh, 1958.

Lockwood, Belva A. "How I Ran for the Presidency." *National Magazine* 27 (Oct. 1902-March 1903): 728–33.

———. "My Efforts to Become a Lawyer." *Lippincott's* (June 1888): 215–29.

Lockwood, Mary Smith. *Yesterdays in Washington,* vol. 2. Rosalyn, Va.: Commonwealth, 1914.

Loewenberg, Bert J., and Ruth Bogin, eds. *Black Women in Nineteenth-Century Life: Their Thoughts, Their Words, Their Feelings.* University Park: Pennsylvania State University Press, 1976.

Logan, Mary. *Our National Government and Life and Scenes in Our National Capital.* Minneapolis: Baldwin, 1908.

———. *The Part Taken by Women in American History.* Wilmington, Del.: Perry Nalle Publishing, 1912.

Logan, Rayford W. *Howard University: The First One Hundred Years, 1867–1967.* New York: New York University Press, 1969.

Loguen, Jermaine. *The Rev. J. Loguen as a Slave and a Free Man.* Syracuse: J. G. K. Truair, 1866.
Loomis, Silas J. "Vitality in American Women." *National Medical Journal* 1 (April 1870): 9–15.
Lopate, Carol. *Women in Medicine.* Baltimore: Johns Hopkins University Press, 1968.
Lovejoy, Esther Pohl. *Women Doctors of the World.* New York: Macmillan, 1957.
Lubove, Roy. *The Professional Altruist: The Emergence of Social Work as a Career, 1880–1930.* Cambridge: Harvard University Press, 1965.
Ludlam, R. "Annual Address: Woman and Homoeopathy." *American Institute of Homoeopathy Proceedings* 1 (March 1869): 77–93.
Lurie, Nancy Ostereich. "Women in Early American Anthropology," in *Pioneers of American Anthropology,* ed. June Helm MacNeish. Seattle: University of Washington Press, 1966, 29–81.
Lutz, Alma. *Created Equal: A Biography of Elizabeth Cady Stanton.* New York: John Day, 1940; reprint, Octagon Press, 1973.
Lutzer, Edythe. *Women Gain a Place in Medicine.* New York: McGraw Hill, 1969.
MacNeish, June Helm, ed. *Pioneers of American Anthropology.* Seattle: University of Washington Press, 1966.
Madsen, David. *The National University.* Detroit: Wayne State University Press, 1966.
Major, Gerri. *Black Society.* Chicago: Johnson Publishing, 1976.
Majors, Monroe. *Noted Negro Women.* Chicago: Donohue and Henneberry, 1893.
Marble, Ella, M. S. "Caroline Winslow's Birthday Party," *Woman's Journal,* 10 Dec. 1892.
———. "The First Pan-American Medical Congress and Some of the Women Who Took Part." *Woman's Medical Journal* 1 (Sept. 1893): 199–200.
———. "National University Welcomes Women." *Woman's Journal,* 17 Dec. 1892.
———. "The Real Facts." *Woman's Medical Journal* 1 (July 1893): 149.
———. "Women and Columbian University: A Reply to the Faculty from the ProReNata Club of this City." *Washington Post,* 29 Jan. 1893.
———. "Women Physicians and Surgeons: "Biographical Series." *Woman's Medical Journal* 5 (March 1896): 69.
———. "Women's Contribution to Medical Literature." *Woman's Medical Journal* 5 (March 1896): 59–63.
Markowitz, Gerald E. and David K. Rosner. "Doctors in Crisis: A Study of the Use of Medical Education Reform to Establish Modern Professional Elitism in Medicine." *American Quarterly* 25 (March 1973): 83–207.
Marritt, Cora Begley. "Nineteenth-Century Associations of Medical Women: The Beginnings of a Movement." *Journal of the American Medical Women's Association* 32 (Dec. 1977): 469–74.
Marzolf, Marian. *Up from the Footnote.* New York: Hastings House, 1977.
Mason, Otis T. *What Is Anthropology? A Lecture Given at the National Museum,*

18 March 1882. Washington: Women's Anthropological Society, n.d., probably 1885.

Mattfield, Jacqueline, and Carol G. Van Aken. *Women and the Scientific Professions.* Cambridge: MIT Press, 1965.

McCracken, Elizabeth. *The Women of America.* New York: Macmillan, 1904.

McGee, Anita N. *General Report of the Recording Secretary.* Washington: Women's Anthropological Society, 25 Feb. 1889.

———. *Organizational and Historical Sketch.* Washington: Women's Anthropological Society, 1889.

———. "Women Nurses in the American Army." *Woman's Medical Journal* 10 (Feb. 1900): 47–53.

McMillan, Lucille Foster. *Women in the Federal Service.* Washington: U. S. Civil Service Commission, 1938.

Meyers, Annie Nathan, ed. *Woman's Work in America.* New York: Henry Holt, 1891; reprint, New York: Arno Press, 1972.

Miller, Kelly. "Historic Background of the Negro Physician." *Journal of Negro History* 1 (April 1916): 99–109.

Miller, M. Sammy. "Slavery in an Urban Area: The District of Columbia." *Negro History Bulletin* 37 (Aug. 1974): 293–95.

"The Minervas of Washington." *Washington Post,* 6 July 1899.

Mohr, James C. *Abortion in America: Origins and Evolution of National Policy.* New York: Oxford University Press, 1978.

Morais, Herbert M. *The History of the Afro-American in Medicine.* Cornwell Heights, Penn.: Association for the Study of Afro-American Life and History, 1976.

Morantz-Sanchez, Regina. "Making Women Modern: Middle Class Women and Health Reform in Nineteenth-Century America." *Journal of Social History* 10 (June 1977): 388–409.

———. "Nineteenth-Century Health Reform and Women: A Program of Self-Help." In *Medicine without Doctors,* ed. Guenter B. Risse et al. New York: Watson Publishing International, 1977.

———. *Sympathy and Science.* New York: Oxford University Press, 1985.

———, and Sue Zschoche. "Professionalism, Feminism, and Gender Roles: A Comparative Study of Nineteenth-Century Medical Therapeutics." *Journal of American History* 67 (Dec. 1980): 568–88.

Morgan, Laura Puffer. "Report on the Status of Women in the Classified Civil Service of the United States Government in the District of Columbia." *Journal of the Association of Collegiate Alumnae* 1 (April 1913).

Morton, Rosalie Slaughter. *A Woman Surgeon.* New York: Frederick A. Stokes, 1937.

Mossell, Gertrude. *The Work of the Afro-American Woman.* Philadelphia: G. S. Ferguson, 1894; reprint, Freeport, N. Y.: Books for Libraries Press, 1971.

Myers, Denys. "Women and the Club." *Cosmos Club Bulletin* 2 (Oct. 1958): 2–5.

Nelson, Bernard. "Miner Teachers' College: The First Century, 1851–1951," M.A. thesis, District of Columbia Teachers' College, 1973.

Nelson, Henry L. "Washington Society." *Harper's New Monthly Magazine* 86 (March 1893): 586–96.

Newcomb, Simon. *Reminscences of an Astronomer.* Boston: Houghton Mifflin, 1903.

Newman, Louise. *Men's Ideas/ Women's Realities: Popular Science, 1870–1915.* New York: Pergamon Press. 1985.

Nichols, John B. *The History of the Medical Society of the District of Columbia,* part 2, *1833–1944.* Washington: The Medical Society, 1947.

Noble, Jeanne. *Beautiful Also Are the Souls of My Black Sisters: A History of Black Women in America.* Englewood Cliffs, N. J.: Prentice-Hall, 1978.

———. *The Negro Woman's College Education.* New York: Teachers College of Columbia University, 1956.

O'Hara, Leo James. "An Emerging Profession: Philadelphia Medicine, 1860–1900," Ph.D. diss., University of Pennsylvania, 1976.

Peck, George B. "Homoeopathy in the United States." *Hahnemannian Monthly* 35 (Sept. 1900): 559–66.

Pivar, David. *Purity Crusade: Sexual Morality and Social Control, 1868–1900.* Westport, Conn.: Greenwood Press, 1973.

Platt, Lois Irene. "Women Doctors in Washington." *Journal of the American Medical Women's Association* 6 (Nov. 1951): 446–49.

Powell, Frances J. "A Study of the Structure of the Freed Black Family in Washington, D. C.," Ph.D. diss., Catholic University of America, 1980.

Prentiss, Daniel W. *Address Delivered at the Opening of the Medical Department of the Columbian University with a Sketch of the Life and Work of Edward T. Fristoe. Oct.1, 1892.* Washington: The National Medical Review, 1892.

Proctor, John C. "Medico-Body More than a Century Old." *Sunday Star* 29 April 1934.

———, ed. *Washington: Past and Present.* New York: Lewes Historical Publishing, 1932.

Rayne, Mrs. M. L. *What Can a Woman Do: Or Her Position in the Business and Literary World.* Petersburgh, N. Y.: Eagle Publishing, 1893.

Reitzes, Dietrich. *Negroes and Medicine.* Cambridge, Mass.: Harvard University Press, 1958.

Rhetta, B. M. "Negro Physicians of Baltimore." *Opportunity* 1 (May 1923): 21–22.

Richardson, Charles W. "Hospitals." In *Washington: Past and Present,* ed. John C. Proctor. New York: Lewes Historical Publishing, 1932.

Risse, Guenter B., ed. *Medicine without Doctors.* New York: Watson Publishing International, 1977.

Rosen, George. *The Structure of American Medical Practice, 1875–1941,* ed. Charles E. Rosenberg. Philadelphia: University of Pennsylvania Press, 1983.

Rosenberg, Charles E. "Inward Vision and Outward Glance: The Shaping of the American Hospital, 1880–1914." *Bulletin of the History of Medicine* 53 (Fall 1979): 346–91.

———. "The Practice of Medicine in New York City a Century Ago." *Bulletin of the History of Medicine* 41 (May-June 1967): 223–53.

———. "Social Class and Medical Care in Nineteenth-Century America: The Rise and Fall of the Dispensary." *Journal of the History of Medicine and Allied Sciences* 29 (Jan. 1974): 32–54.

Rosenberger, Francis C, ed. *Records of the Columbia Historical Society of Washington, D. C., 1966–68.* Washington: The Society, 1969.

Rossiter, Margaret W. "Sexual Segregation in the Sciences: Some Data and a Model." *Signs* 4 (Autumn 1978): 146–51.

———. "Women Scientists in America before 1920." *American Scientist* 62 (May-June 1974): 312–23.

———. *Women Scientists in America: Struggles and Strategies to 1940.* Baltimore: Johns Hopkins University Press, 1982.

Rothstein, William G. *American Physicians in the Nineteenth Century: From Sects to Science.* Baltimore: Johns Hopkins University Press, 1971.

Rottier, Catherine M. "Ellen Spencer Mussey and the Washington College of Law." *Maryland Historical Magazine* 69 (Winter 1974): 361–82.

Ruffin, Josephine St. Pierre. "Presidential Address." *Woman's Era* 2 (May 1895): 14.

Sallume, Xarifa, and Frank Notestein. "Trends in the Size of Families Completed Prior to 1910 in Various Social Classes." *American Journal of Sociology* 38 (Nov. 1932): 398–408.

Samuels, Ernest. *Henry Adams: The Middle Years.* Cambridge: Harvard University Press, 1958.

Savage, Charles C. "Dispensaries, Historically Considered." In *Hospitals, Dispensaries and Nursing,* ed. John S. Billings and Henry M. Hurd. Baltimore: Johns Hopkins University Press, 1894.

Schneider, Margaret. "Survey of Women Graduates from Cincinnati Medical Colleges, 1873–1953." *Journal of the American Medical Women's Association* 9 (Dec. 1954): 400–10.

Scruggs, Lawson A. *Women of Distinction.* Raleigh: L. A. Scruggs, 1893.

Sennott, Mrs. William B., and Mrs. Arthur G. Davis, eds. *History of the District of Columbia Federation of Women's Clubs, 1894–1962.* Washington: District of Columbia Federation of Women's Clubs, 1962.

"Should Professional Women Marry?" *Women's Medical Journal* 2 (Feb. 1894): 38–39.

Shryock, Richard H. *Medicine and Society in America, 1660–1860.* Ithaca: Cornell University Press, 1960.

———. *Medicine in America: Historical Essays.* Baltimore: Johns Hopkins University Press, 1966.

———. *Medical Licensing in America, 1650–1965.* Baltimore: Johns Hopkins University Press, 1967.

———. "Women in American Medicine." *Journal of the American Medical Women's Association* 5 (Sept. 1950): 371–79.

Sklar, Kathryn Kish. "All Hail Pure Cold Water!" In *Women and Health in*

America, ed. Judith Walzer Leavitt. Madison: University of Wisconsin Press, 1984, 246–54.

Slauson, Allan B., ed. *A History of the City of Washington: Its Men and Institutions.* Baltimore: G. M. Rewell, 1903.

Smith, Annie Tolman. "Genetic Development of the Woman's Movement." Women's Anthropological Society. *Proceedings of the 100th Meeting.* Washington: The Society, 1893.

———. "Report Upon the Relation of Women to the Directive Services of the Public Schools." Women's Anthropological Society. *Proceedings of the 100th Meeting.* Washington: The Society 1893.

———. *Scheme of Work of the Committee on the Investigative and Directive Forces in Society.* Washington: Women's Anthropological Society, 1893.

Smith, Thomas C. "History of Medical Colleges." In *Washington: Past and Present,* ed. John C. Proctor. New York: Lewes Historical Publishing, 1932, 57–84.

Smith-Rosenberg, Carroll. "The Female Animal: Medical and Biological Views of Woman and Her Role in Nineteenth-Century America." *Journal of American History* 60 (Sept. 1973): 332–56.

Solomon, Barbara Miller. *In the Company of Educated Women: A History of Women and Higher Education in America.* New Haven: Yale University Press, 1985.

Sorenson, Andrew A. "Black Associations and the Medical Profession, 1930–1970." *Journal of Negro Education* 61 (Fall 1972): 337–42.

Spaulding, Thomas. *The Cosmos Club on Lafayette Square.* Washington: George Bank Publishing, 1949.

Spink, Mary A. "Woman in Medicine." *Women's Medical Journal* 3 (July 1894): 15–19.

Stanton, Elizabeth Cady, et al. "Declaration of Sentiments and Resolutions, Seneca Falls Convention." In *Up from the Pedestal,* ed. Eileen S. Kraditor. Chicago: Quadrangle Books, 1968.

Stanton, Elizabeth C., Susan B. Anthony, and Matilda Gage. *History of Woman Suffrage,* vol. 2. Rochester, N. Y.: Fowler and Wells, 1881.

Starr, Paul. *The Social Transformation of American Medicine.* New York: Basic Books, 1982.

Statistical Sketch of the Women's Anthropological Society. Washington: Women's Anthropological Society, 1893.

Steelman, Joseph, ed. *Studies in the History of the South, 1875–1922.* Greenville: East Carolina College, 1966.

Steelman, Lola Carr. "Mary Clare de Graffenreid: The Saga of a Crusader for Social Reform," In *Studies in the History of the South, 1875–1922,* ed. Joseph F. Steelman. Greenville: East Carolina College, 1966, 53–84.

Stern, Madeline B. *We the Women: Career Firsts of Nineteenth-Century American Women.* New York: Schulte Publishing, 1963.

Steward, Susan Maria McKinney. "Woman in Medicine," a paper read before the National Association of Colored Women's Clubs at Wilberforce, Ohio, 6 Aug. 1914.

Still, William. *The Underground Railroad: A Record of Facts, Authentic Narratives and Letters.* Philadelphia: Pennsylvania State Anti-Slavery Society, 1871; reprint, Chicago: Johnson Publishing, 1970.

Stowall, Charles. "A New College Needed." *National Medical Review* 1 (Oct. 1892): 17.

Studley, W. H. "Is Menstruation a Disease? A Review of Professor King's Article Entitled 'A New Basis of Uterine Pathology'." *American Journal of Obstetrics* 8 (Nov. 1875): 1–26.

Sugg, Redding. *Motherteacher: The Feminization of American Education.* Charlottesville: University Press of Virginia, 1978.

Sumner, Jeanette. "A Puzzling Case of Uterine Disease." Report of the Proceedings of the Eleventh Annual Meeting of the Alumnae Association of the Woman's Medical College of Pennsylvania, 12 March 1882, 52–53.

Sweet, James A. "Recent Trends in the Employment of American Women." In *Women in the Professions,* ed. Laurily Kerr Epstein. Lexington, Mass.: D. C. Heath, 1975, 25–66.

Talbot, Marion, and Lois K. Rosenberry. *The History of the American Association of University Women, 1881–1931.* Boston: Houghton Mifflin Co., 1931.

Tayler-Jones, Louise. "Medicine as a Field for Women." *Journal of the American Medical Women's Association* 31 (April 1938): 152–56.

Terborg-Penn, Rosalyn. "Afro-Americans in the Struggle for Woman Suffrage." Ph.D. diss., Howard University, 1977.

Terrell, Mary Church. *A Colored Woman in a White World.* Washington: Ransdell Publishing, 1940.

———. "History of the High Schools for Negroes in Washington." *Journal of Negro History* 2 (July 1917): 252–66.

———. "The Story of the National Unfolds," *Journal of the National Association of Colored Women* (Feb.–March 1941): 6–23.

Tracy, Martha. "Women Graduates in Medicine." *Bulletin of the Association of American Medical Colleges* 2 (Jan. 1927): 21–28.

Ulrich, Mabel S. "Men Are Queer that Way: Extracts from the Diary of an Apostate Woman Physician," *Scribner's* 93 (30 June 1933): 365–66.

Van Hoosen, Bertha. *Petticoat Surgeon.* Chicago: Pellegrini and Cudahay, 1947.

Van Riper, Paul. *History of the U. S. Civil Service.* Evanston, Ill.: Row and Peterson, 1958.

Vaughan, George T. "Physicians and Surgeons of Washington." In *Washington: Past and Present,* ed. John C. Proctor. New York: Lewes Historical Publishing, 1932, 645–53.

Verdi, Tulio S. "Report on the Committee on Legislation." Chicago: American Institute of Homoeopathy, 1872.

Vietor, Agnes C., ed. *A Woman's Quest: The Life of Maria E. Zakrzewska, M. D.* New York: D. Appleton, 1924; reprint, New York: Arno Press, 1972.

Vogel, Morris. "Boston's Hospital, 1870–1930, " Ph.D. diss., University of Chicago, 1975.

———. "Patrons, Practitioners, and Patients: The Voluntary Hospital in Mid-

Victorian Boston." In *Victorian America,* ed. Daniel W. Howe. Philadelphia: University of Pennsylvania Press, 1976, 121–40.

Waite, Frederick. "Early Medical Service of Women." *Journal of the American Medical Women's Association* 3 (May 1948): 199–203.

Walsh, Mary Roth. *"Doctors Wanted: No Women Need Apply": Sexual Barriers in the Medical Profession, 1835–1975.* New Haven: Yale University Press, 1977.

———. "Feminism: A Support System for Women Physicians." *Journal of the American Medical Women's Association* 31 (June 1976): 247–50.

———. "Selling the Self-Made Woman." *Journal of American Culture* 2 (Spring 1979): 52–61.

Walworth, Ellen Hardin. "Mary Ellen Cabell." *American Monthly Magazine* 1 (Jan. 1892): 119.

———. "Washington, a Literary Center." *Chautauquan* 13 (Sept. 1891): 168–69.

Washburn, Wilcomb E. *The Cosmos Club of Washington, A Centennial History, 1878–1978.* Washington: Cosmos Club, 1978.

Wein, Roberta. "Women's Colleges and Domesticity, 1875–1918." *History of Education Quarterly* 14 (Spring 1974): 31–47.

Weisberg, G. Kelly. "Barred from the Bar: Women and Legal Education in the United States, 1870–1890." *Journal of Legal Education* 28 (1977): 485–507.

Weiskotten, H. G. "Present Tendencies in Medical Practice." *Bulletin of the Association of American Medical Colleges* 2 (Jan. 1927): 29–47.

Weitzman, Louis G. "One Hundred Years of Catholic Charities in the District of Columbia," Ph.D. diss., Catholic University, 1931.

Welsh, Lilian. *Reminiscences of Thirty Years in Baltimore.* Baltimore: Norman Remington, 1925.

"What Becomes of Women Medical Students?" *Woman's Medical Journal* 3 (July 1894): 98.

White, Francis. "American Medical Women." *Woman's Medical Journal* 4 (April 1895): 244.

White, Martha S. "Psychological and Social Barriers to Women in Science." *Science* 170 (Oct. 1970): 413–17.

Whitehill, Walter M. *Dumbarton Oaks.* Cambridge: Harvard Universtiy Press, 1967.

Whiting, Lilian. *Kate Field.* Boston: Little, Brown, 1900.

———. "Women's Organizations in Boston." *Chautauquan* 27 (May 1898): 197–99.

Whyte, James H. *The Uncivil War, Washington during Reconstruction.* New York: Twayne Publishing, 1958.

Wiebe, Robert W. *The Search for Order, 1870–1920.* New York: Hill and Wang, 1967.

Wilkes, Laura E. *The Story of Frederick Douglass.* Washington: Howard University Press, 1889.

Willard, Frances E. *Occupations for Women.* New York: Success, 1897.

Williams, Edwin. "Homeopathy in the District of Columbia." In *Washington:*

Past and Present, ed. John C. Proctor. New York: Lewes Historical Publishing, 1932, 651–53.

Wilson, Dorothy Clarke. *Lone Woman, The Story of Elizabeth Blackwell.* Boston: Little, Brown, 1970.

Wilson, Margaret Gibbons. *The American Woman in Transition: The Urban Influence, 1870–1920.* Westport, Conn.: Greenwood Press, 1979.

Winner, Julia H. "Belva A. Lockwood." *New York History* 39 (Oct. 1950): 321–41.

Wiprud, Theodore. "History of the Medical Society of the District of Columbia." *Medical Annals of the District of Columbia* 39 (July, Aug., Sept. 1970): 379–89, 459–67, 515–26, 695.

"A Woman's Clinic in Washington, D. C." *Woman's Medical Journal* 27 (Jan. 1917): 16.

"Women as Physicians." *The Medical and Surgical Reporter* 44 (March 1881): 354–56.

Women's Anthropological Society. "Catalogue of Books and Periodicals Deposited in the Library of the Bureau of Ethnology." *Bulletin* 1. Washington: Women's Anthropological Society of America, 1890.

———. *Constitution, By-Laws, and List of Members, Revised May, 1886.* Washington: R. H. Darby, 1886.

———. *Organizational and Historical Sketch of the Women's Anthropological Society of America.* Washington: Women's Anthropological Society of America, 1889.

———. *Organization and Constitution of the Women's Anthropological Society.* Washington: Women's Anthropological Society, 1885.

———. *Proceedings of the One Hundredth Meeting, Jan. 28, 1893.* Washington: Gibson Brothers, 1893.

Women's Medical Association of New York City, ed. *Mary Putnam Jacobi, M. D.: A Pathfinder in Medicine, with Selections from Her Writings.* New York: G. P. Putnam and Sons, 1925.

The Women's Medical Fund and the Opening of the Johns Hopkins School of Medicine. Baltimore: Women's Medical Alumnae Association, 1978.

Woodson, Carter G. *The Negro Professional Man and the Community.* New York: Negro Universities Press, 1934.

Woody, Thomas. *A History of Women's Education in the United States*, vol. 2. New York: Science Press, 1929; reprint, Octagon Books, 1966.

Wormley, G. Smith. "Educators of the First Half Century of the Public Schools of the District of Columbia." *Journal of Negro History* 17 (April–July 1932): 124–140, 378–79.

Young, James Allen. "Height, Weight, and Health: Anthropometric Study of Human Growth in Nineteenth-Century American Medicine." *Bulletin of the History of Medicine* 53 (Summer 1979): 214–43.

Zuckerman, Harriet. "Stratification in American Science." *Sociological Inquiry* 40 (Spring 1979): 235–57.

Index

Index

Note on the Author

Gloria Moldow is Associate Dean of Arts and Science and Director of Graduate Studies and Research at Iona College, New Rochelle, New York. She has also served as Coordinator of the Women's Studies Program at that school. Moldow holds a Bachelor's Degree from the University of Wisconsin and Master's and Doctoral Degrees in American Studies from the University of Maryland.